The 'Evil Child' in Literature, F Culture

The 'evil child' has infiltrated the cultural imagination, taking on prominent roles in popular films, television shows, and literature. This collection of essays from a global range of scholars examines a fascinating array of evil children and the cultural work that they perform, drawing upon sociohistorical, cinematic, and psychological approaches. The chapters explore a wide range of characters including Tom Riddle in the *Harry Potter* series, the possessed Regan in William Peter Blatty's *The Exorcist*, the monstrous Ben in Doris Lessing's *The Fifth Child*, the hostile fetuses of *Rosemary's Baby* and *Alien*, and even the tiny terrors featured in the reality television series *Supernanny*. Contributors also analyse various themes and issues within film, literature and popular culture including ethics, representations of evil and critiques of society.

This book was originally published as two special issues of *LIT:Literature Interpretation Theory*.

Karen J. Renner is a Lecturer in American Literature at Northern Arizona University, USA. Her research interests include 19- and 20th-century American Literature, Popular Culture, Childhood Studies, and Horror. She is currently working on two manuscripts: *Perverse Subjects: Drunks, Gamblers, and Prostitutes in Antebellum America* and *Bad Seeds and Injured Innocents: The "Evil Child" in the Contemporary Imagination*.

The 'Evil Child' in Literature, Film and Popular Culture

Edited by
Karen J. Renner

Routledge
Taylor & Francis Group

LONDON AND NEW YORK

First published 2013
by Routledge
2 Park Square, Milton Park, Abingdon, Oxfordshire OX14 4RN

Simultaneously published in the USA and Canada
by Routledge
711 Third Avenue, New York, NY 10017

First issued in paperback 2014

Routledge is an imprint of the Taylor & Francis Group, an informa business

British Library Cataloguing in Publication Data
A catalogue record for this book is available from the British Library

ISBN 978-0-415-53892-3 (hbk)
ISBN 978-1-138-84181-9 (pbk)

Typeset in Times New Roman
by Taylor & Francis Books

Publisher's Note
The publisher would like to make readers aware that the chapters in this book may be referred to as articles as they are identical to the articles published in the special issue. The publisher accepts responsibility for any inconsistencies that may have arisen in the course of preparing this volume for print.

Contents

Citation Information

The following chapters were originally published in the journal *LIT: Literature Interpretation Theory*. When citing this material, please use the original issue information and page numbering for each article, as follows:

Chapter 2
My Baby Ate the Dingo: The Visual Construction of the Monstrous Infant in Horror Film
Steffen Hantke
LIT: Literature Interpretation Theory, volume 22, issue 2 (2011), pp. 96-112

Chapter 3
Monstrous Children as Harbingers of Mortality: A Psychological Analysis of Doris Lessing's The Fifth Child
Daniel Sullivan and Jeff Greenberg
LIT: Literature Interpretation Theory, volume 22, issue 2 (2011), pp. 113-33

Chapter 4
Spoil the Child: Unsettling Ethics and the Representation of Evil
William Wandless
LIT: Literature Interpretation Theory, volume 22, issue 2 (2011), pp. 134-54

Chapter 5
Private Lessons from Dumbledore's "Chamber of Secrets": The Riddle of the Evil Child in Harry Potter and the Half-Blood Prince
Holly Blackford
LIT: Literature Interpretation Theory, volume 22, issue 2 (2011), pp. 155-75

Chapter 6
Terrifying Tots and Hapless Homes: Undoing Modernity in Recent Bollywood Cinema
Meheli Sen
LIT; Literature Interpretation Theory, volume 22, issue 3 (2011), pp. 197-217

Chapter 7
"The Power of Christ Compels You": Holy Water, Hysteria, and the Oedipal Psychodrama in The Exorcist

Notes on Contributors

Holly Blackford (Ph.D., University of California, Berkeley) is Professor of American and Children's Literature at Rutgers University, Camden, USA. Recent books include *Mockingbird Passing: Closeted Traditions and Sexual Traditions in Harper Lee's Novel*, *The Myth of Persephone in Girls' Fantasy Literature*, *100 Years of Anne with an "e"* (ed.), and *Out of this World: Why Literature Matters to Girls.*

Catherine Fowler is a Senior Lecturer in Film at Otago University, New Zealand. She is editor of *The European Cinema Reader*, co-editor of *Representing the Rural: Space, Place and Identity in Films about the Land*, and author of a monograph on the British filmmaker Sally Potter.

Jeff Greenberg received his Ph.D. from the University of Kansas, USA, in 1982. He has co-authored two books, including *In the Wake of 9-11: The Psychology of Terror*, co-edited two books, and published many research articles. He is currently Professor of Psychology at the University of Arizona, USA.

Steffen Hantke has written on contemporary literature, film, and culture. He is author of *Conspiracy and Paranoia in Contemporary Literature* (1994), as well as editor of *Horror*, a special topics issue of *Paradoxa* (2002), *Horror: Creating and Marketing Fear* (2004), *Caligari's Heirs: The German Cinema of Fear after 1945* (2007), with Rudolphus Teeuwen, of *Gypsy Scholars, Migrant Teachers, and the Global Academic Proletariat* (2007), and *American Horror Film: The Genre at the Turn of the Millennium* (2010). He teaches at Sogang University in Seoul, South Korea.

A. Robin Hoffman recently defended her dissertation, which traces the co-evolution of constructions of literacy and childhood in Victorian alphabet books. Her research more broadly addresses representations of childhood, word and image studies, and British print culture in the long nineteenth century. After graduating from the University of Pittsburgh, USA, her teaching will focus on the history of illustrated books.

Rebecca Kambuta is a Ph.D. student in the Media, Film, and Communications Department at Otago University, New Zealand. Her doctoral dissertation traces the figure of the unruly child through film, news media, and reality television. She has also written on the makeover genre in her MA thesis, "Televising Transformation: A Close Analysis of *Extreme Makeover* and *The Swan*."

Karen J. Renner is a Lecturer in American Literature at Northern Arizona University, USA. Her research interests include 19- and 20th-century American Literature, Popular Culture, Childhood Studies, and Horror. She is currently working on two manuscripts: *Perverse Subjects: Drunks, Gamblers, and Prostitutes in Antebellum America* and *Bad Seeds and Injured Innocents: The "Evil Child" in the Contemporary Imagination*.

Meheli Sen is Assistant Professor in the Cinema Studies Program at Rutgers University, USA. Her research area is popular Hindi cinema, commonly referred to as "Bollywood." She is interested in how the filmic registers of genre, gender, and sexuality resonate with specific moments in India's troubled encounters with modernity and globalization.

Daniel Sullivan received bachelor's degrees in psychology and German studies at the University of Arizona, USA, in 2008. He is currently a National Science Foundation Graduate Research Fellow in the Social Psychology program at the University of Kansas, USA.

William Wandless is Associate Professor of English at Central Michigan University, USA, where he specializes in British fiction of the eighteenth century and teaches courses in critical theory and American popular culture.

Sara Williams is a Ph.D. candidate in the English Department at the University of Hull, UK. Her doctoral work concentrates on locating a tyrannical maternal gaze in textual and visual modes of Gothic production from the nineteenth century to the contemporary, and her wider research interests include cultural, feminist, and psychoanalytical (mis)constructions of motherhood and the epistemology of hysteria.

Evil Children in Film and Literature

KAREN J. RENNER

In 2010, Meredith O'Hayre published a book entitled *The Scream Queen's Survival Guide*, which promised to teach us how, if suddenly plunged into a horror movie, we could conquer its clichés and emerge if not unscathed, then at least alive. The subtitle of the book offers three brief directives: to *Avoid Machetes, Defeat Evil Children, and Steer Clear of Bloody Dismemberment*. That "evil children"—and I will discuss that problematic term in a moment—are mentioned alongside machetes and dismemberment speaks to the serious and pervasive threat they have come to represent within the horror genre. But this threat seems largely a contemporary one: we would be hard-pressed, I think, to discover many instances of wicked youngsters in earlier literature, even though plenty of examples existed in the real world.[1] However, during the second half of the twentieth century, such figures began to possess the imaginations of a wide number of writers and filmmakers. A number of scholars have examined the role of children in literature and film, some even focusing upon evil children in particular, but this pervasive plot convention has not been given adequate attention.[2] In fact, this collection is the first book-length study devoted to the subject.

EVIL CHILDREN IN FILM AND LITERATURE: A BRIEF HISTORY

Stories about evil children began to first proliferate with serious regularity in the 1950s. What is noteworthy about these early texts is their tendency to claim that evil children are born bad. In Ray Bradbury's "The Small Assassin" (1946), a newborn emerges with the innate desire and ability to kill; while no motive or reason is confirmed, the baby's father, David, surmises that since "[i]nsects are born self-sufficient" and "most mammals and birds adjust" in a few weeks, perhaps "a few babies out of all the millions born are instantaneously able to move, see, hear, think" (383). Such a child, David muses, would have the capacity to avenge all the perceived wrongs associated with its removal from the womb where it had been "at rest, fed, comforted, unbothered" (384). The implication is that all infants are enraged by their birth but most lack the ability to enact their feelings of anger upon the figures they feel responsible: their parents. If they did, many parents would experience the same vindictive acts of violence that David and his wife suffer. Bradbury's "The Veldt" (originally published as "The World the Children Made" in 1950) explores similar themes but does so in a futuristic world in which technology can transform playrooms into virtual reality spaces that are based upon "the telepathic emanations" of whomever's in the room (268). When the world made by the story's children—the suggestively named siblings Peter and Wendy—takes on a menacing air, their father decides to disengage the room, but the children beg for one last round of play, and he acquiesces. The children then conjure virtual lions to attack and devour their parents. Although the story hints that the parents are much to blame for their children's lack of emotional attachment in that they have allowed many of the gadgets of their futuristic world to take over their child-rearing duties, the overt reference to J. M. Barrie's novel *Peter and Wendy* (1911) also suggests that Bradbury may, like Barrie, have considered children as naturally "gay and innocent and *heartless*," always "ready, when novelty knocks, to desert their dearest ones" (emphasis mine, 148, 100).

Richard Matheson's very short story "Born of Man and Woman" (1950) is narrated by a monstrously deformed child who never clearly details its own appearance, but the fact that it describes its own blood as an "ugly green," refers at one point to "all my legs," and explains how it can "run on the walls" suggests it is a human-sized, spider-like creature (514, 515, 515). The "child" is kept locked away in a basement, is beaten regularly, and thus is an object of some pity. At the end of the story, however, the child alludes to prior acts of aggression and hints that more are soon to come: "I have a bad anger with mother and father. I will show them. . . . I will hang head down by all my legs and laugh and drip green all over until they are sorry" (515). While the creature is incensed by its parents' abuse, it seems to have been quite violent to begin with and certainly born with the most monstrous of appearances.

The tendency to see evil children as inherently so continued to dominate later works from the 1950s, such as Jerome Bixby's short story "It's a Good Life" (1953), William Golding's *The Lord of the Flies* (1954), and one of the most famous stories about an evil child, William March's *The Bad Seed* (1954), all of which were quickly adapted for the screen.[3] Anthony, the three-year-old terror in Bixby's short story, can read the minds of the adults around him, and if they or anything else displeases him, he punishes the perceived transgressor in whatever way he sees fit simply by thinking it so (though on the suggestion of his father, he kindly teleports his victims out to a cornfield, so that the sight of them will not upset the townspeople). In the opening scene of the story, for example, Anthony is controlling a rat with his mind, "making it do tricks" (523); by the end of the scene, the rat has "devoured half its belly, and . . . died from pain" (525). Anthony's abilities and tendency to act on his rage is inborn: "when Anthony had crept from the womb and old Doc Bates . . . had screamed and dropped him and tried to kill him, . . . Anthony had whined and done the thing" (541). Obviously, baby Anthony was reacting in self-defense; however, throughout most of the story, what we witness is a petulant three-year-old who has the magical ability to make his deepest desires come true and who has not yet learned the empathy or self-control to use his powers humanely. Similarly, Golding himself has claimed the boys in *Lord of the Flies* descend into savagery not because of the trauma of being stranded on an island but because they "are suffering from the terrible disease of being human" (Fable 89). In titling his novel *The Bad Seed*, March also implies that evil is a congenital condition, and the book confirms this claim, for Rhoda Penmark, the child at the center of the novel, seems to have inherited her penchant for murder from her grandmother, the accomplished serial killer Bessie Denker.

Interest in evil children continued into the 1960s, though with somewhat less ferocity. During this decade, texts indicate less interest in children who are born bad but rather in those who have been made so. Jack Clayton's adaptation of Henry James's 1898 novel *The Turn of the Screw, The Innocents* (1961), adds details that make the children far more flagrantly malevolent than in the novel but also makes it more obvious that their abnormal behavior is due to their "possession" by the ghosts of former caretakers who corrupted them. During the 1960s, several well known authors, among them Shirley Jackson, Flannery O'Connor, and Joyce Carol Oates, also turned their Gothic eyes upon the subject of children. In Jackson's novel *We Have Always Lived in the Castle* (1962)—the last she was to publish before her death in 1965—we discover that the eighteen-year-old narrator murdered her parents, aunt, and younger brother six years earlier by lacing the sugar bowl with arsenic. O'Connor's short story "The Lame Shall Enter First" (1965) features a street urchin named Rufus who convinces the son of the man who kindly takes him in to hang himself, and Oates's *Expensive People* (1968) opens with the provocative line "I was a child murderer" (3), and the narrator, Richard Everett, goes on to reveal that the act that earned him this designation was committed at the tender age of eleven. Rather than looking to children endowed with special abilities or deviant predilections from birth, these novels are far more interested in how social conditions and adult influences might move a child to murder.

The decade then concluded with Ira Levin's *Rosemary's Baby* (1967), a story about the most evil child of them all: the son of Satan himself. Roman Polanski adapted the novel into a film the following year, and both received popular and critical acclaim. While many narratives in the 1960s had scrutinized the psychological forces and familial dynamics that might produce an evil child, *Rosemary's Baby* took the approach more popular in the previous decade, presenting the evil child as simply born that way. Influenced by and perhaps hoping to capitalize upon the success of *Rosemary's Baby*, authors in the 1970s and early 1980s produced an enormous number of texts about evil kids, many of which were instantly seared into cultural memory, and directors were quick to offer their cinematic renditions. In fact, the 1970s produced so many fictional evil children that one *Newsweek* editorial worried that the era was one of "growing anti-child sentiment," pointing to a recent poll of 10,000 mothers, 70% of whom said that if given the choice again, they would opt not to have children (Maynard 11).

Although *Rosemary's Baby* steered the conception of the evil child in the direction of the demonic, both types of evil child—the satanic and the psychologically deviant—were explored. The most successful venture into the first category was *The Exorcist*.[4] Indeed, William Friedkin's 1973 adaptation of William Peter Blatty's 1971 novel caused such a stir that, according to Nick Cull, many viewers fainted and one even "charged the screen in an attempt to kill the demon" (46). Friedkin's film prompted many imitations, even a Turkish scene-by-scene remake entitled *Seytan* (1974).[5] Richard Donner's 1976 movie *The Omen* gave birth to yet another satanic threat with Damien, whose name has become shorthand for any kind of monstrous youth. Thomas Tryon's bestselling novel *The Other* (1971) offered psychological rather than metaphysical explanations for his evil child. In the book, eleven-year-old Niles commits a series of disturbing and violent acts, which he attributes to his twin, Holland, whom we later discover is dead. *The Other* received a cinematic tribute in 1972, and though neither are well known today, Tryon's focus on insanity rather than demonic possession helped set the stage for later texts that would increasingly examine childhood manifestations of dangerous derangements.

It was also during the 1970s that several writers who would later become virtuosos of horror launched their careers with stories centering on evil children. Dean Koontz started early, publishing *Demon Child* in 1971 under the pseudonym Deanna Dwyer.[6] However, his first big success in the subgenre came with *Demon Seed* (1973), which tells the story of a woman impregnated against her will by the computer that controls her house, Proteus; the book was made into a 1977 film starring Julie Christie.[7] In 1976, Anne Rice published the first and most popular of her *Vampire Chronicles*, *Interview with the Vampire*, a considerable portion of which is devoted to a girl vampire, Claudia. The relish with which Claudia feeds—"I want some more," Claudia says in a petulant voice after feeding on her first human (93)—while all the while exuding the charms of young girlhood is one of the most horrifying aspects of the novel. Stephen King, too, first received serious attention after publishing his novel *Carrie* (1974), and Brian De Palma's 1976 cinematic adaptation only bolstered his reputation. King promptly went on to write several other stories about evil children, including "Children of the Corn" (1977), *The Shining* (1977), *Firestarter* (1980), and *Pet Sematary* (1983), all of which were eventually made into movies. Indeed, the 1984 adaptation of *Children of the Corn* has prompted an unrivalled franchise of evil children films, with six sequels and a recent remake in 2009.

These early horror texts were largely responsible for moving horror from a peripheral genre to a mainstream interest, making room for other lesser-known writers who, at least momentarily, made a career out of books about evil children, including John Saul, Andrew Neiderman, and Ruby Jean Jensen.[8] As a result, the covers of novels from the late 1970s to the early 1990s began to feature a veritable bevy of creepy kids, as Will Errickson has shown in his blog *Too Much Horror Fiction*.[9] Even canonical authors called upon the trope of the evil child, such as Toni Morrison in *Beloved* (1987) and Doris Lessing in *The Fifth Child* (1988). Even television proved eager to get in on the action. Bart Simpson made his debut on the *Tracey Ullman Show* in 1987, and though Bart is more errant than evil, he paved the way for one of the most despicable cartoon children ever to make an appearance: Eric Cartman of *South Park* (1997–).[10] Soon after, the creators of *Family Guy* (1999-2002; 2005–) would offer their own animated evil child in Stewie Griffin.

Nowadays, the evil child is almost a trite plot device. The International Movie Database, imdb.com, lets you search for films using the keyword of "evil child," and Netflix allows you to cater your "Storylines" taste preferences to announce that you "often" watch movies that feature "evil kids," thus ensuring that Netflix will make relevant recommendations for you in the future.[11] The contributions of this century's filmmakers promise to quickly eclipse those of the prior century: of the approximately three hundred films I have identified that portray some kind of evil child, over half have been produced since the year 2000. Television has succumbed to the same phenomenon: it seems that every season of *Law and Order: Special Victims Unit* offers at least one episode that centers upon a wicked adolescent of some kind,[12] and even reality television has ventured into the genre in the US and the UK with *Nanny 911* (2004–) and *Supernanny* (2005–), both of which display a series of badly behaved (though ultimately redeemable) youngsters. A prominent element of video games,[13] evil children have even infiltrated children's literature, most prominently in the form of Tom Riddle in the *Harry Potter* series and in the children who fight to the death in Suzanne Collins's popular trilogy, *The Hunger Games*.[14]

A DISCLAIMER ABOUT TERMINOLOGY

By now, it has probably become obvious that the term "evil children" is far too simplistic to account for the range and complexity of characters to whom I have applied it. To be sure, both parts of the term are problematic. Defining the term "child" poses difficulty since the laws that govern certain rights—voting, drinking alcohol, consenting to sex—vary, each suggesting that a different age marks the boundary between adult and child. And these laws differ again by nation and, within this country, sometimes even by state. For the sake of simplicity, I will rely on markers of citizenship and define a "child" as anyone under the age of 18. Even far more fraught is the word "evil." Problematic enough in its implications, the term becomes even more difficult to apply to children who often lack the maturity and forethought necessary for moral decision-making. Who, out of the crowd of children I've conjured, constitutes a truly *evil* child? Is it *The Bad Seed*'s Rhoda Penmark, who at the age of eight bludgeons a classmate to death with her tap shoes and burns alive a man she fears has evidence of the murder she committed?[15] Is it Damien from *The Omen*, the son of Satan, who, among other evil deeds, wills his nanny to hang herself, pushes his adopted mother over a high balcony, and at the end of the film smiles coyly into the camera to show us just how much he's enjoying himself? Is it Jack and Emily Poe from the 2008 film *Home Movie* who slaughter all of their pets—progressing from goldfish to frog to the family cat and dog —and then butcher their parents? Certainly, each of these children seems to fit the bill of "evil child" pretty straightforwardly.

But applying that label becomes harder when we consider less clear-cut examples. What do we do, for example, with Regan in *The Exorcist*? When demon-possessed, Regan hurls obscenities, violent blows, and pea-green vomit at her mother and the priests who come to help her, but once exorcised, she turns back into the innocent adolescent she was before her possession. Isn't it more accurate to say that Regan is temporarily corrupted rather than evil? Scalpel-wielding Gage of *Pet Sematary* is similarly problematic, for he has returned from the dead and thus is more zombie than boy. The children in John Wyndham's *The Midwich Cuckoos* (1957) are at least half extraterrestrial, the triad of ten-year-old killers in *Bloody Birthday* (1981) have been affected in some way by the solar eclipse during which they were born, and the homicidal adolescents in both the 2006 film *The Plague* and the 2008 film *The Children* appear to have been afflicted by some mysterious disease; all of these children are more "infected" than inherently evil. And what about the carnivorous newborns featured in such films as *It's Alive* (1974) and the 2008 film *Grace*? These babies emerge from their mother's womb with a natural thirst for human blood, but we can't really say that their intentions are "evil" or even malicious. Like any other predator, they are just doing what they need to do to survive.

While "evil children" is admittedly an inadequate catch-all phrase, these figures, I would argue, play a similar role: they force us to consider the age-old question about the nature of humankind. Is the evil child the result of an imperfect environment and thus redeemable, or a sign of inherent corruption? Our understanding of the evil child mirrors the way we view ourselves: is there evil in the world because we have gone astray, or because we have a natural propensity for wickedness and cruelty? Because the answers to these questions are culturally determined and shift throughout time, different categories of evil child have emerged, each offering a response to suit the *zeitgeist*. Even when the dominant type of evil children during a particular epoch cannot easily be labeled "evil," this fact alone tells us much about the predominant ideologies and presumptions that prevent a more straightforward type of evil child from forming in the cultural imagination. Throwing our net wide allows us to determine what sorts of "evil" children prevailed during different eras and why their particular brand of evil was so compelling. Unfortunately, space restrictions do not allow me to cover all of these different categories, so I will focus on two particular types, the possessed child and the feral child, two subtypes that, I will argue, are intimately linked. While the possessed child narrative explores the unique psychological failures of a particular family, the feral child narrative investigates broader social failures that affect children in general.

Possessed children generate horror because they exhibit disturbing behavior—cruel, violent, and, for girls, often sexually suggestive. Possessed child narratives necessarily begin before the point of possession, spending considerable time developing the characters of these victims and their families. As a result, we can see that the behavior the child demonstrates while possessed differs considerably from his or her normal conduct, and therefore we typically transfer blame for the child's wickedness to the offending entity. While the family as a whole might seem like the hapless victims of a supernatural presence, possessed child narratives, as I will show, frequently demonstrate that the child has been made vulnerable because of breakdowns in the family unit. Possession either draws the family back together (though change may not come soon enough to save the child) or magnifies the issues that caused fracture in the first place. Either way, the viewer bears witness to failures in the family that have allowed the child to become the victim of evil forces. I argue that these forces symbolize other nefarious influences commonly cited as taking hold of children when parents are not properly vigilant, such as satanic song lyrics or violent video games. The possessed child narrative thus relies on developing our attachments to particular characters and then using our sympathies to drive home its ideologies about proper familial structures.

Feral child narratives construct a similar critique but on a broader scale. I define the feral child as one for whom base instincts and appetites supersede personal relationships. This subtype includes zombie and vampire children as well as those who have been reared in a primitive or deviant culture in which the humanitarian values of our supposedly civilized society have been discarded in favor of self-centered motives and pleasures. Because feral children are given scant character development and usually appear as part of a larger savage pack, they are rarely individualized enough for us to develop any real sympathy for them. Furthermore, the stories generate revulsion for these children by depicting the terrible acts of brutality, cannibalism, and rape that they commit. These acts make feral children incapable of redemption and ease our acceptance of their bloody annihilation, which typically concludes these narratives. And yet in the background of these tales are hints that the so-called civilized world is quite capable of equivalent forms of savagery. Feral children certainly generate disgust, but as with zombies, with whom they are closely aligned, they are a faceless and thoughtless mob unlike the denizens of the civilized world, whose capacity for forethought and empathy should curtail their cruelties. These narratives often juxtapose the atrocities committed by the enlightened with the mindless savagery of the feral child, with the result being that the civilized look all the more barbaric. In doing so, they launch critiques of the adult world that parallel those of possessed child narratives but which rely on a different emotional logic to impress their ideologies upon viewers.

THE POSSESSED CHILD

Stories of possession have a long history, dating at least as far back as the Bible. However, possession narratives, as I define them, are not always situated within a religious context: although Satan or his minions are often the culprits, just as often the spirits of former humans inhabit or influence the living. Sometimes, ghosts of the wicked linger in order to further their evil reign: in *Fallen* (1998), for example, the spirit of a serial killer lodges in living human beings in order to claim more victims, and in *Child's Play* (1988), the deceased murderer Charles Lee Ray takes up residence in a Chucky doll for much the same reason (though to far more campy effect). But not all possessing spirits have immoral intentions. Some simply seek justice for unpunished wrongs they have suffered while others wish to direct the living to repressed or unknown truths (i.e., that a lover is actually a murderer, as in *What Lies Beneath* [2000]). As I am defining it, in a possession narrative, a supernatural entity of some kind embodies or influences one of the living, compelling the victim to act in malicious, disturbing, or at least uncharacteristic ways.

Children—especially young girls—are frequent victims of demonic possession, and such stories often culminate in an exorcism which may or may not succeed. In other cases, a child is not literally taken over by a spirit but naively falls under its influence, never suspecting that it has insidious intentions. Such narratives play upon the common supposition that children are naturally sensitive to such presences, becoming aware of encroaching spirits long before they are made known to or accepted by adults. Indeed, a standard plot device in horror films shows an innocent child befriending such an entity, and his or her parents mistakenly believing at first that the new playmate is merely a harmless, imaginary friend.

The possessed child narrative, I argue, performs important ideological work that has less to do with the child—who in many ways remains an innocent figure taken advantage of by a more powerful spirit—and more to do with his or her parents. In order to understand the cultural function of the possessed child narrative, I wish to build upon Carol Clover's analysis of possession films in *Men, Women, and Chainsaws: Gender in the Modern Horror Film* (1992). Clover argues that possession films actually contain two narratives occurring in tandem. One is about the travails of the possessed character —typically female. The other focuses on a man who is slowly converted from a purely rational standpoint that scoffs at the existence of supernatural forces—what Clover terms White Science—to a mystical perspective that Clover calls Black Magic, which is commonly embraced by ethnic minorities, women, and "feminized" men, such as creative types or folklorists who rely on emotion, intuition, and imagination. Supporting her claims by drawing upon *The Exorcist* (1973) and *Witchboard* (1987) primarily, Clover argues that these two narrative strands are intertwined in such a fashion because the possession plot is really a story of male crisis, an implicit call for a new masculinity that was "part and parcel of the social changes from the late sixties on, from feminism to the Vietnam experience and the new family" (100). "If action cinema mourns the passing of the 'real man,'" Clover concludes, then horror "urges it along, and occult films go so far as to imagine a new, revised edition" of masculinity (99).

Clover's compelling argument certainly still holds true today, almost twenty years later. *The Last Exorcism* (2010), for example, features a preacher named Cotton Marcus—a name that recalls that of a prominent religious figure involved in the Salem Witch Trials, Cotton Mather. Staged as a documentary meant to expose exorcisms as shams, the film initially shows Marcus playfully boasting about the sway he holds over his disciples and the unabashedly theatrical exorcisms he performs purely for personal profit. However, his encounter with the possessed Nell causes him to rediscover his faith and literally take up the cross to battle a demon. The movie ends up being more about Cotton's slow return to religious belief than it does the exorcism of a possessed teenage girl.

If for Clover, the possession plot is a narrative of male crisis, I would argue that it is also a narrative of *parental* crisis, a probing of the dynamics behind the failure of the family and a proposal for remedy. Possession narratives act as cautionary tales that warn us, in symbolic terms, that children are vulnerable to dangerous influences when traditional family structures are damaged and parents are negligent in their duties. In some cases, if parent figures reassume their proper roles, the child can be saved; other times, it is simply too late.

Let me illustrate my argument by turning now to several literary and cinematic examples. One of the earliest and well-known possession narratives is Henry James's *The Turn of the Screw* (1898), a novella narrated mostly by an unnamed governess who is hired by an attractive bachelor to care for his angelic and orphaned niece and nephew, Flora and Miles, in whom he has little interest. Shortly after arriving at the children's home in the remote country estate, Bly, the governess begins seeing the ghosts of two former servants—the last governess, Miss Jessel, and the uncle's past valet, Peter Quint—who are believed to have been involved in an illicit affair to which the children were exposed. The governess suspects that the children are in secret contact with the spirits, who wish to continue to corrupt and control the children from beyond the grave. The story then traces what the governess believes is her heroic struggle against the evil entities for the children's souls, which ultimately results in Flora's hysterical illness and departure from Bly and Miles's death. *The Turn of the Screw* has generated a great deal of critical debate largely centering on the governess's reliability.[16] Because she is the only person who actually sees the ghosts, many scholars have approached the spirits as manifestations of her psychological instability, possibly the result of repressed desire for the children's uncle or her need as an inexperienced young woman to prove her mettle by constructing for herself an epic battle against evil. Defenders of a supernatural interpretation of the novel claim that our resistance to this reading results from our skepticism regarding the existence of ghosts, a skepticism that James and his original audience members would not have shared.[17]

My purpose here is not to take a side in this debate, for such a determination is unnecessary to my point. Regardless of whether or not the ghosts are real, *The Turn of the Screw* taps into fears about the potential damage that could be done to children raised by hired help; after all, there is no debating that Jessel and Quint were immoral guardians when alive and that they had a pernicious influence upon the children. It is Mrs. Grose, the housekeeper, who says that Quint was "definitely . . . bad" and "too free" with both Miles and everyone else (51). When the governess surmises that Quint was a "hound," Mrs. Grose exclaims in response, "I've never seen one like him. He did what he wished" (58). It is also Mrs. Grose who insinuates that Miss Jessel left her position because she was pregnant with Quint's child. In addition, it is quite clear that the children's virtue *has* been tainted by exposure to the two servants. When Flora falls ill, her language becomes so shocking that Mrs. Grose is driven nearly to collapse: she reports that she heard "'[f]rom that child—horrors. . . . On my honour, Miss, she says things–!' But at this evocation, she broke down; she dropped with a sudden cry upon my sofa" (108). Similarly, Miles himself admits that he was expelled from school because he "said things" that were "too bad" for the masters to repeat in their letter announcing Miles's dismissal (119). Even if the ghosts of Jessel and Quint are not real, their living incarnations have possessed the children in terms of a moral degradation that extends beyond the grave. And the children's initial exposure to these sources of corruption occurred because they lacked proper parental figures to protect them from such influences.

James's text remains ambiguous enough for critics to debate the reality of the ghosts, but many other possession narratives offer definitive evidence that a supernatural entity is indeed at work. For example, William Friedkin's cinematic version of *The Exorcist* gives us visual proof of Regan's possession when her head turns a full 360° and she levitates above her bed. In addition, we see the devil in its actual form during several brief flashes in the film. If possession clearly arises from the presence of an evil spirit, as in Friedkin's film, it would seem difficult to attribute the child's wicked behavior to familial shortcomings. In fact, technically speaking Regan is not evil at all but merely the temporary puppet of a malevolent force, so how could her parents be at fault?

Yet even a work as blatantly supernatural as *The Exorcist* still suggests that failed family structures allow demons to sidle into the home. After all, Regan's parents are divorced, and her father has so shirked his paternal responsibilities that he doesn't even bother to call his daughter on her birthday. Regan's mother, Chris, is a successful actress who employs several people to care for Regan while she works, but it is clear that the girl is often left somewhat unsupervised. Chris only belatedly discovers that Regan has an imaginary friend, Captain Howdy, with whom she communicates via a Ouija board and by then it seems too late: the demon has already gained access to the vulnerable child. Paid childcare, it seems, is no substitute for the careful vigilance of a parent. In the novel, Regan-as-demon even condemns Chris for putting her career above caring for her child: "It is *you* who have done it! Yes, *you* with your career before *anything*, your career before your *husband*, before *her*" (349). Apparently, the sins of a single, successful working mother are worse than those of an almost entirely absent father. Regan's possession ultimately forces her mother to resume duties as a full-time, stay-at-home mom, for her condition requires constant supervision and care. At the end, Chris is "reformed," having learned to put motherhood well ahead of Hollywood, and Regan returns to a state of innocence, a transformation that by extension could suggest that contamination can be removed if the child is given "proper" parental attention in time to rescue him or her.[18]

Other more contemporary films about possession employ similar patterns, linking the child's vulnerability to possession to a disrupted or dysfunctional family. In *The Last Exorcism*, the possessed Nell has lost her mother, whom she proclaims was her best friend, leaving her at the mercy of her overprotective and alcoholic father (as well as the local Satanists). In other films, children are influenced by spirits rather than being literally possessed by them, but this development is still due to rifts in their relationships with their parents. In *The Others* (2001), a film set in England just following World War II, a brother and sister begin communicating with what appears to be the ghosts of former inhabitants of the house. The children seem particularly vulnerable to this communication because they are unhappy in their home life. Both are photosensitive and cannot go out during the day and spend most of their time locked in dark rooms away from the rest of the world in their already isolated mansion. Furthermore, their father has been lost in battle, and their mother, suffering from both the loss of her husband and the strain of raising children alone under such difficult circumstances, is distant and easily angered. Having no meaningful relationships, the children seek company elsewhere.

Other examples abound. In *Hide and Seek* (2005), David Callaway tries to help his daughter, Emily, cope with the recent suicide of her mother. However, Emily is distant and disturbed, and David's attempts to reach her continually fail. It is at this point that Emily announces a new imaginary friend, Charlie, who is either responsible for a series of increasingly violent acts or who influences Emily to commit them. In *Shattered Lives* (2009), a young girl, Rachel, is neglected and verbally abused by her unhappily married mother, who is having an affair and forcing Rachel to collude with her to keep it secret. It is during such a period of familial strain that two of Rachel's harlequin dolls begin communicating with her, eventually convincing her to stab her mother to death. It is never clear whether the dolls are actually demonic spirits masquerading as toys or if Rachel is simply imagining the whole thing as some sort of coping mechanism, but, as with *The Turn of the Screw*, I would argue that the truth is mostly moot. What is important is that the child's vulnerability to this influence, whether real or imagined, is directly due to parental failure.[19]

Possession thus functions, I argue, as an analog for those bad influences that infiltrate children's lives when left unsupervised and which are frequently cited as causing juvenile crime, such as satanic music and violent films and video games.[20] For girls, fears additionally center on sexual promiscuity, though the prime reason cited is much the same: the media—music videos and lyrics, advertising, toys, and films—sexualizes the adolescent girl, leading her to believe that her worth derives primarily from her value as a sexual object for men. That possession narratives symbolize these other forms of corruption seems obvious when we consider for a moment why the possessed child is so horrible in the first place. Miles and Flora swear and while we are not privy to their exact words, they are likely sexual in nature, considering that the children have been exposed to a sexual affair. Regan becomes a physically repulsive creature who secretes all kinds of bodily fluids, but even before that hideous transformation is complete, her behavior disturbs in sexual and violent ways: she screams obscenities and suggestive invitations at her male doctors, then later masturbates with a crucifix, shoving her mother's face into her bloody genitalia before slapping her across the room. In *The Last Exorcist*, Nell, in the throes of possession, suggestively licks the shoulder of a woman who tries to comfort her and shortly after cruelly bludgeons a cat into a bloody mess, thus confirming that she is responsible for the slaughter of her father's livestock as well, whose carcasses had been found earlier. Possessed children exhibit exactly the same type of unchecked aggression and sexuality we fear they would develop if exposed to improper influences.

Possessed children are not always saved, but if the supernatural origins of the behavior are confirmed, then the narrative is at least comforting in that it assures the audience that the child's corruption is due to outside sources from which he or she could be protected by dutiful parents. The problem is, in other words, preventable. The possession narrative thus argues that good parents have control over children's fates and that the moral degradation of children happens only in "those" families that have failed.

THE FERAL CHILD

Tales of feral children have as long a lineage as possession narratives: after all, Romulus and Remus, the founders of Rome, were supposedly suckled by a wolf. While the most famous—and perhaps optimistic—versions of the feral tale focus on stories like this in which children are raised by sympathetic animals, contemporary feral children are more often the victims of shocking abuse and neglect. One of the more notorious cases is that of Genie, who in 1970 was discovered to have been confined to a single room for twelve years.[21] To categorize such unfortunate children as "evil" would seem the height of callousness, but within the horror genre, feral children are transformed into savage creatures whose animalistic behavior—typically, brutal acts of murder, cannibalism, and even rape—negates any capacity for pity.

The feral child of contemporary fiction and film thus demonstrates a far less optimistic view of human nature than that held in previous eras. In the Romantic period, human nature was considered by many to be naturally moral and civilization a contaminating influence that caused its inhabitants to deviate from original virtue. Under such a belief system, the uncivilized child was exalted for its purity and was thought to exhibit more integrity than the cultured, a kin to the so-called noble savage. In his 1841 essay "Self-Reliance," for example, Ralph Waldo Emerson proclaimed, "What pretty oracles nature yields us . . . in the face and behavior of children, babes, and even brutes! . . . Their mind being whole, their eye is as yet unconquered, and when we look in their faces, we are disconcerted" (260). Subsequent authors invented a variety of boy characters who would have received Emerson's praise. Huck Finn, for example, suffers a most degenerate upbringing under the "care" of his Pap—one that could certainly be considered equivalent to that of contemporary feral children. And yet while Huck is never quite as "sivilized" and educated as his companion Tom Sawyer, his capacity for moral reasoning surpasses Tom's and many of the supposedly more sophisticated figures in Mark Twain's 1884 novel. Likewise, in Rudyard Kipling's 1895 collection *The Jungle Book*, Mowgli is depicted as inherently superior to the animals that raise him and later proves to be more advanced than many of the humans with whom he associates once he returns to civilization. Other characters who might fit the positive mold of the feral child include Carlo Collodi's Pinocchio (not Disney's version of the character) and the Lost Boys of *Peter Pan*.[22] As long as human nature was believed to be generally good, the feral child could prove a positive figure.[23]

Soon, the negative potential of the feral child would become the focus, reminding us of the savagery lurking beneath the masks of humanity. Such is the case in Richard Hughes's *A High Wind in Jamaica* (1929), in which children raised in a supposedly primitive Caribbean environment prove at times to be as barbaric as the pirates who take them hostage. Even before their exposure to pirate culture, the children are described as abusing the wildlife around their home, capturing birds and, with each one, "deciding by 'Eena, deena, dina, do,' or some such rigmarole, whether to twist its neck or let it go free" (9). And the narrator further tells us that their mother "meant practically nothing to her children" and that they loved their father "a little more," mostly because when he arrived on horseback, he allowed them "the ceremony of riding home [with him] on his stirrups" (44, 45). Hughes's novel suggests that savagery just might be the natural state of childhood, which will run rampant if children are left to their own devices.

Golding picked up where Hughes left off with *Lord of the Flies* (1954). The plot is familiar to most: a group of schoolboys are stranded on a desert island and for a time they manage to cooperate. However, soon a small band of self-designated hunters led by a boy named Jack form a savage society and turn their aggression on those who resist their authority, seducing or forcing all but two boys—Ralph, the former leader of the entire group, and his self-appointed advisor, Piggy—into their clan. The result is the accidental group murder of an innocent boy they mistook for a marauding beast, followed by the purposeful killing of Piggy, culminating in a final hunt for Ralph, whose head the boys intend to post on a pike. The brutal slaying of Ralph by the feral mob of boys is only prevented by the timely arrival of the cavalry, in the form of the British navy.

Since Golding's novel, few feral child narratives have gained much notoriety. And yet feral child narratives still comprise a considerable portion of the evil child genre. Rarely, however, does the feral child appear alone, for the solitary feral child is not a very intimidating enemy. While unsettling, he or she often poses little threat, bearing some resemblance to a rabid Chihuahua. When the feral child does prove dangerous, it is usually because adults do not expect attack from a supposed innocent and are hesitant to retaliate, even after he or she reveals their murderous intentions.[24] For that reason, feral children, as we will see, are often assembled into far more hazardous hordes.

Feral children also have several incarnations, their defining feature being that their appetites and beliefs supersede the pity and empathy that prevent the "civilized" from operating according to similar desires. Sometimes they appear as animalistic creatures driven purely by base hungers and instincts. Zombie and vampire children are common examples of this type, perhaps one of the earliest examples being young Karen in *Night of the Living Dead* (1968), who, after turning into a zombie, feeds on her dead father and kills her mother with a trowel. In *30 Days of Night* (2007), a small group of people who have survived a vampire attack discover a little girl, pigtails tied up in blue ribbons, feeding on a corpse. She says, "I'm done playing with this one. You want to play with me now?" before viciously attacking the group. Zombie or vampire children are so dominated by their animalistic hungers that they will quite eagerly cannibalize their loved ones or any adults who try to help, which is of course one of the prime reasons why they—and feral children in general—are such disturbing monsters.[25]

Other films employ some unexplained disease or mysterious event in order to transform children into single-mindedly bloodthirsty creatures. Such is the case in the Spanish film *Who Can Kill a Child?* (1976), in which a British couple discover that children have exterminated all of the adults on the island on which they are vacationing. While the exact cause of their spontaneous homicidal impulses is not specified, it is clear that the desire is contagious, for new children are brought into the pack simply through contact with its current members. In *The Children* (1980), a busload of kids are exposed to a toxic cloud that causes them to be able to burn any adult they encounter into a crisp on contact, and they apparently enjoy this newfound ability a great deal. In a 2008 film of the same name, two families sharing New Year's Eve together discover that their children all seem to have caught the same mysterious disease, causing them to vomit, cough up disturbing amounts of mucous (which special effects assures us is simply teeming with bacteria), and finally to plot the vicious murders of their parents. Likewise, in *The Plague* (2006), all children under the age of nine across the globe enter into a deep catatonic state, only to awaken ten years later in a sort of zombie-like trance, motivated solely by a desire to kill all adults.

Feral children are not always zombie-like creatures, though. Quite frequently, they appear as the offspring of a "primitive" society, one whose system of values contrasts sharply with our supposedly more civilized set that purports to value human life and abhor cruelty. Perhaps the most infamous example is King's 1977 short story "Children of the Corn," in which kids in a small town in Nebraska formulate their own religion, which has one central mandate: no one over the age of eighteen is allowed to live. As a result, adults who enter the town are quickly and gruesomely dispatched, most often crucified. In addition, upon reaching their nineteenth birthday, the children willingly forfeit their lives by walking into the cornfield, which is inhabited by a demonic creature that the children refer to simply as "He Who Walks Behind the Rows." The children's religion, which has a decidedly Old Testament flavor, aligns them with other primitive religions that relied on blood-sacrifices to appease the gods.[26]

The feral child as primitive religious fanatic is the subject of the low-budget film *Beware! Children at Play* (1989) as well. The film is set in a small town in New Jersey where kids are being lured away to join a society of savage children in the forest, known to the remaining kids as Woodies. The Woodies, under the leadership of an older boy who refers to himself as Grendel, periodically attack the adults in town and feed on their flesh. Grendel was once a normal boy named Glenn Randall, whose transformation into the leader of this cannibalistic clan is detailed in the opening scenes of the film. As a young boy, Glenn was on a camping trip with his father, whom we later discover was a literary scholar. His father inadvertently stepped into a bear trap from which he could not escape, and Glenn watched him die a slow and painful death. His dying commandment to his son was, "You must do as I say," and then, in an apparent delirium, he recited the words, "Tear it to pieces. Bite through the bones. Gulp the blood. Gobble the flesh." Glenn apparently takes his father quite literally because immediately after he dies, we see Glenn cut into his father's stomach and gleefully fondle his innards, repeating his father's dying words, which then become the mantra that all of the Woodies chant as they kill and devour their human prey. The references to *Beowulf* make it clear that the children should be seen as a sort of ancient tribe.[27]

Offspring (2009) contains a similar group, only this set consists of adults—or at least two parent figures—as well as children. Based on Jack Ketchum's 1991 novel of the same name, itself a sequel to Ketchum's 1980 *Off Season*, the film weaves its opening credits with images of newspaper articles dating from the nineteenth century to the present day. The articles detail various people who have gone missing, some whose remains were discovered later, as well as the disappearances of several children. It seems that a group of savages, descendants of a lighthouse keeper and his family who went missing in 1848, are largely responsible. Dressed in costumes that could have been pilfered from the set of *Clan of the Cave Bear*, the family randomly attack people, chopping off and hauling away body parts that will serve as provisions. The film depicts the family as communicating in a primitive tongue, and clearly they have some sort of religious beliefs as well, for they see babies as a source of power. The children are as brutal as their parents, perfectly adapted to the culture in which they have been reared.

Feral child narratives also include members of inbred families or so-called redneck or hillbilly societies. In many cases, we see only the adult results of such upbringings with the childhoods of such people only a shadowy innuendo, as in films like *Spider Baby* (1968), *Texas Chainsaw Massacre* (1974), *The Hills Have Eyes* (1977), *Mother's Day* (1980), an episode of the *X-Files* entitled "Home" (1996), and Rob Zombie's *House of 1,000 Corpses* (2003) and the sequel *The Devil's Rejects* (2005). Connected to these types of plots are narratives involving "gangs" of children raised in violent or abusive settings who mimic the aggression around them with little remorse for the pain they cause. One of the more recent and disturbing examples of this type of narrative is the British film *Eden Lake* (2008), which narrates the story of a young couple, Jenny and Steve, who take a weekend holiday to a remote lake. Their idyllic getaway is interrupted by a group of young hoodlums whose behavior becomes increasingly disrespectful and threatening. When they steal Steve's car, he finally confronts them and is almost stabbed but instead accidentally kills the beloved Rottweiler of the leader, Brett, an act that escalates the gang's violence to a shocking brutality. For the rest of the film, the young teens stalk Jenny and Steve. *Eden Lake* has precedents in Anthony Burgess's 1962 novel *A Clockwork Orange*, *Devil Times Five* (1974), and *The New Kids* (1985).

Thus, the category of evil child I am terming "feral" rarely resemble the stories of abandoned children raised by animals or those prevented from being properly socialized and nurtured due to extreme forms of neglect and abuse. Indeed, such unfortunate children could not function as subjects for evil children stories. The reason is quite simple: sympathy would interfere with the terror and disgust that the evil child incites and impede our ability to support the violent measures protagonists often need to take in order to survive their encounters with feral children. Within the evil child genre, feral children are incapable of rehabilitation and can only be dealt with through a brutality equivalent to their own.

And yet, at the same time, the feral child narrative does hearken back to these traditional tales by depicting children as reduced to savagery rather than embracing it of their own accord. If feral children can be deemed evil, they do not willingly decide to be so. As horrific as these packs of feral youth are, many of the texts in which they appear suggest that the children ultimately are not culpable for their actions but rather have been corrupted by exposure to adult cruelty. After all, lurking in the background of *Lord of the Flies* is a civilization ravaged by atomic warfare. Similarly, *Who Can Kill a Child?* opens with shocking footage documenting the atrocities done to children during such horrific events as the Holocaust, the Civil War between India and Pakistan, and the Korean War; the implication is that the children are not inherently evil but merely are striking back against a society that has long abused them.[28] And as at least one critic has noted, King's short story is infused with references to the Vietnam War, thus implying that the conflict in Southeast Asia has influenced the children to engage in their own forms of violence; that the children sacrifice themselves to their corn god when they turn nineteen—the average age of the Vietnam soldier—only cements this suggestion.[29] Is it any surprise that the offspring of such a society turn against it? If the feral or savage child represents the basest potential of human nature, these narratives also suggest that children imitate their elders. If adults would learn to treat each other civilly, then perhaps children would follow suit.[30]

Ultimately, feral children are horrifying because they remind us of the animalistic nature that all humans share and would be reduced to if placed in similar circumstances. But what is even more grotesque is witnessing human acts of savagery committed by one as supposedly innocent as a child, a savagery so appalling that it is beyond redemption. It is for this reason—and the fact that the feral child often appears in a horde and thus is not individualized to an extent that promotes much sympathy—that so many narratives can kill off feral children without causing much moral quandary on the part of the viewer. As Tom Shankland, director of the 2008 *The Children*, noted about his own film, "In society we're not supposed to harm children, but in the movie, by the second half, everyone seems to get a little bloodthirsty towards them because of how evil they are" ("Tom Shankland Talks"). His description holds true for feral children in general. The offenses they commit are just too repulsive, too inhuman, for forgiveness to be an option, and thus the texts can glory in providing readers or viewers with the catharsis of bloody retribution but not before planting some haunting suspicions about the role the adult world plays in creating such monsters.

Ultimately, though, there is something relatively simple and safe about the message behind the feral child narrative. After all, it's not too hard to accept that societal failings—war, careless pollution, adult violence—create roving packs of "savage" children. And we must wonder, too, if the social critique proffered is sincere or merely included in an attempt to elevate a film marked by graphic atrocities to one with a moral purpose. At the same time, the possessed child narrative seems in many ways more insidious, conjuring demons to punish families for not adhering to culturally dominant (i. e., white, middle-class) ideologies of parenting. What is remarkable is that both types of narratives depict evil children who are the unfortunate products of a faulty family or society and so, in the end, are not really so evil after all.

THE ESSAYS

Space has not allowed me to examine other important subtypes of evil children, which include psychics and superkids, monstrous newborns, and child killers. Nor have I been able to give much attention to the ways in which gender, race, nationality, and class figure into the conventions of the subtype and the genre as a whole. Fortunately, many of the topics that I am unable to cover in my introduction have been taken up by the contributors to this collection.

In "My Baby Ate the Dingo: The Visual Construction of the Monstrous Infant in Horror Film," Steffen Hantke explores a technique he terms *visual reticence*—a director's refusal, for at least most of the film, to provide viewers with a clear visual image of the creature (a technique used to its fullest potential in *The Blair Witch Project* [1999]). Hantke argues against the common perception that visual reticence is a more sophisticated and effective means of creating terror and instead examines other factors that influence its deployment, using *Rosemary's Baby* and *It's Alive* to illustrate his points. *Rosemary's Baby*, Hantke argues, is more interested in exploring the pressures of motherhood and the delusions it may cause the isolated and possibly hysterical Rosemary than it is in the physical being of the antichrist, and this partly explains Polanski's decision to withhold a final visual disclosure of the eponymous child. By contrast, Cohen's *It's Alive*, which features a lethal newborn, is more interested in the way that society responds to monsters that actually exist; therefore, the creature must be displayed. CGI has become refined and inexpensive enough today to be used within even relatively low-budget films, and Hantke concludes his essay by considering the developments that may occur within the monstrous infant subgenre as a result by analyzing two recent films, a 2008 remake of *It's Alive* by Joseph Rusnak and Vincenzo Natali's *Splice* (2009).

If Hantke is interested in the factors that affect how (and if) a monstrous infant is displayed in film, in "Monstrous Children as Harbingers of Mortality: A Psychological Analysis of Doris Lessing's *The Fifth Child*," Daniel Sullivan and Jeff Greenberg are more concerned with why certain infants are perceived as monstrous in the first place. In the novel, Ben, the fifth child of Harriet and David Lovatt, seems more animal than human, not only in his appearance and eating habits, but also in his tendency to inflict harm on those around him. To understand why Ben's particular characteristics prove especially disturbing, both to readers and to his family, Sullivan and Greenberg take an approach informed by their backgrounds in psychology: terror management theory (TMT). A theory that has been validated empirically by experiments, TMT holds that humans are motivated to transcend their mortal limits via various types of "immortality striving"; the two most pertinent to *The Fifth Child*, Sullivan and Greenberg claim, are the biological mode—a drive to produce offspring who will preserve not only their parents' genes and deepest held values—and the cultural mode, a desire to achieve immortality through culturally-validated accomplishments, such as a legacy of artistic achievements or philanthropic deeds. The Lovatts' need to produce a large family— they had aimed to have six children until Ben arrived—in spite of their inability to financially and emotionally handle such a horde and in the face of family disapproval, demonstrates their rejection of the cultural mode of immortality striving in favor of the biological. According to Sullivan and Greenberg, Ben is monstrous because he points out that the Lovatts' immortality striving is ultimately a doomed venture. Not only does Ben's "creatureliness" remind the Lovatts and readers that, like all animals, we will one day die, but he also demolishes his parents' hopes to achieve symbolic immortality through the biological mode: he breaks up their immediate family, disrupts their ties with their extended family, and refuses to function as a vehicle through which the Lovatts could transmit their moral values and beliefs into the future, finding instead a more suitable set of companions in a local biker gang. Thus, Sullivan and Greenberg conclude, Ben is monstrous because, in these various ways, he represents the doomed nature of immortality striving.

Sullivan and Greenberg offer a psychological explanation for why a savage and inassimilable child like Ben could prove monstrous. By contrast, the evil children that William Wandless studies in "Spoil the Child: Unsettling Ethics and the Representation of Evil" are far different in nature. Strange, certainly, but hardly sub-human, the children in the films Wandless scrutinizes—Rob Zombie's 2007 adaptation of John Carpenter's *Halloween* (1978), *Joshua* (2007), *Home Movie* (2008), and *Orphan* (2009)—are psychological and moral abominations whose brand of "evil" frustrates facile psychological explanations. The four movies Wandless considers all offer potential explanations that help viewers dismiss the distressing possibility that an evil child could emerge from "normal" and "healthy" situations, but those provided by *Joshua* and *Home Movie* offer only a modicum of comfort. Zombie's decision to give Michael Myers a dysfunctional childhood *seems* to suggest that the seemingly random acts of violence we know he will later commit as an adult are legible psychological responses to his early experiences. Not all of the murders Michael commits as an adult, though, can be explained as resulting from Michael's childhood experiences: as Wandless points out, Michael kills people whom—according to the film's psychological logic—he should have no desire to murder. However, the brutalities Michael commits as a child are extenuated to a large degree, thus making Zombie's film perhaps "the second most comforting film of the new millennium," according to Wandless. Likewise, the movie *Joshua* initially *seems* to establish family dynamics that, while different from that of Michael Myers, still promise to account for the title character's bizarre and malicious behavior. A cold, distant, and yet uncannily mature child, nine-year-old Joshua appears to get pleasure (or at least satisfaction) from the fact that his new baby sister, Lily— once the apple of her parents' eyes—has become a cantankerous infant, much as he was as a child; there is even evidence that Joshua is inciting Lily's discontent. Even though Joshua proves abnormally devious and cruel—responsible for his mother's descent into madness, his grandmother's death, and his father's false imprisonment for child abuse—viewers initially assume that Joshua's behavior is an extreme version of sibling rivalry And yet at the end of film, what we find is that Joshua actually has been arranging matters so that he can end up with his beloved uncle. That he has a motive at all is comforting; that he also commands the powers of manipulation necessary to get his way is not.

As my earlier description of the children in *Home Movie* made clear, Jack and Emily Poe are much more disturbing figures, killing numerous animals and ultimately murdering and likely cannibalizing their parents. In stark contrast to their gregarious parents, the twins are, even from the beginning, almost entirely devoid of affect and affection except for a brief interlude during which they seem miraculously healed and freely gambol with their parents, behavior later revealed to be a ruse. But while we could diagnose the Poe children as sociopaths and thus attribute their alarming aberrations to psychological disorder, Wandless shows that the film provides reason to believe that their appetite for human flesh may have been inspired by various stimuli to which they were exposed by their parents, especially a bedtime story featuring a dragon who earns the trust of children only to devour them.[31] Even if we decide to attribute their penchant for human fare to misinterpreted cues, we ultimately cannot forget the "performative self-awareness" that the children demonstrated. Wandless concludes his essay with a discussion of *Orphan*, which, he claims, incites none of the anxiety prompted by Joshua or the Poe children, for its evil child Esther is revealed to be a 33-year-old homicidal woman named Lena, a fact that explains away her strange behavior, her sexual interest in her adoptive father, and her hostility toward her mother. In addition, since she is adult, Lena is entirely accountable for her actions, and thus we can cheer for her death at the end of the film without any reservation. For these reasons, *Orphan* is the most reassuring of the four films and perhaps even, as Wandless declares, "the most comforting film of the new millennium."

We might expect evil children to appear in horror films such as those that Wandless studies, but they also have invaded children's literature, as Holly Blackford makes clear in her essay entitled "Private Lessons from Dumbledore's 'Chamber of Secrets': The Riddle of the Evil Child in *Harry Potter and the Half-Blood Prince*." Blackford focuses on Tom Riddle, who, as the child precursor of the evil Lord Voldemort, is defined by many of the wizard adults as innately evil. However, Blackford demonstrates that in many ways Tom is merely a reflection of a "hidden curriculum" that Hogwarts School of Witchcraft and Wizardry refuses to acknowledge. Blackford demonstrates that Tom's tendency to hoard objects, to assemble a questionable group of peers, and to manipulate could all be seen as behaviors encouraged at the school. Tom is thus the embodiment of unacknowledged lessons at Hogwarts that its officials wish to deny; in labeling Tom as evil, teachers and administrators can avoid culpability for the demonic figure he became. Blackford also calls upon queer theory to further explain Tom's development. Noting that Harry displays many of the same characteristics as Tom, she asks why Harry's story is one of success and Tom's that of moral failure. Blackford concludes that the best way to approach *Half-Blood Prince* is to view Tom's narrative as a failed coming-out story that creates "a very closeted monster."

Meheli Sen's "Terrifying Tots and Hapless Homes: Undoing Modernity in Recent Bollywood Cinema" reminds us that interpretations of evil children narratives must take into consideration the conventions of the genre within which the text is situated as well as the status of children within the culture from which the story arises. For that very reason, Sen begins her essay with a brief history of Hindi horror and Bollywood's recent engagement with the genre. Sen takes as her texts three films—*Vaastu Shastra* (2004), *Phoonk* (2008), and *Gauri* (2007). While these films may appear to support the "modern, metropolitan ethos" to which their targeted viewers likely adhere, Sen claims that instead they dismantle it, and children are the site upon which these ideological critiques are constructed. An exemplary possessed child narrative, *Vaastu Shastra* implicitly condemns modern evolutions in the family that leave the child vulnerable to the presence of nefarious forces. In the film, traditional gender roles are reversed: the mother, Dr. Jhilmil Rao, and her live-in sister, Radz, leave the home to work while father, Viraag, acts as primary caretaker to their son, Rohan. By the end of the film, Radz and Viraag are dead and—worse—have become members of the undead horde that haunts the house. While Jhilmil and Rohan survive the onslaught, Rohan's final smile into the camera at the film's conclusion, reminiscent of Damien's smirk at the end of *The Omen*, lets us know that Rohan remains a minion of evil, forever damaged by the lack of traditional family structures.

If *Vaastu Shastra* is ultimately a tragic film, *Phoonk* proves much more optimistic. *Phoonk* precisely illustrates Clover's theory that possession films contain two entwined narratives: the story of the possession and the story of male conversion from White Science to Black Magic. This transformation is exemplified by father and husband, Rajiv, whose daughter's possession forces him to embrace more mystical aspects of his culture which he has hitherto rejected. Of all three films, *Gauri* is the most conservative. The film charts the return of married couple, Sudeep and Roshni, and their daughter, Shivani, to the home in which they lived before Shivani's birth, where they conceived and later decided to abort their first child. Upon arriving at the home, the couple discovers that it is haunted by the ghost of their unborn daughter, who attacks the family and possesses Shivani, whom she threatens to kill. In the end, however, Gauri relents when the family promises to give her the love that the film suggests she rightly deserves. As with *Vaastu Shastra* and *Phoonk*, then, *Gauri* undermines a modern ethos in its anti-abortion stance.

Sara Williams traces similar themes in a more well-known Western text in "'The Power of Christ Compels You': Holy Water, Hysteria, and the Oedipal Psychodrama in *The Exorcist*." Her subject is not the infamous Friedkin film which overtly attributes Regan's possession to a supernatural entity but Blatty's original novel, which, Williams claims, purposefully links Regan's condition to the history of hysteria and the Freudian concept of the Oedipus complex. Williams starts by tracing the study of hysteria from Jean-Martin Charcot's work with his patient Augustine to Sigmund Freud and Josef

Breuer's interactions with Dora and Anna O., respectively. Williams demonstrates that the behavior of Regan while possessed—her unnatural bodily contortions, her sexually-suggestive behavior—bear an uncanny resemblance to those hysterical patients who came before her. But if Regan has deluded herself into believing she is possessed, she is certainly not the only character in the novel who does. Her mother, for one, embraces the supernatural explanation. Williams argues that Chris's beliefs can be explained as an instance of Shared Psychotic Disorder, or *Folie à Deux*. The other priests involved in the case, Merrin and Karras, also have good reason to invest in the idea that Regan is possessed: Merrin has made the defeat of Pazuzu, the specific demon supposedly inhabiting Regan, his life's work, and Karras is having a crisis of faith. Thus, a case of *Folie à Deux* becomes one of *Folie à Plusieurs*, a mass hysteria that seems to have spread to audience members of the film as well, for whom the film, in the words of one critic, "scared" back to church in droves.

As the title of Robin Hoffman's essay "How to See the Horror: The Hostile Fetus in *Rosemary's Baby* and *Alien*" makes clear, her piece shifts us away from the possessed child and toward another significant type: the monstrous unborn. According to Hoffman, in the years surrounding these two films, technological advancements dramatically altered society's sense of the fetus. In 1965, just a few years prior to the release of *Rosemary's Baby* (1968), *Life* magazine published Lennart Nilsson's famous *in vitro* photography series "Drama of Life before Birth." Although this technology would not become available to the average pregnant woman for some time, the event foreshadowed developments in her treatment to come: specifically, her increased subjugation to both her fetus and to the medical professionals who controlled the technology that would increasingly be seen as necessary to ensuring the fetus's wellbeing. The decade leading up to *Alien* (1979) saw the passing of *Roe v. Wade* (1973), the increasing availability of ultrasound technology, and also the birth of the world's first test-tube baby in 1978—thus, even the zygote had become visible, constructed under the eyes of laboratory technicians rather in the womb. Although *Rosemary's Baby* arrived when the prospect of visibility was still an innovation, *Alien* appeared when such technology had become a familiar aspect of life. Hoffman argues that both films address complex reactions to the availability of this new medical technology.

Catherine Fowler and Rebecca Kambuta's essay "Extreme Human Makeovers: *Supernanny*, the Unruly Child, and Adulthood in Crisis" brings us back to a more familiar domestic space. Though the children in *Supernanny* are not as wicked as those we find in quintessential evil child narratives and certainly not supernaturally so, one can hardly deny that they are, as Fowler and Kambuta put it, "tiny terrors." Fowler and Kambuta begin by discussing *Supernanny*'s place within the genre of makeover television. They argue that *Supernanny*, with its supposed focus on family dynamics, appears to differ from other makeover shows more concerned with amending surface appearances—unshapely noses, unflattering wardrobes, or unsuitable home décor—in order to improve people's lives. However, as Fowler and Kambuta point out, *Supernanny* also remains on the surface, fixing children's behavior rather than investigating the root causes of it. This characteristic, among others, makes *Supernanny* very much a member of the makeover genre, the originary show of a third wave of makeover television that Fowler and Kambuta say focuses on renovating relationships via the help of allegedly more knowledgeable authorities, such as the star of *Supernanny*, Jo Frost. Fowler and Kambuta demonstrate that ultimately *Supernanny* proclaims that it is not so much the misbehaving children who need to be madeover but rather their guardians, who have relinquished their parental authority and, in the process, become like children themselves. Bizarrely, *Supernanny* in many ways resembles a possessed child narrative: a terrible force has been allowed to take over the household because of parental shortcomings, but instead of inviting an exorcist, the family consults Jo Frost. Judging by online reviews of the show, though, it seems that some viewers would prefer to struggle with Satan than to face the judgments of a smug British nanny.

CONCLUSION: A NEW TURN TO THE GENRE?

The title of the 1976 film about a pack of homicidal youngsters asked a provocative question, *Who Can Kill A Child?* The question at first seemed rhetorical: by inter-weaving opening credits accompanied by the eerie sound of children singing with shocking footage documenting a variety of wartime atrocities done to children, the movie supplies an obvious answer—well, apparently *lots* of adults can. However, the movie also shows that outside of the world of war, killing a child, regardless of how evil and dangerous he or she may be, is no easy undertaking. In one scene, for example, a father allows his tearful daughter to lead him off by the hand toward the horde of her savage compatriots, even though he is well aware that they have killed all the adults on the island and that he will certainly face the same fate, he simply cannot resist the tug of paternal protectiveness. Violence against children is difficult for both the fictional characters who face this prospect and the audience members who witness the con-sequences of their decisions. Certainly one of the most dangerous weapons that evil children wield are our presumptions of their innocence and reluctance to deal them a fatal blow.[32]

But the protagonists of *Who Can Kill a Child?*—Tom and his pregnant wife, Evelyn —learn from the devoted father's mistake: when a young child threatens to kill Evelyn, Tom shoots him without hesitation. Although both husband and wife are appalled by what Tom has done, the gang of children threatening them temporarily disbands. "Nobody dared to attack a child, to kill one of them," Tom says. "That's why they weren't afraid, but now they are." Other protagonists also kill off the evil children who plague them. In *It Lives Again* (1978), Cohen's sequel to *It's Alive*, parents decide that they must shoot their monstrous newborn when they see him slaughter yet another person. In *The Good Son* (1993), a mother has the choice to save either the nephew she knows to be good or the son she knows to be evil and opts to save her nephew. And in *Pet Sematary*, the father gives his son Gage a lethal injection, even though it was his overwhelming grief over Gage's death that led him to bury the child in the supernatural cemetery in the first place, thereby enabling his unnatural resurrection.

Contemporary films express far greater hesitation about punishing even the vilest child with death. The subtitle of O'Hayre's book, which I mentioned at the beginning of this introduction, tells us, after all, to "*defeat* evil children," a word carefully swab-bed clean of all bloody implications. And yet directors have found ways to have their cake and eat it, too. As Wandless's essay demonstrates, *Orphan* sanctions the pleasure viewers get from watching adopted mother Kate kick Esther in the face and send her to her death by reassuring them that Esther is, in fact, a woman. But Isabelle Fuhrman, the actress who played Esther, was just twelve when the movie *premiered*, and regard-less of how hard the film tries to convince us that she's a grown woman, what we wit-ness is an adult attacking a child.

Other more recent films have found similar ways for us to savor the fatal punishments inflicted on children without any pangs of conscience. In *Case 39* (2010), the main character, Emily kills her villainous foster daughter, Lilith, but her actions are endorsed because Lilith is not really a little girl at all but some sort of demon. Throughout most of the film, however, the demon cloaks itself in Lilith's body, and it is a little girl we see Emily try to kill, and we root her on. *The New Daughter* (2009) unfolds according to a similar logic, but in this film, the daughter, Louisa, is not a demon but rather has been selected to become the queen of a hive of all male, human-sized creatures. Unable to help, all her father, John, can do is watch her descend into stranger and more hostile behavior. In the middle of the film, John encounters another man, Roger Wayne, whose granddaughter suffered a similar fate. Rather than stand idly by, Roger killed the child, he says, because "[s]he wasn't my granddaughter anymore. I had to do it. So will you. . . . A father will do anything for his daughter, even the worst thing." Roger's prediction comes true: John causes an explosion that destroys the hive, Louisa, and himself. Although a very brief moment of CGI confirms that Louisa indeed has become one of the creatures, what we actually *see* for the bulk of the film is a young girl who becomes so evil that the only choice left is to kill her. Films like *Case 39* and *The New Daughter* operate according to the logic that even though it looks like a child, talks like a child, and acts like a child, it really isn't a child at all, and thus violence is warranted. What strikes me as further noteworthy about *Case 39* and *The New Daughter* is that both feature very familiar faces: Renee Zellweger takes on the role of Emily, and Kevin Costner plays the part of John James. Both actors have a history of playing relatively likeable and trustworthy characters and their squeaky clean appearances lend a special authority to the executions they carry out.

Interestingly, these films mirror a conflict embedded in our justice system. Recent Supreme Court decisions that ruled death penalties and life sentences for minors unconstitutional suggest that United States policy toward juvenile criminals, at least at the most official levels, is moving away from punishment and toward rehabilitation.[33] While these decisions may indicate a shift toward leniency, one cannot assume that they reflect public opinion or the attitudes of judges and juries. Jeffrey Fagan, for example, has shown that the number of juveniles serving time in adult jails between 1990 and 2004 rose 208 percent even though juvenile crime decreased dramatically during that time (95). That more minors ended up in jail though fewer were committing crimes can only indicate an increased tendency to punish minors with stricter sentences than juvenile courts allow. Likewise, recent films about evil children have found ways to dispatch them without any qualms. Lilith and Louisa may be unwitting vessels for external sources of evil, but nevertheless these films imply that once the child is corrupted (or has committed a crime), she cannot be redeemed. Death, not rehabilitation, *is* the only option, and the fictional contrivances of the films allow us to witness the acting out of this belief with an entirely clean conscience. Perhaps in an era so entirely child- and family-focused, resentment is being secretly harbored about the expectations that children require never-ending devotion and bring complete fulfillment, and perhaps these films are expressing it.

NOTES

1 In 1874, for example, Jesse Pomeroy was convicted of killing a ten-year-old girl and four-year-old boy; he was 14 at the time of the murders. For discussion of British child murderers, see Loretta Loach's *The Devil's Children*.

2 Numerous articles have been written about the major works in the genre, but I've not yet discovered a book-length study on specifically *evil* children. Some noteworthy single-author studies that contain important discussions include Sabine Büssing's *Aliens in the Home: The Child in Horror Fiction* (1987), Ellen Pifer's *Demon or Doll: Images of the Child in Contemporary Writing and Culture* (2000), and Lynn Schofield Clark's *From Angels to Aliens: Teenagers, the Media, and the Supernatural* (2003), but as their titles suggest, these authors examine child as both demon and doll, angel and alien. Barbara Creed's *The Monstrous-Feminine: Film, Feminism, Psychoanalysis* (1993) also focuses on other matters than evil children, as the title suggests, but her book does examine several important films in the genre, including *Alien* (a film about monstrous births if there ever was one), *The Exorcist* (1973), *The Brood* (1979), and *Carrie* (1974). Evil children also are discussed at some length throughout the introduction of David J. Hogan's *Dark Romance: Sexuality in the Horror Film* (1986) and within his chapter entitled "Turgid Teens," pp. 122–37; in a chapter entitled "It's Alive, I'm Afraid" in David J. Skal's *The Monster Show: A Cultural History of Horror* (1993), pp. 287–306; and in William Paul's *Laughing Screaming: Modern Hollywood Horror and Comedy* (1994), pp. 255–380. Various edited collections, such as Gary Westfahl and George Slusser's *Nursery Realms: Children in the Worlds of Science Fiction, Fantasy, and Horror* (1999) and Steven Bruhm and Natasha Hurley's *Curiouser: On the Queerness of Children* (2004), contain relevant work as well.

3 Bixby's short story became a 1961 episode of *The Twilight Zone*; Golding's novel led to a 1963 movie; and stage and screen versions of *The Bad Seed* appeared in 1954 and 1956, respectively, and the latter was nominated for four Academy Awards. All of these would be revisited again in later years as well: "It's a Good Life" resurfaced in *Twilight Zone: The Movie* (1983) and a sequel entitled "It's Still a Good Life" was included in the first season of a new *Twilight Zone* series (2002–2003); Golding's novel would be adapted again in 1990; and a made-for-television version of *The Bad Seed* starring Lynn Redgrave and David Carradine aired in 1985. That all of these texts have seen multiple film adaptations suggests that these narratives—and the evil children they involve—struck a resounding chord that has reverberated across time.

4 While *Rosemary's Baby* was nominated for Best Adapted Screenplay and Ruth Gordon received an Oscar for her supporting role as Minnie Castevet, *The Exorcist* easily surpassed that success with eight nominations and two Academy Awards.

5 I have yet to view it for myself, but the description on Netflix, which remarks that *Seytan's* "highlights include the green-vomit scene, which has been transformed to a mustard-spitting sequence, and a demonic voice that sounds more like a drunken pirate than Satan," suggests that this film is hardly a flattering homage.

6 The book is out of print and hard to find, but the cover proclaims that the story is about "a child accursed" who summons the protagonist to "a house of terror—and an appointment with death!"

7 In the 1980s, Koontz penned *Twilight* (1984), later re-released as *The Servants of Twilight* (1990) and made into a film the next year. The novel and film portray a child suspected of being the antichrist.

8 Featuring children who are both victims of and portals for evil, Saul's almost annual contributions during this period include *Suffer the Children* (1977), *Punish the Sinners* (1978), *Cry for the Strangers* (1979), *Comes the Blind Fury* (1980), *When the Wind Blows* (1981), *The God Project* (1982), *Nathaniel* (1984), *Brainchild* (1985), *The Unwanted* (1987), and *Second Child* (1990). The titles of Neiderman's novels—*Brainchild* (1981), *Child's Play* (1985), *Imp* (1985), *Perfect Little Angels* (1989), *Playmates* (1987), *Teacher's Pet* (1986), *Surrogate Child* (1988), *Unholy Birth* (2007)—proclaim his similar interests. Though Ruby Jean Jensen began her prolific writing career in the 1970s, her most notable works in this genre are *Hear the Children Cry* (1981), *Such a Good Baby* (1982), *Best Friends* (1985), *Jump Rope* (1988), *Vampire Child* (1990), *Lost and Found* (1990), *The Reckoning* (1992), and *The Living Evil*

(1993). Jensen is also responsible for contributions to the "evil doll" genre, which became popular during this time and which bears an obvious connection to evil children. Jensen's *Mama* (1983), *Annabelle* (1987), *Victoria* (1990), and *Baby Dolly* (1991) likely inspired such films as *Dolly Dearest* (1992), *Demonic Toys* (1992), and, of course, a series of films featuring the most famous evil doll of all—Chucky. Since *Child's Play's* appearance in 1988, four sequels have been produced, and there have been rumours of a remake.

9 See, for example, Errickson's entries entitled "*Pin* by Andrew Neiderman (1981): The Kids Want Something to Do," "*Tricycle* by Russell Rhodes (1983): Out of His Way, Mister, You Best Keep," "William W. Johnstone: The Paperback Covers," "Ruby Jean Jensen: The Paperback Covers," and "*The Next* by Bob Randall (1981): Mommy, Can I Go Out and Kill Tonight?" The URL for Errickson's blog is http://toomuchhorrorfiction.blogspot.com/.

10 In one particularly memorable episode, "Scott Tenorman Must Die," Cartman takes revenge on the title character, who throughout the episode has humiliated him in various ways. Cartman ultimately wins the duel between them by killing Scott's parents and mixing their corpses in with a vat of chili, a portion of which he offers to Scott. When Scott begins to eat, Cartman asks, "Do you like it? Do you like it, Scott? I call it, 'Mr. and Mrs. Tenorman Chili.'" Scott paws through the bowl, only to find a finger with his mother's wedding ring still on it. Realizing what Cartman has done, Scott breaks down into hysterical tears, and Cartman begins licking the tears from Scott's face, exclaiming, "Oh, let me taste your tears, Scott. Mmm. Your tears are so yummy and sweet."

11 Thanks to Gregory Colón Semenza for pointing this out.

12 See, for example, "Prodigy" (Season 3, Episode 13, 8 Jan. 2002), "Juvenile" (Season 4, Episode 9, 22 Nov. 2002), "Damaged" (Season 4, Episode 11, 10 Jan. 2003), "Soulless" (Season 4, Episode 25, 16 May 2003), "Mean" (Season 5, Episode 17, 24 Feb. 2004), "Sick" (Season 5, Episode 19, 30 Mar. 2004), "Conscience" (Season 6, Episode 6, 9 Nov. 2004), "Game" (Season 6, Episode 14, 8 Feb. 2005), "Web" (Season 7, Episode 21, 9 May 2006), and "Unorthodox" (Season 9, Episode 13, 15 Jan. 2008).

13 The examples are endless. The first of the six *Silent Hill* games, which appeared in 1999, features "grey children," child-like monsters who carry small knives and attack the player's avatar, and one possible ending to the game involves a monstrous, demonic birth. *American McGee's Alice* (2000) transforms Lewis Carroll's character into a young girl wielding a butcher knife, whose apron is splattered with blood. The covers of *F.E.A.R.* (2005) and *F.E.A.R. 2: Project Origin* (2009) display a creepy little girl with dark hair hanging in her face; this character, Alma, menaces players throughout the game. In *Bioshock* (2007) and *Bioshock II* (2010), players must decide whether to "harvest" or rescue the Little Sisters they encounter, genetically-altered little girls who have been trained to extract a valuable substance called ADAM from corpses and who are guarded by destructive Big Daddies, humans in armored diving suits. A third video game in the series is scheduled for 2013. A society of girls named the Red Crayon Aristocrats terrorizes players in *Rule of Rose* (2006), and in *Limbo* (2010), small shadowy children take inventive measures to try to kill the main character as he navigates through a series of dangerous and puzzling obstacles.

14 Collins's trilogy consists of *The Hunger Games* (2008), *Catching Fire* (2009), and *Mockingjay* (2010). See also, for example, Lynn Reid Banks's *Angela and Diabola* (1997) and Nancy Farmer's *The House of the Scorpion* (2002).

15 Later in the novel, we discover that these are not Rhoda's first murders. Not only did she push a puppy out her window when caring for it interfered with playtime, but she also shoved an elderly woman down the stairs in order to claim the opal pendant that the woman has promised her in her will.

16 For a succinct and helpful overview of criticism on *The Turn of the Screw*, see "A Critical History of *The Turn of the Screw*" in the most recent Bedford edition of the novella, edited by Peter G. Beidler.

17 Such critics point out that at the time of the novel's publication, ghosts were taken so seriously that formal societies had been formed to study the phenomenon systematically. James's preface to the 1908 edition of the story alludes to these "factual" reports of ghosts and describes the ghostly characters of his tale as supernatural rather than psychological entities. The pervasive belief in ghosts was not merely a background cultural influence for James: his brother William, the eminent psychologist, was an active participant in the field.

18 For these reasons, Gary Hoppenstand has argued that Regan functions "as a type of moral symbol warning of the dire consequences of an evolving family structure" resulting from a "rising divorce rate and the [putative] drawbacks of single-parent household" (38).

19 I have simplified the storylines of these films considerably in order to avoid giving away certain plot twists, but the general point still remains.

20 See Buckingham for discussion of the blame placed upon the film *Child's Play 3* for instigating ten-year olds Robert Thompson and Jon Venables to kill two-year-old James Bulger in 1993. In 1996, the death metal band Slayer was sued by the parents of murder victim Elyse Pahler after one of the killers claimed that Elyse's "sacrifice" was inspired by one of Slayer's songs; see Weiner. See Leavy for an explanation of how and why the Columbine shootings in 1999 were linked to, among other factors, singer Marilyn Manson, the video game *Doom*, and the movie *The Matrix* (1999). The video game *Grand Theft Auto* has also been implicated in the trials of several child murderers; see Leung.

21 For a history of Genie and feral children in general, see Michael Newton's *Savage Boys and Wild Girls*. For discussion of one of the more recent discoveries of a feral child, see Lane DeGregory's article on Danielle Crockett.

22 In Collodi's novel, Pinocchio is much more mean-spirited, at least until he learns how to be a "real" boy. In fact, when the Cricket tells Pinocchio that he needs to go to school to learn a trade, Pinocchio retorts that the only trade that fancies him is "[t]o eat, drink, sleep, and amuse [him]self, and to lead a vagabond life from morning to night" (27). The Cricket then says that he pities him for having a wooden head, and Pinocchio throws a hammer at him. Collodi's following description allows for the act to have been accidental, but stresses its brutality as well: "Perhaps he never meant to hit him; but unfortunately it struck him exactly on the head . . ., and then he remained dried up and flattened against the wall" (27). Yet by the end of the book, Pinocchio has successfully transformed into a good boy, suggesting that savagery is a natural part of child development, a claim that would be affirmed by psychologist G. Stanley Hall in *Adolescence* (1904).

23 This was true only for white boys from the West, of course. Tarzan, who sounded his first barbaric yawp in 1912, affirmed author Edgar Rice Burrough's sense that the civilized races were naturally superior to all others: as Gail Bederman has made clear, it was because Tarzan was originally an "aristocratic Anglo-Saxon [that he] always triumphs over beasts and savage black Africans" (222). See also Kenneth Kidd's *Making American Boys: Boyology and the Feral Tale*.

24 In *28 Days Later*, the protagonist fends off and then only reluctantly kills a frenzied boy zombie. A similar scene occurs in the Spanish film *REC* (2007) and its faithful American adaptation, *Quarantine* (2008), when a young girl, clearly infected with a mutated rabies virus that reduces people into a zombie-like condition, bites her mother's face and runs upstairs. When she is discovered, the police officer leading the group still approaches her as if she is an innocent child. His inability to view her as anything other than a sweet girl allows her to attack him viciously.

25 This is not to say that all vampire children fit the mold of the feral child. Claudia in *Interview with the Vampire*, for example, kills in a very controlled manner and is civilized enough to fit into polite society even when still a young vampire. Similarly, Eli, the vampire in *Let the Right One In* (2008) and the American rendition *Let Me In* (2010), very successfully acts the part of the twelve-year-old girl she appears to be – unless she hasn't fed in several days or is in the presence of blood – solving a Rubik's cube and leaving affectionate notes that incorporate Shakespearean references. Both characters are also developed in a way that is uncharacteristic of the feral child.

26 In fact, as the protagonist of the story Burt discovers, most of the New Testament has been expurgated from the Bible the children use, but "the Old Testament was intact" (267). In addition, the children's church includes a portrait of Christ that "looked like a comic-strip mural done by a gifted child—an Old Testament Christ, or a pagan Christ that might slaughter his sheep for sacrifice instead of leading them" (266).

27 Through a ludicrous plot contrivance, this mantra leads the main characters of the film to discover the origins of Grendel, the leader, for one recognizes in the chant the device of Anglo-Saxon alliteration and directs the investigators to *Beowulf*. The chant also obviously

bears a close resemblance to that used in the most famous feral child narrative, *Lord of the Flies*, in which the hunters intone, *"Kill the beast! Cut his throat! Spill his blood!"* (135).

28 *The Plague* explicitly connects the condition of its zombie children to adult perfidy. At the end of the film, as the protagonist and his ex-wife face a hostile gang of the children, he realizes that the corruption of the adult world is ultimately responsible for their condition —"It's not just what we say and do. . . . It's everything we are. Everything we think and feel. That's what they take from us," he tells her—and willingly offers himself up as a sacrifice. As a result, the children allow her to live.

29 See Tony Magistrale's "Inherited Haunts: Stephen King's Terrible Children" and "Stephen King's Viet Nam Allegory: An Interpretation of 'The Children of the Corn.'"

30 At the end of *Beware! Children at Play*, a group of vigilantes from town shoot all of the Woodies, regardless of age, without much hesitation, even though such an action is protested by the protagonist. As with the ending of *Night of the Living Dead*, this conclusion seems to suggest that the Woodies are no more horrible than the adults. In *Offspring*, the cruelty of the savage clan is juxtaposed with that of a "civilized" character, Stephen, who is willing to offer up his ex-wife and children to save his own skin. *Eden Lake* also shows that the members of the young gang are from households in which violence and abuse is common. The French film *Them* (2006) is perhaps one exception to this rule. Like *The Strangers* (2008), it features a group of youths who terrorize a couple simply because they seem to enjoy doing so, though *Them* is considerably more disturbing since the children are markedly younger.

31 Of course, in doing so, the viewer must assume that the story inspired their cannibalistic tendencies, not that it appealed because it reflected their already deepest desires and instincts.

32 In *The Omen*, Damien's adopted father, Robert Thorn, is just about to kill the adopted son he knows to be the antichrist, but the sight of the boy squirming and begging for his life causes him to hesitate long enough for the police to shoot him before he can complete his mission to save the world. As a result, Damien continues his reign of terror for two more sequels, whereupon his daughter Delia takes over in *Omen IV: The Awakening*, and in 2006, Damien was resurrected for a remake and started all over again. One can only wish that Robert would have been more decisive. At the end of the French film *Them* (2006), the female protagonist refuses to smash a boy's head with a rock, even though his gang has been terrorizing her and her husband for an entire night; in fact, she just witnessed this particular boy cause her husband's death. However, when the boy covers his face with his hands and exclaims, "Don't hit me! I didn't do anything! We just want to play," she drops the rock and instead tries to escape. She fails.

33 *Roper v. Simmons* (2005) banned death sentences and *Graham v. Florida* (2010) life sentences for crimes committed by juveniles.

WORKS CITED

Barrie, J. M. *Peter and Wendy*. 1911. Peter Pan: Peter and Wendy *and* Peter Pan in Kensington Gardens. Ed. Jack Zipes. New York: Penguin, 2004.

Bederman, Gail. *Manliness and Civilization: A Cultural History of Gender and Race in the United States, 1880–1917*. Chicago: U of Chicago P, 1996. Print.

Beidler, Peter G. "A Critical History of *The Turn of the Screw*." *The Turn of the Screw*. Case Studies in Contemporary Criticism. Ed. Peter G. Beidler. Boston: Bedford/St. Martin's, 2010. Print.

Beware! Children at Play. Dir. Mik Cribben. 1989. Troma, 1998. DVD.

Bixby, Jerome. "It's a Good Life." 1953. *Science Fiction Hall of Fame: The Greatest Science Fiction Stories of all Time*. Ed. Robert Silverberg. New York: Avon, 1970. 523–42. Print.

Blatty, William Peter. *The Exorcist*. 1971. New York: Harper Paperbacks, 1994. Print.

Bradbury, Ray. "The Small Assassin." 1946. *The Stories of Ray Bradbury*. New York: Knopf, 1980. 372–86. Print.

——. "The Veldt." 1950. *American Gothic Tales*. Ed. Joyce Carol Oates. New York: Plume, 1996. 264–77. Print.

Bruhm, Steven, and Natasha Hurley, eds. *Curiouser: On the Queerness of Children*. Minneapolis: U of Minnesota P, 2004. Print.

Buckingham, David. "Child's Play: Beyond Moral Panics." *Moving Images: Understanding Children's Emotional Responses to Television*. Manchester: Manchester UP, 1996. 19–56. Print.

Büssing, Sabine. *Aliens in the Home: The Child in Horror Fiction*. Contributions to the Study of Childhood and Youth. Vol. 4. New York: Greenwood P, 1987. Print.

Case 39. Dir. Christian Alvert. 2010. Paramount, 2011. DVD.

Clark, Lynn Schofield. *From Angels to Aliens: Teenagers, the Media, and the Supernatural*. New York: Oxford UP, 2003. Print.

Clover, Carol. *Men, Women, and Chainsaws*. Princeton: Princeton UP, 1992. Print.

Collodi, Carlo. *Pinocchio: The Story of a Puppet*. 1883. Philadelphia: J. P. Lippincott, 1914. *Google Books*. Web. 28 Feb. 2011.

Creed, Barbara. *The Monstrous-Feminine: Film, Feminism, Psychoanalysis*. New York: Routledge, 1993. Print.

Cull, Nick. "*The Exorcist*." *History Today* 50.5 (May 2000): 46–51. PDF File.

DeGregory, Lane. "The Girl in the Window." *Tampabay.com*. St. Petersburg Times, 31 July 2008. Web. 31 May 2011.

Eden Lake. Dir. James Watkins. 2008. Weinstein Company, 2009. DVD.

Emerson, Ralph Waldo. "Self-Reliance." 1841. *Emerson: Essays and Lectures*. New York: Library of America, 1983. 257–82. Print.

Errickson, Will. "*The Next* by Bob Randall (1981): Mommy, Can I Got Out and Kill Tonight?" *Too Much Horror Fiction*. 7 June 2010. Web. 7 Mar. 2011.

——. "*Pin* by Andrew Neiderman (1981): The Kids Want Something to Do." *Too Much Horror Fiction*. 18 Nov. 2010. Web. 7 Mar. 2011.

——. "Ruby Jean Jensen: The Paperback Covers." *Too Much Horror Fiction*. 16 Aug. 2010. Web. 7 Mar. 2011.

——. "*Tricycle* by Russell Rhodes (1983): Out of His Way, Mister, You Best Keep." *Too Much Horror Fiction*. 26 Oct. 2010. Web. 7 Mar. 2011.

——. "William W. Johnstone: The Paperback Covers." *Too Much Horror Fiction*. 23 Sept. 2010. Web. 7 Mar. 2011.

Fagan, Jeffrey. "Juvenile Crime and Criminal Justice: Resolving Border Disputes." *The Future of Children* 18 (Fall 2008): 81–118. *JSTOR*. Web. 31 Dec. 2010.

Golding, William. "Fable." *The Hot Gates and Other Occasional Pieces*. New York: Harcourt, 1966. 85–101. Print.

——. *Lord of the Flies*. 1954. New York: Penguin, 1999. Print.

Hogan, David J. *Dark Romance: Sexuality in the Horror Film*. Jefferson: McFarland, 1986. Print.

Hoppenstand, Gary. "Exorcising the Devil Babies: Images of Children and Adolescents in the Best-Selling Horror Novel." *Images of the Child*. Ed. Harry Edwin Eiss. Bowling Green, OH: Bowling Green U Popular P, 1994. 35–58. Print.

Hughes, Richard. *A High Wind in Jamaica*. 1929. New York: New York Review of Books, 1999. Print.

The Innocents. Dir. Jack Clayon. 1961. Twentieth Century Fox, 2005. DVD.

James, Henry. *The Turn of the Screw*. 1898. Boston: Bedford/St. Martin's, 2010. 22–120. Print.

Kidd, Kenneth B. *Making American Boys: Boyology and the Feral Tale*. Minneapolis: U of Minnesota P, 2004. Print.

King, Stephen. "Children of the Corn." 1977. *Night Shift*. New York: Signet, 1979. 250–78. Print.

Leavy, Patricia. *Iconic Events: Media, Politics, and Power in Retelling History*. Lexington Books, 2007. Print.

Leung, Rebecca. "Can a Video Game Lead to Murder?" *CBSnews.com*. CBS Interactive, 11 Feb. 2009. Web. 31 May 2010.

Loach, Loretta. *The Devil's Children: A History of Childhood and Murder*. London: Icon, 2009. Print.

Magistrale, Tony. "Inherited Haunts: Stephen King's Terrible Children." *Extrapolation* 26 (1985): 43–49. Print.

——. "Stephen King's Viet Nam Allegory: An Interpretation of 'The Children of the Corn.'" *Cuyahoga Review* 2 (1984): 61–66. Print.

Matheson, Richard. "Born of Man and Woman." *The Dark Descent*. Ed. David G. Hartwell. New York: Tor, 1987. 513–15. Print.

Maynard, Joyce. "The Monster Children." *Newsweek* 26 July 1976: 10–11. PDF File.

The New Daughter. Dir. Luis Berdejo. 2009. Anchor Bay, 2010. DVD.

Newton, Michael. *Savage Girls and Wild Boys: A History of Feral Children*. 2002. New York: Picador, 2004. Print.

Oates, Joyce Carol. *Expensive People*. 1968: New York: Modern Library, 2006. Print.

Offspring. Dir. Andrew van den Houten. Lionsgate, 2009. DVD.

O'Hayre, Meredith. *The Scream Queen's Survival Guide: Avoid Machetes, Defeat Evil Children, Steer Clear of Bloody Dismemberment, and Conquer Other Horror Movie Clichés*. Avon, MA: F+W Media, 2010. Print.

Paul, William. *Laughing, Screaming: Modern Hollywood Horror and Comedy*. New York: Columbia UP, 1994. Print.

Pifer, Ellen. *Demon or Doll: Images of the Child in Contemporary Writing and Culture*. Charlottesville: UP of Virginia, 2000. Print.

The Plague. Dir. Hal Masonberg. Sony, 2006. DVD.

Rice, Anne. *Interview with the Vampire*. 1976. New York: Ballantine, 1997. Print.

"Scott Tenorman Must Die." *South Park*. Comedy Central. 11 July 2001. Television.

"Seytan." *Netflix*. Web. 8 Mar. 2011.

Skal, David J. *The Monster Show: A Cultural History of Horror*. New York: Norton, 1993. Print.

Them. Dir. David Moreau and Xavier Palud. 2006. Dark Sky Films, 2008. DVD.

Thirty Days of Night. Dir. David Slade. 2007. Sony, 2008. DVD.

"Tom Shankland Talks the Children." *Dreadcentral.com*. Dread Central Media, 6 Oct. 2009. Web. 15 May 2011.

Weiner, Allison Hope. "Facing the Music." *EW.com*. Entertainment Weekly, 24 Aug. 2001. Web. 18 May 2011.

Westfahl, Gary, and George Slusser, eds. *Nursery Realms: Children in the Worlds of Science Fiction, Fantasy, and Horror*. Athens: U of Georgia P, 1999. Print.

Who Can Kill a Child? Dir. Narciso Ibáñez Serrador. 1976. Dark Sky Films, 2007. DVD.

My Baby Ate the Dingo: The Visual Construction of the Monstrous Infant in Horror Film

STEFFEN HANTKE

INTRODUCTION: MAGGIE, STEWIE, AND OTHER PREPOSTEROUS MONSTROUS INFANTS

Among the many horror films that feature "evil children," a small cycle of films deal specifically with monstrous, murderous, carnivorous, predatory infants—babies that, rather than being eaten by the proverbial dingo, turn the tables on a harsh and hostile world by preying on those who conventionally prey on them. While the larger cycle of films with a child in the role of the monster has produced numerous horror classics—highly respected films even outside the genre, ranging from Mervyn LeRoy's *The Bad Seed* (1954) and Wolf Rilla's *Village of the Damned* (1960), to Jack Clayton's *The Innocents* (1961), William Friedkin's *The Exorcist* (1973), Nicholas Roeg's *Don't Look Now* (1973), Richard Donner's *The Omen* (1976), David Cronenberg's *The Brood* (1979), and, more recently, Tomas Alfredson's *Let the Right One in* (2008) and Vincenzo Natali's *Splice* (2009)—the smaller sub-cycle of horror films about monstrous newborns has remained as limited in size as in reputation. With the notable exception of Roman Polanski's *Rosemary's Baby* (1968), the other entries in the cycle are decidedly marginal in terms of budget and prestige: Donald Cammel's *Demon Seed* (1977), Larry Cohen's *It's Alive* (1974), with its two sequels (1978, 1987) and a recent remake directed by Josef Rusnak (2008), and Rodman Flender's *The Unborn* (1991).[1] As a thematic adjunct to these few films, which form the core of the subgenre, we should also consider the sizable body of horror films in which aspects of procreative sexuality—from conception, pregnancy, and childbirth to early parenthood—are used figuratively, as visual or topical metaphors of monstrosity; one might think of the elaborate procreative mythology developed throughout the films in the *Alien* franchise, with their perverse oral inseminations and explosively lethal births. Films that deal directly and literally with monstrous babies, however, are few and far between.[2]

At first glance, this is surprising. To the same degree that horror films succeed in transforming children of all ages into frightening creatures, why would films dealing with newborns rather than, say, five-year-olds, perform this task so much less successfully? From Christian doctrines of natural depravity, which suspect the newborn in its cradle to be "seething with sin," to Freud's view of "the newborn as a 'seething cauldron'—an inherently selfish creature" (Shaffer 39), cultural conventions have laid an ideological foundation for understanding early infancy that plays into the hands of the horror genre, especially if one considers the degree of surplus repression by which infants have been sentimentally transformed, concurrently, into paragons of innocence and cordoned-off sites of extreme anxiety.[3] Dominant contemporary conceptions of the infant's body privilege it as a site upon which external forces impinge, a passive, docile, inert object, incapable of action yet constantly acted upon. Horror films reverse this conception—in fact, monstrous infants in horror films command alarming degrees of agency. In the reversal, they liberate the repressed archaic notions of the infant as a seething cauldron of aggression, selfishness, and sin—a notion which, like everything we pride ourselves on having "overcome" and cast off, returns in frightening, demonic guise.[4]

Nonetheless, within the public consciousness, films about monstrous infants are often indistinguishable from their own parodies. For a variety of reasons, there seems to be something inherently ridiculous about a baby as monster. Take, for instance, the episode of *The Simpsons*, entitled "A Streetcar Named Marge," in which baby Maggie has led an uprising of infants at her daycare center, heroically retrieving everyone's pacifiers from a grouchy attendant (Season 4, Episode 2). When Homer arrives to pick her up, he discovers that the babies have taken over the facility. He must tread carefully in between scores of impassive infants, the sucking sounds of their pacifiers grotesquely enhanced against a backdrop of ominous silence; on one occasion, a baby weakly paws at his shoe when nudged as if to suggest the potential infant fury waiting to be unleashed. By way of the intertextual projection of the final sequence of Hitchcock's *The Birds* onto a group of infants, the humor in the scene derives from the lack of proportionality between the ominous threat of predatory animals before the moment of attack on the one hand and a group of toddlers happily sucking on their binkies on the other.[5]

While the satire in *The Simpsons* is relatively gentle and largely a matter of limited intertextual play, Seth McFarlane's animated series *Family Guy*

(Fox, 1999-), with its recurring character Stewie Griffin, goes to much greater lengths to explore the comedic potential inherent in the figure of the monstrous baby. Cleverly depicting Stewie as alternating between infantile and fully adult characteristics, the show's writers frequently depart into intertextual asides during which he is cast as a serial killer, a Chicago mobster, a member of the Brat Pack, a science fiction mutant, and so on. Unlike Maggie Simpson, who is turned into an uncanny creature by way of intertextual superimposition, Stewie Griffin functions as a fully conscious engine of cultural disambiguation. Those negative concepts about early infancy which might have been moved into the collective cultural unconscious (e.g., the infant's aggression and sexual fixation on its mother, its polymorphously perverse sexuality, its anti-social selfishness, etc.) are constantly and explicitly articulated in the show's surface text. Stewie Griffin provides a form of satire that demystifies the cultural dynamics of the monstrous infant to the degree that it shares the show's general approach to sublimation, i.e., to shock or startle by saying out loud the very thing that, when concealed by genuine repression or merely by decorum, retains the charisma of the dangerous and illicit.[6] Consequently, when it comes to Stewie, *Family Guy* undermines the uncanny effect the monstrous infant possesses by articulating openly why Stewie wants what he wants. *Family Guy*'s approach to early infancy depends upon and, in equal measure, generates and confirms a sense that the monstrous infant is ultimately a preposterous figure—a subject for satire rather than horror films.

While this explanation may sound persuasive in its broader application, it fails to account for the fact that, among the few films that constitute the cycle about monstrous infants, only *Rosemary's Baby*—a well respected canonical horror film if there ever was one—seems to have transcended the debilitating yet inescapable inherent preposterousness of its subject matter. While Cammel's *Demon Seed*, Cohen's *It's Alive*, and Flender's *The Unborn* are, by and large, dismissed as camp and banished to the margins of the genre's cinematic canon, Polanski's film commands respect even outside the horror film community. *Rosemary's Baby* raises a number of questions: are all horror films about monstrous infants preposterous and thus doomed to a shadowy existence in the cultural margins? Or is the success or failure of a horror film about monstrous infants a matter of intelligence and skillful execution? In order to untangle these questions, I would like to take a closer look at the core texts within this small sub-cycle of films, especially at the cinematic iconography they mobilize and the ways in which they visualize the infant body, a body densely encoded through cultural interdictions and taboos. A critical examination of the visual strategies brought into play during the cinematic representation of this body will, I hope, provide insights into the larger representational politics at work when horror film takes on a subject matter that is, simultaneously, as serious and preposterous as the monstrous, predatory infant. The most efficient way into the minutiae of these films is to look at the climactic closing scene in the key film of the cycle—the final few minutes of Polanski's *Rosemary's Baby*—released to great popular and critical acclaim in 1968.[7]

"WHAT HAVE YOU DONE TO HIS EYES?": SEEING IS BELIEVING

In this closing sequence of the film, Mia Farrow's eponymous character, alerted to the presence of an infant in the neighboring apartment, enters a room in which all those who have conspired to have her impregnated with the devil's own child are gathered. In an alcove by the window, fussed over by a viciously protective elderly woman, stands a cradle draped in black from which the crying of a fussy baby emanates. Rosemary goes over and peeks inside, only to be startled by a sight Polanski decides to withhold from his audience. Instead of a reverse-angle shot or a downward camera tilt, which would reveal what Rosemary sees, the film provides a medium close-up of Rosemary backing away from the cradle in horror asking, "What have you done to his eyes?" Having raised the audience's curiosity with this conspicuous visual ellipsis—we want to see what causes this paroxysm of fear—Polanski follows the moment with a lengthy sequence of shots in which the assembled group of Satanists reassures the distraught mother that "He has his father's eyes," that is to say, yes, the child is not her husband's but that of the devil himself. "Look at his hands," one of them prompts. "Or at his feet," another chimes in. Disregarding these visual prompts ("Look at . . . "), the camera instead follows Rosemary, observing her mounting hysteria as she staggers around the room in a state of shock. Finally, in a medium frontal shot, Farrow raises her hands to her eyes, and only then does Polanski provide a superimposed image which shows, in a blurry extreme close-up double exposure, the same pair of yellow eyes, surrounded by mottled grayish skin that were visible during the sequence in which Rosemary barely registers, in a drug-induced haze, that she is being raped by the demonic creature in the guise of her husband that is to be the father of her child.[8]

The most striking feature of this scene is the curious visual restraint Polanski exercises when he withholds the sight of the monstrous infant the audience has been anticipating for most of the film. After all, the sight of this baby would let us determine whether Rosemary is delusional or whether there really is a Satanist conspiracy. While the decision to never let the audience see Rosemary's eponymous baby is a deliberate attempt to frustrate expectations, the visual ellipsis also functions paradoxically as a confirmation of the crucial significance of the (withheld) visual experience. In other words, the most important thing is what we do not see. It is this conspicuous visual gap in the fabric of the diegesis on which the entire narrative ultimately hinges—a fact driven home by the curious overdetermination of the scene, the densely layered presence of a variety of discourses that all converge upon this crucial moment.[9]

The most obvious explanation for why Polanski never allows the audience to see Rosemary's baby is a straightforward diegetic one. What Polanski substitutes for an unobstructed shot of the monstrous infant—visualizing what we already know as his abnormal eyes, hands, and feet—is a repetition of the superimposition we see during the earlier scene in which the child is conceived. Significantly enough, the repeated use of the image at this moment fails, in the final instance, to disambiguate the events mimetically; just as the Satanists may simply be a group of deluded eccentrics, Rosemary's rape fantasies, as well as her abhorrence of what she perceives as the infant's physical abnormality, may simply be the product of a heightened state of hysteria, which the film reproduces on a visual level, marking the images as subjective by their lack of clarity and persistence and their unmooring from the diegesis. In other words, whatever bodily abnormality the film shows exists in Rosemary's mind; we never see the monstrous infant because there *is* no monstrous infant.

This cognitive dimension of the film is also reiterated in Rosemary's panicky prompt, "What have you done to his eyes?" It is hardly difficult to see this statement as a self-reflexive move on Polanski's part. To the degree that the film is concerned with the difference between the empirical veracity of events as distinct from their subjective perception and interpretation—a difference which translates into the paranoid plot that asks the audience to decide whether Rosemary really is the target of a satanic conspiracy or whether her imagination is getting the better of her—it asks its viewers to examine the visual evidence placed before them. As we test the boundaries of our own credulity, Polanski asks us to indulge, to one degree or another, in the same hysterical hyper-interpretive mode as Rosemary herself.

This explanation, grounded pragmatically in the narrative and thematic logic of the film, fits in with considerations of Polanski as auteurist filmmaker. To the degree that *Rosemary's Baby* is ultimately the story of an isolated single protagonist sequestered in an apartment in which she quietly yet inexorably goes insane, the film reiterates a thematic constant Polanski has been pursuing in other films, most notably *Repulsion* (1965) and *The Tenant* (1976). Both films explore just this central thematic conceit—the individual isolated within the larger community of the apartment building and the city surrounding it—suggesting that the domestic space is especially confining and debilitating to women.[10] In the context of these overarching concerns in Polanski's work, it would appear that the film's psychologizing of Rosemary's troubled marriage to her husband Guy, as well as her ambivalence toward her pregnancy, transfers the child's demonic nature and monstrous appearance from empirical truth to neurotic/hysterical symptom. The very fact that we never see the monstrous infant allows us to determine, as observers outside the grasp of Rosemary's distorting hysteria, the state of her troubled mind, by way of recognizing the cause of her rejection of the infant in the sexual trauma that occurs during the act of conception.

But then again, as idiosyncratic as Polanski's reasons as an auteurist film-maker might be in withholding the sight of Rosemary's baby from the viewer, they are also perfectly attuned to the conventions of the horror film. This applies not only to the baby only making an appearance within the final few minutes of the narrative, the lion's share of which is devoted to the pregnancy and the period preceding it during which Guy and Rosemary are trying to conceive. It also applies to the broader use of visual strategies that withhold the monster from the audience's view. *Rosemary's Baby* is a perfect example of what Noël Carroll has called the "complex discovery plot" underlying many horror films—a narrative model in which a lengthy period of intense paranoia (driven by, on the one hand, the cognitive uncertainty whether a threat exists or not and, on the other hand, the delayed collective social confirmation of the lone protagonist's suspicion that, yes, the threat does exist) leads up to a crucial scene in which, in a moment of open confrontation with the monster, its very existence is finally and undeniably confirmed.[11] Bluntly put, horror films tend to make us wait for the monster, just as they tend to grow less and less coy about displaying the monster. Even though the monster in *Rosemary's Baby* is Rosemary's baby, Polanski's film abides by the rules of its chosen genre, treating the infant in the same manner James Whale treats Boris Karloff in *Frankenstein* and Elsa Lancaster in *The Bride of Frankenstein*, Ishiro Honda treats Godzilla, Steven Spielberg treats the shark in *Jaws*, or Jan DeBont treats CGI tornadoes in *Twister* (a monster if there ever was one).

For further discussion, it is important to note here that the horror film's idiosyncrasy of making the audience wait for the monster stems from a dialectic of practical expediency and deliberate ideology. For example, as the Universal horror films from the 1930s demonstrate, the classic Hollywood style demands full visibility, fetishizing the monster within the overarching discourse of stardom, the product of both actors like Karloff, Lugosi, or Chaney and make-up designers like Jack Pierce. Overdetermined by this discourse, the monster's entry into the film became a matter of strategic delay early on. Aside from the monster's "star entrance," however, visual reticence—a term that will figure prominently in the discussion to come—is also grounded in the practical inability to showcase a monster convincing enough to match audience expectations inflated by prolonged periods of anticipation. The best example here might be Val Lewton's series of classic horror films produced for RKO in the 1940s, which are frequently cited as having made a stylistic virtue of their minuscule budgets by keeping the monsters they had no money to manufacture almost entirely invisible. Cognitive uncertainty *can be* but does not *have to be* a thematic corollary of this strategy. Visual reticence as it appears within the dynamics of post-classical horror films, like the ones discussed here, must be understood as the complex product of expedience, ideology, and tradition.

Nonetheless, common wisdom about horror films has it that films which refuse to show the monster tend to terrorize their audiences more effectively than films that do. Our imaginations, so the story goes, conjure up monsters far more frightening us than any creature that writers, directors, and special effects wizards could possibly create. What *have* they done to the child's eyes, we are asked to wonder; what *could* one do to a child's eyes so that its mother would be *this* horrified? Affectively speaking, then, Polanski's refusal to grant us full view of the monstrous child increases the (self-induced) horror of the scene (and keeps the film on the safe side of an R-rating at the same time).

Obviously, there is an element of playful but masterly audience manipulation in Polanski's handling of the scene. But then the same considerations for the effectiveness of the film's affective aesthetic—that is, the ones that motivate the decision never to point the camera into the black crib in the closing scene (and to substitute a far more ambiguous image instead of the conventional "money shot" of horror cinema)—may also be at work when Polanski decides to place the scene at the very end of the film. Thematically speaking, the scene articulates the social horrors about motherhood and pregnancy that the film has been exploring all along—loss of individual agency and self-determination. In facing and accepting her baby, one might say that Rosemary completes the transformation from being Rosemary into being "Rosemary's baby's mother," a social entity re-defined by its relationship to its progeny. The horror of the film lies not in the sight of a grotesquely anomalous infant body. It lies in this reversal—from having the infant be the adjunct to her own body as its grounding biological and ideological reality, to becoming an adjunct to the infant as *her* grounding reality, turning her from an autonomous person into "the baby's mother."

PREPOSTEROUS PREMISES: BARING THE PROSTHETICS

While *Rosemary's Baby* may come across, in turn, as a fairly conventional horror film and an original, deliberately overdetermined, and highly ambiguous piece of auteurist filmmaking, its significance as a film about a monstrous infant becomes visible only in comparison to other films in the same genre. In order to situate the film within that cycle, let me retrace some of my earlier arguments in the light of Larry Cohen's *It's Alive* (1974), a film with marked differences to Polanski's. Most notably, Cohen has the birth of the monstrous infant occur within the first third of the narrative, which is then followed by a lengthy sequence in which the child's father—not the mother—must come to terms with the fact that it is his very own offspring which is, police in pursuit, prowling the streets of Los Angeles, claiming one bloody victim after another. As much as the shift from female paranoia in Polanski's film to the male experience of early parenthood marks a move away from what one might call the feminist agenda of *Rosemary's Baby*, it is the adjustment of the narrative trajectory—from the birth as the culmination of the plot to the birth as the point of departure of the plot—that makes all the difference. The earlier in the story the birth occurs, the more opportunities the film has to grant its audience a glimpse of the monstrous infant—opportunities which, as their number increases, start amounting to an imperative to pay up or shut up, so to speak. Polanski's maneuvering to keep the monster out of sight would be exceedingly difficult for Cohen to emulate, given the structure of his film's plot.

Surprisingly enough, Cohen pursues the same strategy of visual reticence as Polanski. Scattered throughout the film are scenes in which the monstrous infant, lurking in the bushes or the undergrowth, watches adults going about their daily business. Throughout, Cohen is exceedingly fond of the shaky and imperfect fluidity of movement accomplished by the subjective camera, commonly associated with the 1970s slasher films, beginning with Bob Clark's *Black Christmas*, released the same year as *It's Alive*, and later popularized by John Carpenter's *Halloween* (1978). Cohen often substitutes the movement of plant life or inanimate objects as physical markers of the baby's presence. The strategy also extends to the scenes in which the baby goes on the attack: carefully staged stalk-and-slash set pieces, first of animals and pets, then of random passers-by, eventually menacing members of its own family and immediate social circle. Together with the conspicuous absence of that same reverse-angle shot anticipated yet omitted from *Rosemary's Baby*, fast editing and subjective camera angles help to create an infant monster more agile and aggressive than Rosemary's baby, though no less invisible.

Cohen abandons the visual reticence prized by Polanski because his thematic interests are different. Just as he shifts the point of view from that of the mother to that of the father, he also moves away from those deliberations about individual psychology so important to Polanski—whether Rosemary is sane or not, and, hence, whether the infant really *is* monstrous or not—so that it can function as a sociological meditation on parental responsibility, the ambiguous allegiances between family and community, and the hardships that occur when children alienate parents from the larger community rather than entrenching them more deeply within it. Moving the story from psychological interiority further out into the world of social, economic, and political relations, Cohen also inserts into the dialogue references to the role of environmental pollution and pharmaceutical experimentation as possible, albeit unconfirmed, explanations for the infant's monstrosity. Cohen's decision to link these social issues with a masculine point of view moves the film further away from Polanski's feminist agenda than does his choice to write the mother out of the narrative after she has given birth.[12] In order to carry this thematic burden, there can be no doubt, no cognitive ambivalence, about whether the infant is an empirical reality. Consequently,

Cohen makes relatively little of the conventional uncertainty, listed by Carroll's "complex discovery plot" under the rubric of "onset," which tends to accompany the first subtle manifestations of the threat in horror films. From the moment the infant enters the world—during a gory scene in the delivery room that leaves all medical staff in attendance of the birth in a pool of their own blood—its existence is not in question.

Given the narrative pressures that result from the monster's early entry into the narrative, as well as the thematic conceptualization of the infant as an empirical reality, it is hardly surprising that most viewers will remember *It's Alive* less for Cohen's indulgence in visual reticence than for showing them what Polanski wouldn't. Over a sequence of scenes designed incrementally to increase the visibility of the infant, Cohen reveals a creature produced largely by special effects. For a series of extreme close-ups, he uses an adult mouth, made up and equipped with a pair of prosthetic fangs. In medium shots, he alternates between what looks like a dummy, which allows him to handle the body roughly and put on display the infant's veined, disproportionately enlarged head, and a genuine human infant, which allows him to generate a certain degree of visual verisimilitude as long as the shot is not sustained for too long.

Cohen's move toward the visualization of the monstrous infant does not contradict my earlier assertion that *It's Alive* functions basically within the same regime of visual restraint as *Rosemary's Baby*. As both representational strategies align themselves with each other throughout the film, an intermediate strategy emerges that stands in sharp contrast to the full visualization of the monster in horror films as a moment of visual spectacle. Though Cohen gradually reveals the monstrous infant, there is no single climactic moment in the film comparable to, for example, the revelation of the monster's bride in James Whale's *The Bride of Frankenstein* or the revelation of Nola Carveth's monstrous external womb in David Cronenberg's *The Brood*. Even at the very end of *It's Alive*, which culminates with a long sequence in which the LAPD chases the baby through the storm drains and sewer tunnels underneath the city, Cohen has the infant covered in a blanket when its father discovers it, tries to carry it to safety, and is cornered by the police who unload a barrage of gunfire into the barely animated bundle of blankets. By and large, long and medium shots of this bundle prevail throughout the scene.

Given Cohen's willingness to show the infant throughout the film, this final scene is puzzling but points to yet another reason why both Polanski and Cohen might have resorted to visual reticence: the state of special effects at the time both films were shot. Like Polanski, Cohen must have wondered how exactly to translate the concept of the monstrous infant into a concrete visual signifier, even if he had at his disposal the then yet unknown special effects wizard Rick Baker, who, in the course of a long and distinguished career (with groundbreaking work on such horror film classics as John Landis's *An American Werewolf in London* [1981] and David Cronenberg's

Videodrome [1983]), was to become a star comparable to Frank Pierce—a detail that, more than anything else about *It's Alive*, might draw horror fans to Cohen's film. Respectively, in 1968 and in 1974, body effects consisted primarily of make-up altering skin tone and surface morphology of the body, of prosthetics altering the size of the actor's body and the proportionality of its parts in relation to each other and their environment. Camera work and editing supplemented these physical transformations. By the late 1960s, molded latex casts also became increasingly available, which combined effects of both body surface and proportion. Aside from the actor's own body movements, this prosthetic assemblage had to remain largely static, oriented primarily toward the camera rather than its direct physical environment or, at best, discouraged sudden or expansive movement, lest they betray their presence to the camera. Digital effects—so-called CGI—were not, needless to say, anywhere on the horizon quite yet.

Since Polanski forgoes body effects almost completely and Cohen indulges in them only to a limited extent, the earlier question about the effectiveness of either showing or not showing the monster resurfaces in this context. Instead of comparing the affective impact of confronting viewers with the sight of the monster to letting viewers fill in the visual ellipsis, it is more helpful to consider each approach as based upon a fundamentally different aesthetic model, each eliciting a different set of viewer emotions, interpellating viewers into a radically different interactive and interpretive relationship with the image in front of them. The common wisdom that conceives that the elliptical approach is more effective—and, conversely, that opting for full visibility is less aesthetically refined, more bluntly direct, and less sophisticated—translates, at best, into a reflection of class prejudice; in other words, sophisticated auteurist psychological drama leaves its audience to imagine the monster—lowbrow splatter films leave little or less to their audience's atrophied imagination.[13]

While *Rosemary's Baby* occupies a far more exalted position within the cinematic canon than Cohen's *It's Alive*, I would like to argue that the difference in both films' respective treatment of the problem of visualization is a representational strategy consistent with the theme of each film. While Polanski is interested in a cognitive uncertainty and diegetic ambiguity arising from the monstrous infant as a potential manifestation of Rosemary's mental state, Cohen focuses on the social consequences that come with being the parent of a monstrous infant; consequently, little of the narrative dwells upon Carroll's "onset" stage, in which cognitive uncertainty triggers paranoia in a protagonist isolated from the community by being the only one aware of the rising threat. Most of *It's Alive* is devoted to the public panic over the rampaging monstrous infant and the authorities' ensuing "man hunt" for it, as well as to the devastating social consequences for the father who first cannot deny that the baby is his but who later embraces his role as parent. For these issues to gain credibility, there must be no doubt that the infant is real.

Both films, one could argue, are interested in the infant as the reification of a larger issue; that is to say, like all well-made monsters that have made a lasting impact on the popular imagination, Polanski's and Cohen's monstrous infants are, first and foremost, metaphors. Given the weight that these metaphors must carry, it is important that the concrete reification of the metaphor, the material signifier of the abstract signified, is both empirically convincing and poetically fertile enough to carry this weight. The cinematic monster's prosthetically enhanced body, as a material signifier of the abstract ideas it represents, tends to elicit an evaluative response from the audience geared primarily toward its empirical, and not its poetic, persuasiveness; in other words, the more a film foregrounds the concrete materiality of the signifier, the more it predisposes the audience toward an evaluation of what the monster looks like or how it moves than of what it represents. Though the relationship between the actor's concrete material body, prosthetically enhanced, and the themes it symbolizes is essentially no different than the relationship between the monster conjured up in the viewer's imagination and the abstract idea *it* represents, bad special effects are more likely to sever this relationship than a limited imagination. They reduce audiences to laughter even, or especially, when they try for pathos; they make willing suspension of disbelief impossible; with devastating effect, they—to quote the Russian formalists—"bare the device."

The anxiety that the affective and ideological structure of a horror film might collapse because of the insufficiency of its representational apparatus seems all the more urgent when it comes to monstrous infants in horror films: while incredulity, as Carroll argues, is a necessary condition of the traditional horror film plot, its complete and utter refutation is, too. Both contravening, complementary movements within the text must at the time of their occurrence be so convincing as to override the audience's awareness that the premise of the text is fundamentally preposterous. While the audacity of the horror film premise might be relatively easy to overlook when the creature is of overpowering size, speed, and strength, it moves right to the forefront when the opposite is true—as in the case of the monstrous infant, which is one of *the* most preposterous monsters in horror film.

Polanski never needs to confront this problem fully because of his focus on subjective experience and cognitive uncertainty: of course, the very idea of Rosemary giving birth to a satanic spawn is preposterous—this is exactly why nobody would want to believe her in the first place. Hence, with the sight of the monstrous infant meticulously withheld, there is little the film has to be apologetic about. Cohen, however, has a fairly unconvincing special effects creature to account for, not to mention the far-fetched visualizations of this infant attacking and brutalizing anything from the family cat to the obstetrician and his crew who aid the mother in the birth. Cohen is no less aware than Polanski that his mutant baby, cobbled together from diverse special effects, is, in the final instance, an untenable cinematic construction.

Cohen inserts a few key scenes in which the film pre-emptively signals its awareness of how preposterous its own premise really is. In one scene, a heavily armed police unit surrounds a suburban home and then, with ruthlessly efficient paramilitary moves, storms the building's back yard—only to discover a normal toddler playing on a blanket staring at the intruders with big, uncomprehending eyes. From those eyes, Cohen cuts to a reverse-angle shot straight into the barrels of a dozen or so guns pointed at the hapless infant, visually exploiting the discrepancy between threat and response for all its comical potential as a moment of camp.[14]

What makes the issue of camp so difficult to decide, however, is that in the final instance, *It's Alive* is at the core a deeply serious film, and its visualization of the monstrous infant matches its ambitions. To the same degree that psychology demands an immaterial, invisible, internal manner of representation, the sociological dimension of monstrosity Cohen takes measure of calls for a monster that represents, in its essential nature, the materiality of the social world. Cobbled together in a collaborative effort by designer Rick Baker, with the help of cinematographer Fenton Hamilton and editor Peter Honess, the monster represents exactly that materiality which tends to undermine the mimetic seamlessness of the film—very much in the same manner in which the monstrous infant within the diegesis has the uncanny power to tear open the seemingly seamless social fabric of upper-middle-class suburban Los Angeles. In other words, the materiality of the monster is its very point.

CONCLUSION: CGI AND THE FUTURE OF THE MONSTROUS INFANT

The further development of this subgenre will undoubtedly be influenced by the revolutionary changes that computer-generated imagery has brought to creature effects in horror film. Because budget no longer determines the deployment of this technology—its application occurs in post-production and thus does not affect the costliest aspects of production—even small independent films have the ability to render a wider variety of effects with the highest degree of mimetic verisimilitude.[15] The two films I would like to introduce briefly are examples of how new technology might affect the representational strategies of horror films about monstrous infants.

First, there is the 2008 remake of *It's Alive*. Director Josef Rusnak shifts the narrative back from the male point of view to the female; the film's protagonist is the monstrous infant's mother. The film tracks her development from accepting the child and covering up the havoc that it wreaks, to her final insight that she and her child, in the famous words of Karloff in *The Bride of Frankenstein*, "belong dead." Accordingly, she and the infant exit the film in the fire that destroys her house in the film's closing scene. That this house happens to be located on at the edge of the woods, far removed from the nearest small town, forecloses the social dimension in which the original film was so interested and returns it instead to the intense psychological interiority of *Rosemary's Baby*, albeit an interiority lacking, as Cohen's original would have it, the paranoia pervading Polanski's film.

Given the wide availability of digital effects, Rusnak's refusal to make use of them except in one particular scene—a digitally modulated infant hand creeping up over her mother's shoulder as she hugs the child—is clearly a deliberate strategy. Assuming that it was the camp status of *It's Alive* that attracted investors to the idea of producing a remake, it is not very likely that Rusnak decided to rely more heavily on the visual concealment of the monstrous infant out of respect for Cohen's original film; the radical change of location, from urban California to rural New Mexico (doubled unconvincingly by Rumania), and of social milieu from (middle-aged) upper-middle class to (late teenage) lower-middle class, bordering on working class, also point in that direction. Instead, it seems like Rusnak is acting out of the unexamined conviction that he can elevate the film by using the elliptical approach, make it "classier" somehow than its campy original. However, because all the changes to the original script eliminate the opportunity for retaining social relevance, the stylistic choice remains just that—a matter of style over substance. As a result, the film thematically never comes into focus, displaying exactly that uncertainty Cohen knew to avoid.

In the final instance, one might argue that, despite having the means for visualizing the monstrous infant at his disposal, Rusnak decides to eschew such visualization because he is ultimately more interested in his female protagonist's inner life than the social consequences of the monstrous infant. To the degree that Rusnak actually moves the remake in its ideological concerns further away from Cohen's original and more closely toward those embraced by *Rosemary's Baby*, one might conclude that the film's intends to refocus upon Polanski's gender politics (even if the element of cognitive ambiguity, which is so crucial to *Rosemary's Baby*, is entirely absent from the remake of *It's Alive*). With the female perspective replacing the male one, Rusnak's film arrives at exactly the same final plot twist as Polanski's, which may be the expression of a specifically *male* horror in the face of maternity—that the mother of the monstrous infant will embrace her hideous progeny despite its monstrous nature and heinous acts (an act more horrifying than that of Rosemary's husband Guy, who chooses to become an accomplice in the demonic conspiracy against his own wife because it furthers his professional advancement; maternal love lacks such immediately pragmatic motivation). The difference between how both films end—Polanski's ends with a shot that shows Rosemary and her child disappearing into the anonymity of the modern metropolis, while Rusnak's concludes with the willing self-destruction of the mother who, in accepting the monstrous nature of her child, accepts that she, like it, must not be allowed to live—marks the difference between

Polanski's ironic deconstruction of maternity as an essentially immoral force and Rusnak's serious imposition of a tragic morality which confirms, albeit without James Whale's sarcastic overstatement, that all monsters "belong dead."

The long shadow of James Whale also falls over the second recent horror film about a monstrous infant, Vincenzo Natali's *Splice* (2009). Like *It's Alive*, which, after all, takes its title from Colin Clive's hysterically elated line in Whale's film, *Splice* also makes reference to *Frankenstein* and *The Bride of Frankenstein*, featuring a couple of scientists named, tongue-in-cheek, Clive (as in Colin Clive) and Elsa (as in Elsa Lancaster). Both create a human infant whose DNA has been interspliced with that of a variety of other species, producing a creature, nicknamed Dren, who undergoes infancy, childhood, adolescence, and maturity within a matter of weeks, revealing along the way unsuspected bodily traits which are, in turn, sublime and horrific.

Unlike Rusnak's remake of *It's Alive*, Natali decides to go all out on digital body effects. Though the creature in its older incarnations is played by an actress—Delphine Chaneac, her body worked over in post-production with digital enhancements—its early infant self is entirely a product of computer-generated imagery, combining avian, mammalian, and human traits in an unsettling manner. The result is a creature that looks like a rabbit combined with a plucked uncooked chicken, whose agility, mobility, and three-dimensional plasticity are excessively on display. As with some recent productions that rely heavily on CGI, there is a vague sense that the technology itself is on display, celebrated or even fetishized. However, the risk of this re-directing of the film's visual attention into self-referentiality, which is then often dismissed as a form of authorial or industrial self-indulgence, hardly applies to a film of such modest dimensions. Unlike the excesses of, for example, a James Cameron production, Natali has other intentions. As Clive and, especially, Elsa encounter the monstrous infant, the film is firmly rooted in their perspective, alternating between interactions between Dren and Elsa in the role of its mother (as observed by Clive), and vice versa—a dynamic that illuminates both human characters and their relationship to each other through the catalyst of their collaborative project. Against this interpersonal dynamic, and more in keeping with Mary Shelley's original novel, the film follows the arc of a Bildungsroman, if seen from the monster's point of view. From Clive's and Elsa's point of view, however, it offers a surface onto which both can project their own complex and conflicted parental experiences, which, especially in Elsa's case, suggest that *Splice* is a film in which parenthood and family are not the solution but the problem. The darkest enactments of Freudian family romance are played out when Elsa repeats physical and psychological abuse upon Dren that used to be inflicted upon her by her own mother, while Clive increasingly drifts toward incestuous scenarios as Dren moves from early infancy toward sexual maturity in leaps and bounds. What matters to Natali's film, however, is that the surface upon which both characters project their psychodrama is not an inert, passive object lacking in agency but, as a concrete material body, the engine that drives the film's tragic vision. To have the audience see the infant *act upon* its parents and its environment, while being acted upon by the social forces of family and the apparatus of technoscience, is the most compelling aspect of Natali's film.

That neither Rusnak's nor Natali's film manage to extricate themselves entirely from the aesthetics of visibility and/or visual reticence which dominated their predecessors suggests that horror films about monstrous infants have not been substantially affected by the availability of new and improved technologies for visualizing these monstrous creatures. Whatever the representative tricks up the filmmaker's sleeve, it seems as if nothing will dispel the suspicion that films about monstrous infants are, at their very core, preposterous. And yet, technological progress does not seem to alter the basic fact that monsters in horror films are, essentially, metaphors requiring from their audiences the conceptual leap from the image to what it signifies. As with technologies predating the arrival of CGI, that leap can be made easier or harder by how visually arresting, compelling, or persuasive the material representation of that metaphor happens to be. In other words, CGI itself will not decide which horror films get away with the premise of the monstrous infant, but the difference between good and bad CGI surely will—as will the weight that each film's metaphor carries.

What remains, thus, as a measure of each film's sense of relevance or even urgency is the historical context that gives weight to the metaphor of the monstrous infant. Polanski's *Rosemary's Baby* and Cohen's *It's Alive* were released on the heels of events that focused public attention upon matters of reproductive technology and its social consequences: the birth control pill became available in the United States during the early 1960s; the sedative Thalidomide was withdrawn from the market around the same time after it was revealed to cause severe birth defects; and the Supreme Court ruling on *Roe vs. Wade* in January of 1973 increased women's control over their own bodies in matters of reproduction. That these events took place within the larger context of the women's movement added that undercurrent of male paranoia that runs so strongly through *Rosemary's Baby* and *It's Alive*. Even a horror film with the most preposterous premise could claim a certain sense of urgency against this historical background.

While feminist discourse may not be preoccupied with exactly the same issues in 2008 and 2009, Rusnak's and Natali's films suggest that matters of reproductive technology have lost none of their urgency. Fears of monstrous offspring induced by a drug like Thalidomide and anxieties about procreative processes detached from the traditional social contexts of parenthood and family have realigned themselves with the ongoing debate about human cloning and, more specifically, the controversy regarding human stem cell research played out to great media effect by the Bush administration during its second term. More broadly speaking, economic anxieties triggered by the most recent cycle of boom and bust comport themselves readily with horror film scenarios in which procreation is not a source of social stability but its opposite. Under these conditions, cinematic technologies might advance, just as genre conventions might change, but monstrous infants will most certainly continue to show up in horror films to come.

NOTES

1. Though not a remake, the 2009 film by David Goyer under the same title also happens to feature a demonic infant.

2. In his discussion of *The Exorcist*, Kendall Phillips determines that the common theme in all of these films is "a fear of children themselves," which he attributes, somewhat too broadly, to "the rebellious nature of the children of the sixties and an underlying concern that the next generation might wreak even more cultural destruction" (109–10).

3. The mid-1980s saw the most recent upsurge of this phenomenon, in the tidal wave of "recovered memory" cases, which invariably featured early childhood abuse, often with themes borrowed directly from the generic inventory of horror film: satanic worship, ritual human sacrifice, and so on. Discourse surrounding recovered memories frequently condensed concepts of early infancy as both a site of innocence, vulnerability, and victimhood, and a site of danger, contamination, and corruption. For further information, see Jon Trott, "Interview with Sherill Mulhern," and Hollida Wakefield and Ralph Underwager, "Recovered memories of alleged sexual abuse: Lawsuits against parents."

4. An argument made persuasively by Freud in his essay on "The Uncanny."

5. The reference is reinforced by a cameo of Hitchcock himself, walking two lapdogs, glimpsed briefly when Homer steps outside the daycare center with Maggie on his arm. A similar intertextual nod to *The Birds* also appears in James Cameron's *Aliens*, when the film's heroine discovers that she has unwittingly stumbled into the monster's nursery, demonic offspring being the connecting theme of each reference.

6. At their most effective, these moments of desublimation fail to shock and startle and instead flatten out affect as only a "bad" or "lame" joke can because *Family Guy* suggests that repression and/or decorum do not *conceal* the illicit but, in fact, *produce* it.

7. To focus, as I will in the course of my discussion, on canonical horror films only—that is, on films well-known and associated most strongly with the theme of the demonic child—may not be particularly original; neither may it take properly into account the critical, subversive, or revisionist responses issued by lesser known films in response to the canonical power of these "classics." But then this discussion is concerned with a basic typology, an organizing principle behind the visual conventions within the genre, and in this regard, it is, without doubt, the canonical films that have helped to establish and entrench these conventions.

8. Or, doubting the veracity of her perceptions, she is seeing her husband, as a sexually repressed Catholic girl would, transformed by lust into a demonic creature availing himself with impunity of her body for the fathering of his child. This reading is supported by the fact that, in the same scene, she also envisions herself on a yacht where John F. Kennedy may or may not be the seducer.

9. It is important to note, though, that the reference in the scene to the (invisible) infant's eyes, hands, and feet still point to the body as the site where monstrosity manifests itself—a fact embraced and even celebrated, for example, by Cohen's *It's Alive*. Monstrosity, as I have argued elsewhere, "never really leaves the body as its preferred site of manifestation, though it may become detached from any particular bodily characteristic" (35). In the absence of such bodily markers of monstrosity, most narratives resort to action as an index of monstrosity, a category that remains useless in the case of infants without significant bodily agency. As a last resort, horror films construe the very absence of all markers of overt monstrosity, bodily and behavioral, as pathological. While horror films like *The Omen* or *The Bad Seed* resort to this strategy, scrutinizing their child protagonists incessantly and suspiciously for a slipping of the mask, I have not been able to discover a single horror film about a monstrous infant which pursues this option: all films about monstrous infant, in other words, sooner or later refer back to the baby's body

as a site of abjection. For a full discussion of these representational patterns, see Steffen Hantke, "Monstrosity without a Body."

10. Though the central character in *The Tenant* is male—played, incidentally, by Polanski himself—his descent into insanity leads him to assume, by way of clothing and wig, the identity of the previous tenant of his apartment, a woman who had tried to commit suicide by jumping out her window. Like *Repulsion*, *The Tenant* features scenes that exquisitely render the character's mental state as distortions of the material world around him.

11. For the full discussion, see Carroll, *The Philosophy of Horror*, pp. 97–128.

12. It is important to note here that the film does not treat the mother's erasure from the narrative as the result of social formations, which would thematize her exclusion as a social phenomenon, but simply asserts the father's dominance over the narrative by authorial fiat.

13. One category that must be mentioned here—because it is strongly connected to taste as an expression of social class and because it has the ability to transcend the absolute claim verisimilitude tends to exercise upon these films and their affective impact—is that of camp. As a specific viewer attitude, camp would redeem, so to speak, Cohen's badly, bluntly, inelegantly visualized infant monster from being dismissed as B-movie fodder. To the extent that Cohen seems to have *intended* his film to be camp—that is, to the extent that viewers would not freely *chose to perceive* it as camp but be lead toward that conclusion by the film itself—issues of social class recur not only on the side of the audience but also as deliberate choices on the part of the filmmaker in terms of how the film is positioned.

14. See note 12.

15. Though their price has decreased considerably over the past twenty years, CGI are still more expensive than conventional prosthetic effects. This is especially true for effects designed to be highly visible, to be visible for prolonged on-screen visibility, and/or to be visible in highly complex interactions with other elements of the *mise en scene*; examples of how low-quality CGI lends itself to newly adapted forms of camp would be Global Asylum's 2010 *Mega Piranha*, which, in all its glorious awfulness, provides a tongue-in-cheek commentary upon Alexandre Aja's glossy, CGI-heavy remake of *Piranha* from the same year.

WORKS CITED

Carroll, Noël. *The Philosophy of Horror, or, Paradoxes of the Heart*. New York: Routledge, 1990. Print.

Hantke, Steffen. "Monstrosity without a body: Representational strategies in the popular serial killer film." *PostScript* 22.2 (2003): 34–54. Print.

It's Alive. Dir. Larry Cohen. Perf. John P. Ryan and Sharon Farrell. Warner Bros., 1974. Film.

It's Alive. Dir. Josef Rusnak. Perf. Bijou Philips and James Murray. Alive/Amicus, 2008. Film.

Phillips, Kendall R. *Projected Fears: Horror Films and American Culture*. Westport, CT: Praeger, 2005. Print.

Rosemary's Baby. Dir. Roman Polanski. Perf. Mia Farrow, John Cassavetes, and Ruth Gordon. Paramount, 1968. Film.

Shaffer, David R. *Social and Personality Development*. 2005. Sixth Ed. Belmont, CA: Wadsworth, 2009. Print.

"A Streetcar Named Marge." *The Simpsons*. Fox. 1 Oct. 1992. Television.

Splice. Dir. Vincenzo Natali. Perf. Adian Brody and Sarah Polley. Gaumont/Dark Castle, 2009. Film.

Trott, John. "Interview with Sherill Mulhern." *Cornerstone* 20.96 (1991): 8, 20, 26. Print.

Wakefield, Hollida, and Ralph Underwager. "Recovered memories of alleged sexual abuse: Awsuits against parents." *Behavioral Sciences & the Law* 10.4 (Fall 1992): 483–507. Print.

Monstrous Children as Harbingers of Mortality: A Psychological Analysis of Doris Lessing's *The Fifth Child*

DANIEL SULLIVAN
JEFF GREENBERG

> She woke to see Ben standing silently there in the half dark, staring at them. The shadows from the garden moved on the ceiling, the spaces of the big room emptied into obscurity, and there stood this goblin child, half visible. The pressure of those inhuman eyes of his had entered her sleep and woken her.
>
> —Doris Lessing, *The Fifth Child*

Images of deformed or malevolent children have a particular power to disturb us. To understand why this is the case, we must first acknowledge the popular view of children as innocent and good. This conception of children is a social construction that has grown in popularity in recent history. Since the eighteenth century, the rise of Enlightenment philosophies of education, as epitomized by Jean-Jacques Rousseau's *Émile*, along with the blank-slate hypothesis of the British empiricists have generated idyllic images of children as dependent, uncorrupted, and precious in industrialized societies, a trend documented by Chris Jenks and Peter N. Stearns. The prototypic child of "Western" modernity is the opposite of evil.

The contradiction between the evil child and the prototypic innocent child of modernity suggests that aversion to monstrous children can be accounted for partly by theories such as those of Noël Carroll and Julia Kristeva which trace horror to ambiguous stimuli that cannot be placed into clear, natural categories. In the context of the modern cultural understanding of childhood, children who exhibit tendencies towards cruelty or subversive self-assertion represent a category violation that turns conventional knowledge of human behavior on its head. As Eric Ziolkowski has shown, images of evil children have had a place in culture since Antiquity, but they are an extreme departure from the Post-Enlightenment view of the innocent child that is popular in modernity. The contradiction between the evil child and the Post-Enlightenment prototype may help explain the relative explosion of examples of monstrous children in literature and film that has occurred in the past half-century, noted by such diverse thinkers as anthropologist George Boas and author Joyce Carol Oates. Increasingly, the modern view of the child as innocent is accompanied by the sinister archetype of its opposite: the child who is thoroughly evil.

The fact that monstrous children are an affront to a modern understanding of what childhood *should* be cannot entirely account for their unique power as horrific figures. Many ambiguous creatures and sources of malevolence have the power to frighten. Monstrous children stand out among the rest in the uncanny disturbance they generate, as if they arouse a more primordial terror than that of expectancy violation or anxiety at the subversion of innocence. Sigmund Freud's theory of the uncanny, which argues that we are uniquely disturbed by entities that are simultaneously familiar and unfamiliar, captures something of the feeling but fails to adequately explain the source of the modern aversion to evil children. What is required to explain this aversion is a post-Freudian account of the importance of children in our symbolic lives. We propose that one such account is offered by terror management theory, an empirically supported social psychological theory of human behavior formulated by Sheldon Solomon, Jeff Greenberg, and Tom Pyszczynski (*TMT*; see Greenberg, Solomon, and Arndt, 2008). TMT argues that fear of personal mortality is a primary motivating force behind human behavior. From this perspective, children have a special importance for their parents and the preceding generation as guarantors of a form of what Robert Jay Lifton called *symbolic immortality*: the sense that one will leave behind some kind of legacy after death. Children thus provide psychological equanimity in the face of the potential for paralyzing death anxiety. According to TMT, then, fear of monstrous children is inseparable from fear of mortality and the breakdown of cultural strategies for repressing this fear.

To demonstrate the applicability of TMT to the case of monstrous children in the horror genre, we will use the theory to analyze Doris Lessing's novel *The Fifth Child* (1988). We argue that the horror manifested by the novel's evil child, Ben, has two sources, both of which are rendered psychologically explicable by TMT. First, the birth and development of the monstrously ambiguous Ben acts as a potent reminder of human creatureliness. Because animals are mortal, humans prefer not to think of themselves as animals and instead seek refuge in symbolic constructions. A child such as

Animalistic ~ Werewolf ~ doesn't live to wash

Ben who is animalistic in both appearance and behavior makes it difficult for his parents to deny their animality and therefore their mortality. Second, Ben's status as the fifth child of parents psychologically committed to obtaining symbolic immortality through their offspring makes both his perversity and his dangerousness symbols of the ultimate failure of our strivings to overcome death. By highlighting these two aspects of the horror of monstrous children—the deformed child as symbol of human creatureliness and the corrupt child as a subversion of the use of children to secure symbolic immortality—Lessing's work serves as an apt demonstration of the unique terror engendered by such children, a point made clear by applying TMT to the text.

Before turning to a brief presentation of TMT and our application of the theory to *The Fifth Child*, we must acknowledge that this theory (like any other) is necessarily limited in its explanatory scope and that there are other post-Freudian accounts which also help illuminate the psychological import of the monstrous child. One such perspective may be found in the writings of Julia Kristeva on *abjection*, which, in contrast to TMT, is more closely rooted in both traditional Freudian ideas and the aforementioned claim that horror's essence lies in ambiguity. In order to clarify both the limitations and the potential unique contribution of a TMT account, we will foreground our analysis with a short discursion into Kristeva's theory, which offers an interpretation of monstrous children that both diverges from and complements the present TMT analysis. We hope that by comparing these two theories throughout this essay, we will shed light on the complexity of the monstrous child as a symbolic figure as well as the richness of Lessing's novel.

A THEORY OF ABJECTION

In her essay *Powers of Horror*, Kristeva argues that many of the figures that terrify (and captivate) us in life and art can best be understood in terms of the process of abjection.[1] Abject things are interstitial entities that do not present themselves as true "objects" for the individual in the psychoanalytic sense of object-relations because they exist in the boundaries and margins between conventional categories (Kristeva 1–4, 15–17). Although these entities are generally repellent to us in our lives as enculturated beings, Kristeva proposes that the process of abjection—positing abject elements outside the self—marks a crucial and primal step in the establishment of one's ego. The infant defines herself over and against the abject before she develops the cognitive ability to grasp true objects through the schemas provided by language and symbolic self-awareness. Thus, echoing Otto Rank's reformulation of Freudian theory in *The Trauma of Birth*, Kristeva argues that the prototypic site of all abjection is the mother-child dyad, and the mother's body is the first abject thing against which the individual defines herself in the initial act of separation at birth (12–14, 61–63). Importantly, the abjected mother both repels and compels the individual, who learns to define herself in opposition to the mother (and all abjected material) but nevertheless retains a desire to return to the undifferentiated state of "egoless-ness" experienced in the womb (see Sara Beardsworth's informative, extended discussion of this point).

Kristeva argues that concepts of the abject—especially the abjected maternal—have had a marked influence on human cultural history. She asserts with Freud that understanding a culture means understanding those acts and ideas that are most strongly forbidden by it and follows him further by acknowledging that the two taboos present at the origins of human society are those against killing and incest. As Rank has noted in *Psychology and the Soul*, the taboo against killing posited by Freud can be interpreted as a consequence of, and an attempt to control, the fear of mortality. Kristeva seems to share this interpretation (57–58). While Freud builds his theory of the origins of repressive culture around this taboo and its connection to the murder of the "father of the primal horde," Kristeva focuses instead on the dread of incest. She contends that extreme dread of mother-son incest, manifested in the form of a taboo, is the cultural analogue of the individual's abjection of the mother (61–64). The incest taboo symbolizes each individual's necessary separation from their mother and the fact that patriarchal culture forbids any return to the "primary narcissism" of a fetal, pre-individuated state. At the same time, the taboo reflects a fear of the "archaic mother"—of the generative power of women, which is both vital to and potentially disruptive of the patriarchal order—and this fear in turn reinforces the motivated abjection of women.

Kristeva's theory of abjection provides a possible explanation of the power of monstrous children as symbolic figures, an explanation rooted in the importance of gender, sexuality, and uncertainty as characteristics of our psychological experience. Not only are monstrous children themselves abject and ambiguous (a point we will explore in more detail later in this paper; see also Barbara Creed's analysis), but they also may be seen as an incarnation of the abjection of the mother, a concretization (in reverse) of the psychological process of separation from the mother. The abject infant lays bare the typical process, operating at both the individual and societal level, of the mother's abjection. In this way, the monstrous child exposes typically hidden aspects of individual repression (the need to psychologically distance from one's mother) and of societal oppression (of the generative power of women). Just as scholars from Antiquity through the Renaissance interpreted deformed children as a direct consequence of their mother's untoward and powerful desires (a body of literature reviewed by Marie Hélène Huet), a Kristevan reading suggests that monstrous children represent fear of the ambiguous power of the archaic mother.

This approach provides a useful framework for understanding novels such as *The Fifth Child*. Ruth Robbins, for example, has directly applied Kristevan ideas to an analysis of the novel. We do not wish to deny the unique insights offered by such an analysis; indeed, as should become apparent throughout this paper, there are many points of convergence between a Kristevan and a terror management analysis of monstrous children, driven by their mutual roots in Freudian thought. Nevertheless, we hope to show in the remainder of this paper that a full understanding of the power of both stories of monstrous children in general and *The Fifth Child* in particular requires recognition of the role played by awareness of mortality in human psychology. In other words, while Kristeva develops her cultural theory from a focus on the incest taboo discussed by Freud, we will instead return to the other primary taboo—that against death—to show that a doomed desire to overcome mortal limits motivates the characters in *The Fifth Child* and fuels the terror of the monstrous child at the novel's center. But before elaborating on this analysis of Lessing's novel, it is necessary to first briefly introduce the theoretical perspective that will serve as its foundation.

TERROR MANAGEMENT THEORY

TMT is an empirically supported social psychological theory that has roots in the works of cultural anthropologist Ernest Becker (such as *The Denial of Death*), who in turn took inspiration from the post-Freudian psychoanalysis of Rank. The theory posits that humans share with other animals strong biological predispositions for continued survival but, unlike other animals, are burdened with an understanding of their own inevitable mortality. This awareness of death conflicts with a basic drive towards continued survival. As a result of this basic conflict, humans have a unique capacity to experience terror at the mere thought that their existence will end. Despite this, the majority of humans seem to function without being constantly paralyzed by fear of death. TMT offers an explanation for how this is possible. The theory posits that humans deny the reality of death as an insurmountable problem by imbuing the world with symbolic webs of meaning referred to as cultural worldviews. Worldviews such as the Christian faith, Stoic philosophy, and logical positivism serve many purposes, but from the perspective of TMT, two of their most important functions are to allow us to deny our animal (and therefore mortal) nature and to provide us with routes to symbolic immortality.

Lifton has identified a set of primary modes of what he calls *immortality striving*, which is the pursuit of symbolic immortality through culturally supported philosophies and life projects. The most basic mode, perhaps, is the literal immortality strategy encoded in the majority of the world's religious faiths: the reassuring metaphysical belief that death is not, in fact, the end of existence. Two other modes are the "creative" or cultural-symbolic mode and the "biological" mode. In the cultural-symbolic mode of immortality striving, individuals shield themselves from the threat of death by accruing culturally validated accomplishments that will (hopefully) be honored after their demise. Authors seek publications, politicians strive to make world-changing decisions during their terms, business executives gain fame and respect by rising up the corporate ladder before immortalizing their names in the form of philanthropic endowments, and so on. Alternatively, in the biological mode, individuals seek a sense of immortality through their offspring. Parents know that, upon death, they will leave behind one or more individuals who will not only carry on their memory and family name but who will also (given the proper socialization) transmit their most cherished beliefs and values to subsequent generations.

Terror management research has demonstrated the appeal of these strategies as symbolic defenses against thoughts of death. In support of the cultural-symbolic mode, over 400 empirical studies conducted in such countries as China, India, Israel, Germany, Japan, the Netherlands, and the United States have shown that concerns with death partly underlie our adherence to cultural worldviews and our proclivity to behave in ways that will guarantee our symbolic immortality (for recent reviews of this work, see Greenberg, Solomon, and Arndt; see also Greenberg and Arndt). In one line of supportive experiments, participants asked to reflect on their death (as opposed to a variety of other topics, many of them aversive) engage in more rigorous defense of their national culture or exhibit greater effort on tasks relevant to their sense of self-worth. For example, Greenberg, Kosloff, and colleagues demonstrated that writing about thoughts associated with one's death (relative to another aversive topic) leads individuals to report greater desires to be famous. Supporting the biological mode, Immo Fritsche, and colleagues showed that induced thoughts of death increase reported desire to have offspring in both men and women.

In addition, such experimentally-induced reminders of death increase efforts to psychologically distance ourselves from other animals and to deny or sublimate our animal and sexual nature. For example, participants who are asked to contemplate death subsequently show a greater tendency to conceptualize sex in less physical and more romantic terms. Thoughts of death also lead to stronger disgust reactions to animals and animal-like human behaviors (such as excretion; for a review of this research, see Goldenberg, Kosloff, and Greenberg). In addition, as these studies demonstrated, the effects of death reminders operate outside of conscious awareness. In other words, participants are not explicitly aware that thoughts of death are causing them to cling more rigidly to their worldviews or to become more averse to the thought that humans are animals. Finally, several studies, which were recently reviewed by Hayes, Schimel, Arndt, and Faucher, have shown that threatening people's faith in their worldview or their self-worth or reminding them of their animal nature all bring thoughts of death to the fringes of consciousness.

While traditional Freudian psychoanalysis has received mixed empirical support, TMT is an empirically validated theory that stands to enhance our understanding of common existential themes in literature and art, and themes of horror or tragedy in particular.[2] TMT posits that much of human behavior and cultural creation reflects a non-conscious desire to transcend our animal and mortal limitations by imbuing our lives with a broader sense of social connectivity and purpose. From this perspective, children play an important role in the psychological lives of adults as symbols of immortality: they bear our genes, names, memory, and culture into the future. It is little wonder that their corruption elicits reactions of horror, for evil and monstrous children represent both a reminder of our own physical animal nature and a failure in our attempts to overcome death through the next generation. Consequently, they are potent symbols of our mortality. We begin our TMT analysis of *The Fifth Child* with a discussion of the significance of the monstrous child and particularly the evil fetus or infant as an ambiguously powerful symbol of disturbing human creatureliness.

THE ABJECT CHILD AND HUMAN CREATURELINESS

Doris Lessing is a prolific author whose oeuvre spans a number of themes and genres. She is perhaps best known for her 1962 novel *The Golden Notebook*, which has been both positively and critically received as a major work of twentieth-century feminism (see, for example, Mona Knapp's discussion of the novel). Louise Yelin has observed that child characters do not figure prominently in some of Lessing's early realist and semi-autobiographic works, such as *The Golden Notebook* and *In Pursuit of the English* (1960), despite the works' centering around female protagonists who have children. Yelin interprets Lessing's reluctance to bring children to the fore in these realist works as a kind of resistance to patriarchal expectations.

Interestingly, however, as Roberta Rubenstein has noted, abject children have figured continually in Lessing's more fantastic works. *The Four-Gated City* (1969) features an island of children who are gifted with unusual psychic powers; *The Memoirs of a Survivor* (1976) depicts feral, violent children who roam a post-apocalyptic city. Lessing understands the simultaneously compelling and repelling nature of the abject child and weaves this source of ambivalence into the heart of many of her science fiction novels. Because the narrative of *The Fifth Child*—monstrous children excepted—operates within the boundaries of everyday reality (the novel might well be characterized as magical realist), it stands out among Lessing's depictions of abject children as an attempt to work out the meaning of these figures for our own lives. Indeed, while Rubenstein notes that Lessing's fantastic child characters often call into question conventional understandings of reality for both their fellow protagonists and her readers (72), we will argue that the monstrous *Fifth Child*, Ben, instead functions to highlight the harsh realities of human animality and mortality.

In the novel, the conservative, family-oriented British couple Harriet and David Lovatt plan to have a bevy of children and an ideal household full of life, despite meager financial resources and their relatives' skepticism. They buy a very large house, have four children in quick succession, and are seemingly well on their way to the life they envisioned. Then Harriet gets pregnant again, this time unintentionally, and eventually gives birth to the monstrous Ben. Ben has a sinister, violent nature that defies conventional modern associations of infants with innocence. Even while he is in her womb, Harriet is overwhelmed with the feeling that Ben is an enemy figure with whom she is locked in a physical struggle (42–47). Not only is Ben a sinister presence, but once he is born, he is also physically abnormal. Ben has an alien, "gnome"-like (71) appearance and enough physical strength to strangle a dog within months of his birth. Almost from the moment of his conception, Ben is described as an ambiguous creature who is not entirely human. While discussing her child with a doctor, Harriet suggests that Ben might be a "throwback" to an earlier stage of human evolution, a member of a more animalistic subspecies whose genes somehow survived hidden in the human pool (106). While pregnant with Ben (a pregnancy that causes her tremendous discomfort), Harriet imagines herself the victim of some botched scientific experiment mixing "the products of a Great Dane or a borzoi with a little spaniel; a lion and a dog; a great cart horse and a little donkey; a tiger and a goat. Sometimes she believed hooves were cutting her tender inside flesh, sometimes claws" (41).

In Kristevan terms, Ben is a perfect example of the abject as he blurs the line between existing natural categories and brings disorder into the highly ordered system of the Lovatt's household. The abject child as a source and symbol of horror has been chronicled in the beliefs of both industrial and pre-industrial peoples by anthropologist Mary Douglas. Douglas observed that in many cultures even normally developing children become symbols of potential power and danger, to be feared and avoided, when they are transitioning to different stages of life. In the frameworks of Douglas and Kristeva, people associate undefined or interstitial others with broader sources of disorder that threaten to undermine their worldviews, which are based on the coherent structuring of reality. For example, the Nyakyusa and Lele peoples of Africa have traditionally associated fetuses with the power to bring about suffering, because of their ambiguous, undetermined state (for instance, their gender is not yet known). Similarly, developing children are often viewed as possessing dangerous powers traceable to their protean condition.

Part of the terror of the monstrous child, then, lies in its existence in transitional life-phases already charged with the anxiety of the abject. The character of Ben blurs and deviates from expected developmental stages. His delivery is induced at eight months, and yet he is already at birth muscled and almost able to stand on his own, like a much older child; in later child-hood, he is described as being much older than he appears (113). Though even normal fetuses and children may represent transitional figures about whom we feel a certain ambivalence, the disturbing ambiguity of evil chil-dren is reinforced by their deviation from cultural norms of youthful inno-cence. Thus, Ben's uncanny appearance is made all the more disturbing by the monstrous acts he undertakes, which mimic the dangerous powers asso-ciated with transitional figures in the superstitions chronicled by Douglas. The Nyakyusa people do not allow pregnant women to stand near store-houses of grain, for fear that the hungry fetus inside will cause the grain to disappear. Similarly, while inside his mother, Ben forces Harriet to devour food with an untiring voracity (43).

Once out of the womb, Ben continues to eat voraciously, so much so that he bruises Harriet's breasts, prompting her to quickly abandon breast-feeding. Throughout the novel, Ben is portrayed as devouring food with little or no conformity to civilized rules of etiquette. Consider this parti-cularly vivid example:

> Harriet had come down one morning . . . to see Ben squatting on the big table, with an uncooked chicken he had taken from the refrigerator, which stood open, its contents spilled all over the floor. Ben had raided it in some savage fit he could not control. Grunting with satisfaction, he tore the raw chicken apart with teeth and hands, pulsing with barbaric strength. He had looked up over the partly shredded and dismembered carcass at Harriet, at his siblings, and snarled. (97)

In short, to use a popular expression, Ben eats "like an animal."

From a TMT standpoint, Ben's physical ambiguity and his animalistic nature are inseparable. TMT asserts that reminders of human animality are disturbing because they imply our ultimate sameness with all other mortal creatures on the earth. Douglas gives many examples of feared ambiguous entities that make it difficult to deny our animality. For instance, menstruation is commonly reviled because menstrual blood represents a paradoxical being that is dead without ever having lived. Menstruation also implies our com-monality with other fluid-secreting, physically limited beings, a stark contrast to the symbolic beings inhabiting worlds rich with meaning that we imagine ourselves to be. Similarly, Ben's abject nature reinforces the connection between humanity and other forms of organic life. As a "throwback" to an earlier evolutionary phase, Ben is a disturbing reminder that all humans are animals at base, evolved in a world of violence and death.[3]

Ben is not the only abject child who serves as a reminder of human creatureliness in *The Fifth Child*. One of the most impactful and horrifying sequences in the novel occurs when Harriet arrives at an institution for disabled children in which Ben has been placed. She unwittingly enters a ward of the institution, only "to see that every bed or cot held an infant or small child in whom the human template had been wrenched out of pattern, sometimes horribly, sometimes slightly. A baby like a comma, great lolling head on a stalk of a body...then something like a stick insect, enormous bulging eyes among stiff fragilities that were limbs" (81). Fetuses and infants are inherently associated with the animalistic act of procreation. When they develop normally, these transitional beings do not typically arouse death-related anxiety; rather, as symbols of our transcendence of death through the creation of new generations, they can help us cope with mortality concerns. Yet evil or deformed children, and monstrous infants like Ben in particular, seem to pervert this process, corrupting our wish for immortality into a reminder of our doomed nature as procreating animals.

Robbins has interpreted *The Fifth Child* as a parable exposing the darker side of fertility. Drawing on Douglas and Kristeva, Robbins highlights Lessing's attention to the painful aspects of Harriet's pregnancy with Ben, concluding that the novel serves in many ways as a corrective to culturally sanctioned narratives of the birthing process. In such narratives, human procreation is often cast as a route to immortality, with children providing the salvation of their mortal parents. But such reassuringly symbolic stories are counteracted by the animalistic aspects of pregnancy: blood, milk, the swollen belly, unbearable pain, and the umbilical cord. Harriet's physical pain, as well as her feelings of isolation and animosity during her pregnancy, undermine conventional narratives of the "miracle" of birth and externalize the typically hidden process of the mother's abjection noted by Kristeva. Furthermore, because the physical aspects of pregnancy highlight humanity's condition as a procreative animal species, they can serve as a psychologically problematic reminder of mortality and thereby elicit negative reactions. This contention is supported by the experimental work of Goldenberg and colleagues, which shows that reminding people of the similarity between humans and animals induces more negative attitudes towards pregnant women and bodily fluids and brings death-related concerns to the fore. By making our animality salient, Harriet's brutally physical pregnancy with Ben transforms procreation from a symbolic victory over death to a concrete reminder of mortality.

It is important to note that neither a TMT nor a Kristevan perspective on the potential ambivalence of pregnancy justifies or excuses the abjection of the mother's body. As feminist scholars like Jane M. Ussher have noted, the (pregnant) female body is not inherently abject; rather, it has been positioned as such in different cultures at different times in history. The association of pregnancy with death and animality is largely culturally conditioned and part of a repressive ideological link between death and sexuality that is stronger in certain epochs than others (for more on this association, see, for example, Phillipe Ariés 369–81). Furthermore, TMT suggests that any reminder of human animality has the potential to trigger unconscious death anxiety: this is as true of male ejaculate as it is of female menstruation. Pregnancy is neither uniquely nor inherently associated with fear of death according to the theory, and, as we have mentioned, it often stands as a symbol of victory over death. Indeed (and possibly for this reason), the pregnant female body was the first human form commonly represented in some of humanity's earliest artifacts (or so some scholars have argued; for a review of this work, see Peter Watson 53–73). It is quite possible, as suggested by Ussher (7–8), that the positioning of pregnancy as an abject state in later periods of history has stemmed partly from male envy of female generative power. Regardless, our intention in applying a terror management analysis to Lessing's portrayal of Harriet's pregnancy is not to frame aversive reactions to pregnancy as natural, but rather to illuminate one dimension of the powerful symbolic role played by the birthing process in cultural thought. When pregnancy is problematized as a biological event (as it is in the novel), the unease that results is due in part to the general double-edged potentiality of human sexual nature, which serves as both a route to immortality and a reminder of our mortal biology.

This mixed potential for sexuality to be both a problematic reminder of and (when properly sublimated) a symbolic means of overcoming death is apparent in Harriet's ambivalent attitudes about sex, described early in *The Fifth Child*. For Harriet, the sexual act has an inherent association with death: when she and David first engage in intercourse, their bedroom becomes "a black cave that had no end" with "a smell of cold rainy earth" (10). Yet she is able to overcome the fear of mortality implied by sex by embracing the notion that her children will become her life's transcendent purpose: she sublimates David's sexual advances by considering them "his taking possession of the future in her" (10). Harriet's sublimation of sex as procreation brings us to the core of the unique contribution offered by a TMT account of the problem of monstrous children. While the Kristevan and TMT perspectives largely converge on the power of the monstrous child as a symbol of animality and the psychological ambivalence generated by pregnancy, a TMT account goes further in its insistence on the importance of the child as a symbol of the parents' immortality. We will now examine the motivation and psychology of the parental figures in *The Fifth Child*, as well as its numerous references to mortality and its socio-historical context in an attempt to show that the monstrous child is always, among other things, a denied bid for immortality.

THE CHILD AS DOUBLE AND THE HUBRIS
OF IMMORTALITY STRIVING

Born in Persia, raised in Rhodesia, yet a self-declared "English writer," Doris Lessing has a multifaceted sense of personal identity and, as Yelin has observed, many of her novels portray characters attempting to fashion a coherent identity out of the conflicting ideologies available in globalized (post-)modernity. *The Fifth Child* can also be understood as a narrative about conflicting worldviews or, from a TMT perspective, about a conflict of opposing routes to symbolic immortality. As previously mentioned, Lifton distinguishes between, among other modes of immortality striving, the cultural-symbolic mode, through which immortality is secured by accruing culturally sanctioned accomplishments for oneself, and the biological mode, whereby one achieves immortality through one's children. *The Fifth Child* can be read as the story of two individuals who reject the cultural-symbolic (arguably the favored mode of the modern, largely secular "Western" milieu) in favor of the biological mode and the consequences of doing so.[4]

The Lovatts are alienated from the dominant cultural beliefs of their generation (that of the radical 1960s) and are not interested in pursuing the routes to accomplishment and happiness collectively endorsed by that generation, namely, self-expressionistic careers and a sexually liberated, hedonistic lifestyle. Lessing begins the novel with a description of the protagonists' feelings of alienation from the cultural worldview in which they are immersed: "They defended a stubbornly held view of themselves, which was that they were ordinary and in the right of it, should not be criticized for emotional fastidiousness, abstemiousness" (3). Indeed, Robbins has pointed out that Harriet, who longs for a life of simple domesticity during the height of the second-wave feminist movement, is in many ways as anachronistic as Ben, the evolutionary throwback. Similarly, David also rejects what he perceives to be the normative goals of his radical generation. He actively deviates from the career-oriented life of his wealthy father, choosing an obscure existence marked by financial insecurity over the temptation of culturally validated personal success. Instead of embracing the cultural-symbolic mode of immortality striving through work and achievement, the Lovatts pursue the biological mode, investing their savings and energy in "the dream" of six prospective children.

Throughout the opening pages of the novel, this plan to deviate from the cultural norm and sacrifice career interests for an idyllic family life is perceived by both the Lovatts and those around them as a kind of selfish rebellion. When they purchase a large house beyond their means to accommodate the planned family, Harriet and David are concerned that their parents will disapprove. This pattern is repeated with each of Harriet's pregnancies up until Ben's conception, which follow one another in rapid succession (five children are born in seven years; 25, 31). With each new pregnancy, the Lovatts fear that their friends and relations (who gather at the house annually for holiday parties) will chastise them for expanding their family despite David's inadequate salary and Harriet's struggle to adequately tend to the present children. Such criticism is repeatedly voiced, to the extent that Harriet begins to consider herself "a criminal" on account of her desire for continuous propagation (25).

The Lovatts' transgression lies in their defiance of the normative mode for immortality striving of their epoch, their rejection of the cultural-symbolic in favor of the biological mode. The conflict between these modes is expressed in Lessing's description of a remark made by David's mother in criticism of an exclusive family orientation: "she [David's mother] was standing up for a life where domesticity was kept in its place, a background to what was important" (27). Refusing to give the career life pride of place, the Lovatts pursue biological immortality with defiant zeal. This pursuit is characterized by those around them as thoughtless and arrogant. The negative reaction on the part of their family and friends to Harriet and David's "alternative" lifestyle fits well with many of the TMT studies summarized by Greenberg, Solomon, and Arndt which show that people are threatened by and respond negatively to others who choose paths to immortality discrepant with their own.

There are multiple possible interpretations of Lessing's emphasis on the conflict between career-oriented and family-oriented worldviews in the novel. From a Kristevan perspective, this emphasis can be taken to suggest that the ritualized abjection of the mother is most pronounced in cultural settings where procreation is only minimally necessary and largely discouraged (Kristeva 78). In relatively affluent, established societies where the number of offspring required to sustain the community has been reduced, the abject maternal is less tolerated and monstrous children become a symbol of warning and taboo against female generative power.

Alternatively, one can understand the worldview conflict in *The Fifth Child* as a commentary by Lessing on the cultural tensions present in Britain at the time of the novel's publication (1988). Yelin and Susan Watkins have noted the significance of the fact that Lessing wrote the novel during Margaret Thatcher's tenure as Prime Minister. The "return to family values," for which the Lovatts yearn, was also an ideological aspect of Thatcher-era conservatism and the popular reaction of the 1980s against 1960s radicalism. In this reading, Ben (and his family's reactions to him) can be alternately seen as supporting and problematizing a return to conservative politics. For example, through its portrayal of the treatment Ben and Harriet receive at the hands of various social institutions, *The Fifth Child* highlights issues made prominent by the political initiatives of the Thatcher era. On the one hand, Harriet is horrified by the inadequate (even cruel) treatment Ben receives during his brief stay in the hospital for abnormal children. As John Mohan pointed out in a review of the privatization of health care in 1980s England, Thatcher's administration often relied on such portrayals of mental health and senior care facilities as inferior and inhumane to marshal support for the "Care in the Community" policy, which was designed to cut spending on public care for long-stay patients. At the same time, several passages in

the novel that depict Harriet feeling like she is being held personally responsible for Ben's problematic nature by experts (doctors and teachers; Lessing
99–101, 103–104) call to mind the conservative rhetoric of individual culpability in healthcare matters that was part of the Thatcherian agenda. Rather
than offering a clear solution to the political debate on care for the elderly
and mentally disordered, the novel touches on the conflicts surrounding this
issue while also questioning whether either institutional or family-based,
private care is sufficient in as extreme a case as Ben's.

TMT offers an additional interpretation of the novel which builds on and
moves beyond a historically situated clash of worldviews. In a more univer-
sally applicable sense, the monstrous child also symbolizes punishment for
(counternormative) biological immortality striving. Several references to mortality in the first section of the novel suggest that the Lovatts are pursuing their
procreative dream as a defense against insecurity and death. In response to the
news that David will need three decades to pay off the house in which he and
Harriet plan to make their dream home, David's father replies, "I'll be dead by
then" (14). Later, Harriet's mother accuses the couple of acting rashly by having children so early in their married life, saying, "You two go on as if you
believe if you don't grab everything, then you'll lose it" (15). David replies
strangely and with conviction: "Everything *could* very well be taken away"
(16), while news of death and chaos in the wider world blares from a radio
in the background. The Lovatts' general understanding of the world "outside
their fortress, their kingdom, in which . . . precious children were nurtured" as
it is conveyed through news media is of a hostile place full of "wars and riots;
killings and hijackings; murders" (107). In this mortal and dangerous world,
the Lovatts are pursuing constancy, security, and ultimately immortality
through their children. This is made clear when Lessing describes their
planned offspring as their "demands on the future" (8), language that
parallels Harriet's sublimation of sex as a procreative act.

The symbolism of the child (and the son in particular) overcoming the
mortality of the parent is perhaps universal and has had a particular significance in the Christian worldview, as noted by Rank in his discussion of the
common theme of the Double. In *Psychology and the Soul*, Rank amassed
several examples from the anthropological literature to demonstrate that,
across cultures and time, people have commonly believed in a Double or
Doppelgänger, which is essentially a second self that transcends individual
mortality by existing beyond the self's physical decay. In the early stages
of human cultural evolution, Rank argues, the idea of the Double was primarily conveyed through soul-concepts or in the special reverence given to
twins in many cultures. However, with the decline in animism and the rise
of sexual awareness that has occurred over the course of cultural history,
Rank asserts that increasingly the child has come to serve as the Double of
the parent in cultural texts. The story of Jesus Christ is only one of many such
allegories connecting the figure of the son with the promise of immortality.

Thus, in the modern era, many people (like the participants in the afore-mentioned empirical study by Fritsche and colleagues) have dealt with the threat of death by psychologically investing in biological children who serve as Doubles, guaranteeing the Self's immortality.[5] Rank noted that the rise of the biological mode of immortality striving brought about an important change in the power of the child as a symbol. In his cultural studies, Rank observed that a common theme in world literature, perhaps best epitomized in the Greek tragedies, is that striving after personal immortality is doomed. In "animistic" or pre-industrial societies, folk stories often depict personal death as the punishment warranted by hubristic pursuit of immortality. How-ever, with the elevated importance of the child as Double in the modern era, Rank argues that modern literature contains far more numerous examples of the child's destruction or perversion as the penalty incurred by the parent's desire to transcend mortal fate.

In *Beyond Psychology*, Rank highlights the moralistic use of the Double motif in modern literature to warn against the desire for immortal life—particularly when that desire manifests in a mode of immortality striving that runs counter to that of the mainstream worldview. Thus in the nine-teenth-century European cultural milieu, when, according to Ariés, dom-estic life, romantic relationships, and procreation reached the zenith of their symbolic value as paths to immortality, Gothic characters like Victor Frankenstein and Henry Jekyll reject domesticity and instead strive cre-atively to overcome death by "birthing" fiendish Doubles characterized to varying degrees as the "children" of their creators. In the following century, in the anti-domestic radical 1960s, Harriet and David's rebellious pursuit of biological immortality is punished through the corruption of their fifth child: the monstrous Double, Ben. Isabel Gamallo has commented on the Gothic style and structure of *The Fifth Child*, and Watkins also character-ized the work as "urban Gothic"; these stylistic elements underscore its kin-ship with past works in which the Double heralds death for those who transgress against the dominant worldview in pursuit of their own immor-tality. While the Double initially made its way into culture as a sign of immortality (e.g., the ideology of the soul), the monstrous Double-child of modern literature is an image of inescapable mortality.

As in the ancient stories chronicled by Rank, the Lovatts defy their mortal condition and the cultural norms of their era by investing their lives in the promise of biological immortality. But their efforts are brought to an end by Ben, who emerges as a symbol of the Lovatts' mortality. Ben brings mortality to the fore with his deadly actions, uncontrollable fits, teeth-baring snarls, and fearsome stares. He kills a dog and a cat and becomes such a threat while still a toddler that the Lovatts have their other children, who live in fear of their savage brother, locked safely in their rooms at night. As Ben grows up, the Lovatts age with unnatural celerity, and they begin to look much older than they are physically, suggesting that Ben is a harbinger of their demise.

There are other, subtler ways in which Lessing's writing suggests an inherent association between Ben and mortality. For one, Harriet frequently imagines and even longs for Ben's death (63). Yet she cannot bring herself to kill him or allow her own child, the central biological basis of her immortality striving, to die. So she rescues Ben from the institution where he had been hidden away by her husband and where he certainly would have soon died. She picks up his cold, drugged body and suddenly realizes the meaning of the expression "a dead weight" (84). Each mutant child in the institution stands for the mortality of its parent, patently denied by sequestering the disturbing creatures away in a hospital. In the prison for perverse children, Lessing fashions a metaphor for the modern "institutionalization" of death. As Ariés explains, in modern industrial societies, the experience of death has become increasingly remote and mediated: though we are exposed to plenty of safe media images of death, the deaths of those around us occur primarily in hospitals, removed from the immediate experience of all but a few caretakers and experts. Similarly, the monstrous Double-children that represent the mortality of their parents are locked away from society and never seen again in Lessing's novel.

Ben embodies not only the Lovatts' physical death but, more importantly, the destruction of its symbolic cure: he kills their dream of conquering mortality. The presence of Ben has "dealt the family a mortal wound" (93). After returning with Ben from the institution, Harriet's relationship to her husband and other children is irrevocably altered. When the Lovatts make love, it is now as if "the ghosts of young Harriet and young David entwined and kissed" (112). There is no question of further procreation, despite the fact that they originally planned for six (rather than only five) children. The Lovatts begin using "the Pill," which was once for them a despicable symbol of the modern attitude toward domesticity they shunned (92). Ben's siblings grow emotionally distant and distrustful of their mother, spending increasingly more time away from home with relatives (when they are at home, Harriet's sense of alienation from them is increased by the fact that they must be locked in their rooms for safety; 95). Ben's destruction of the Lovatts' dream is no better conveyed than in the sequence, contained in the final pages of the novel (128–29), in which an aging Harriet stares into the glossy surface of the large dining room table in her now lifeless home and sees idyllic images of her other children gathered around when they were young, before a dark vision of Ben overshadows the tableau and all other pictures vanish.

It is not only Ben's ambiguous animal nature and violent potential that puts an end to the Lovatts' bid for immortality, but also his attraction and ultimate conversion to a symbolic worldview that is the antithesis of their own. Ben's status as cultural Other—of a foreign worldview connected to both immigration and deviance—becomes a central idea of the novel's third act. As Ben grows older, he ingratiates himself with the local biker gang the Lovatts always associated with the hostile world beyond their cocoon of domesticity.

By the time Ben reaches adolescence, with all her other children preferring boarding school to their ruined home, Harriet is often left alone in the house with Ben and his hooligan compatriots, who stay uninvited between raids on local stores and riots at seaside towns. The youths do little to hide the joy they take in violence and commonly speak of the day when they will rise in "revolution" against the Lovatts and the rest of their generation (124).

Though the Lovatts hoped to raise children in whom they could instill their conservative love of domesticity and traditional English values, Ben's rejection of this worldview in favor of its deviant antithesis is clear. It extends even to the gang's preferred cuisine: Ben and his friends litter the Lovatts' suburban English home with exotic take-out of every variety, Chinese, Mexican, Turkish (128). As his life begins to center around the gang, Ben's systematic destruction of his parents' traditional dream reaches its final stage. He has discovered a sense of belonging his parents could never give him among the "outsiders" (the immigrant and criminal groups) they had always feared and from whom they had tried to shelter their family. As scholars such as Gamallo and Yelin have noted, the ultimate identification of Ben with foreign, deviant forces characterizes *The Fifth Child* as a product of Thatcher-era Britain, when an ideological push towards reviving the old values and virility of the Empire was accompanied by ever-increasing concerns with unemployment, immigration, and crime.

To summarize, Ben symbolizes the mortality of his parents in three ways illuminated by TMT. First, his physical ambiguity, blurring the line between humanity and animality, serves as a reminder of the Lovatts' status as mortal creatures. Second, he destroys the Lovatts' relationship with their other children, their primary basis for symbolic immortality. Third, his conversion to a deviant worldview implies the futility of the Lovatts' bid for symbolic immortality. Parents invest in their children as vehicles for projecting themselves into the future and thus overcoming death. But children, of course, do not always passively assimilate to their parents' cultural beliefs. Even biologically normal children, like the other members of Ben's biker gang, are not guaranteed to become vessels for the transmission of their parents' cherished values. In these ways, the dream of immortality through children, which the Lovatts hubristically pursued in defiance of contemporary cultural conventions, was destroyed by the birth of the monstrous child, a potent instantiation of the mortal Double.

CONCLUSION

Throughout this paper, we have attempted to demonstrate how a TMT analysis uniquely contributes to an understanding of the symbolic significance of monstrous children by bringing parental desire for immortality into focus. At the same time, we have pointed to some common ground, and some divergences, between TMT and more conventional contemporary approaches to literary analysis—Kristeva's theory of abjection in particular. There are doubtless aspects of *The Fifth Child* which a Kristevan perspective is better suited than TMT to explain. For example, the concept of the abjected mother is useful in understanding Lessing's relative prioritization of Harriet's point of view over that of any of the other characters. Throughout the novel, we are encouraged to sympathize with Harriet as she is made to feel like a "criminal" by those around her: firstly, for having children at all; secondly, for feeling like something is wrong with Ben when doctors and educators refuse to acknowledge his ambiguous status; and finally for keeping Ben alive at the cost of her family's happiness. Harriet's experience as the mother of an abject child is outside the scope of a TMT analysis but is revealed as a rich literary exploration of the socially conditioned nature of maternity when viewed through Kristeva's lens (an example of this type of approach may be found in Robbins's writing on the novel).

Although TMT does not provide the only framework for understanding monstrous children in modern literature, Lessing's emphasis on Ben's animal nature and the Lovatts' dream of immortality support the importance of incorporating the problem of death into a complete explanation of this phenomenon. By exposing the monstrous child as a symbol of punishment for doomed immortality striving, the present analysis illuminates the persistence in the modern era of the common cultural belief that abnormal children are the outcome of parental sins. This theme is expressed early in *The Fifth Child* when Harriet tells David she believes her niece's Down Syndrome to be the result of an unhappy marriage: "Sarah and William's unhappiness, their quarreling, had probably attracted the mongol child" (22). The fact that the deformed Ben will be the Lovatts' own genetic retribution for their relentless propagation is presaged by an early description of their first four children as four "challenges to destiny" (27). Towards the end of the novel, Harriet even acknowledges her feeling that Ben was their punishment for desiring too much for themselves: "We are being punished, that's all . . . . For presuming. For thinking we could be happy. Happy because *we* decided we would be" (117).

Lessing's focus on the counternormativity of the Lovatts' zeal for biological immortality foregrounds a work in which the monstrous Double-child warns against the hubris of death defiance. Simultaneously, her attention to Ben's physical ambiguity highlights the evil child's power to disturb by reminding us of our animal, and thus mortal, nature. An application of TMT to *The Fifth Child* allows us to combine these important strains in the novel in a coherent framework, which yields the insight that monstrous children are a particularly disturbing source of terror because they transform what is normally a basis of parents' striving for immortality into an incarnate symbol of the mortality of the parents, and by implication, of us all.

NOTES

The authors wish to thank Guest Editor Karen J. Renner and two anonymous reviewers for their comments on earlier versions of this manuscript. We also thank Leah L. Kapa and Tara Harney-Mahajan for proofreading the final manuscript.

1. Kristeva's theory of abjection has yielded many different interpretations and has been used in a variety of different ways. We fully acknowledge that ours is only one possible reading of her nuanced writings, which offer alternate interpretations. Our reading has been largely influenced by Sara Beardsworth's *Julia Kristeva: Psychoanalysis and Modernity*.

2. For example, Daniel Sullivan, Jeff Greenberg, and Mark J. Landau have recently used the theory to analyze horror and ultraviolent films.

3. In her article "Reproduction, Genetics, and Eugenics in the Fiction of Doris Lessing," Clare Hanson discusses Ben as a symbol of the link between humans and animals and explores the possibility that this link is disturbing and typically repressed. However, her account differs from a TMT perspective insofar as it suggests that repression of the connection between humans and other species is a phenomenon unique to modern societies, rather than a longstanding aspect of human culture designed to mitigate the psychological threat of death. It should be noted that Kristeva also suggests that the abject is inherently connected to fear of our animality and distancing from the body (12–13, 77–79).

4. It is interesting that Lessing wrote a novel about a couple rejecting the cultural-symbolic to embrace the biological mode of immortality striving, given that one could interpret Lessing's biography as an example of the opposite: a woman who pursued the cultural-symbolic path of the writer in an era (1950s England) when women were highly encouraged to embrace the biological mode. As noted, a more in-depth discussion of Lessing's relationship as an author to issues of maternity and patriarchy is provided by Yelin.

5. Jenks's sociological work also shows that children increasingly have come to serve as symbols of their parents' "futurity" (immortality), particularly in the last century and in industrialized nations. He writes of the modern era: "The dreams and the promise embedded in our children, was to reach for the stars, to control more and more of the wantonness of the cosmos, and to produce human culture as the triumph of finitude over infinity" (102–03). Jenks traces this tendency to, among other factors, the decline of traditional religious beliefs as guarantors of immortality, the diminished importance of community and the rise of ideological individualism, the accompanying elevated belief in historical progress, and the decline in birth rate in modern societies.

WORKS CITED

Ariés, Phillipe. *The Hour of our Death*. New York: Knopf, 1981. Print.

Beardsworth, Sara. *Julia Kristeva: Psychoanalysis and Modernity*. Albany, NY: State U of New York P, 2004. Print.

Becker, Ernest. *The Denial of Death*. New York: Free Press, 1973. Print.

Boas, George. *The Cult of Childhood*. London: Warburg Institute, 1966. Print.

Carroll, Noël. *The Philosophy of Horror, or Paradoxes of the Heart*. New York: Routledge, 1990. Print.

Creed, Barbara. "Baby Bitches from Hell: Monstrous Little Women in Film." Paper delivered at the Scary Women Symposium. UCLA: January, 1994. Print.

Douglas, Mary. *Purity and Danger*. Baltimore: Penguin Books, 1970. Print.

Freud, Sigmund. "Das Unheimliche." *Das Unheimliche: Aufsätze zur Literatur*. Hamburg: Fischer, 1963. Print.

Fritsche, Immo, Eva Jonas, Peter Fischer, Nicolas Koranyi, Nicole Berger, and Beatrice Fleischmann. "Mortality Salience and the Desire for Offspring." *Journal of Experimental Social Psychology* 43.5 (2006): 753–62. Print.

Gamallo, Isabel C. Anievas. "Motherhood and the Fear of the Other: Magic, Fable, and the Gothic in Doris Lessing's *The Fifth Child*." *Theme Parks, Rainforests and Sprouting Wastelands: European Essays on Theory and Performance in Contemporary British Fiction*. Eds. Richard Todd and Luisa Flora. Atlanta, GA: Rodopi, 2000. 113–24. Print.

Goldenberg, Jamie L., Spee Kosl
off, and Jeff Greenberg. "Existential Underpinnings of Approach and Avoidance of the Physical Body." *Motivation and Emotion* 30.2 (2006): 127–34. Print.

Goldenberg, Jamie L., Joanna Goplen, Cathy R. Cox, and Jamie Arndt. "'Viewing' Pregnancy as an Existential Threat: The Effects of Creatureliness on Reactions to Media Depictions of the Pregnant Body." *Media Psychology* 10.2 (2007): 211–30. Print.

Greenberg, Jeff, and Jamie Arndt. "Terror Management Theory." *Handbook of Theories of Social Psychology*. Eds. Arie Kruglanski, Edward Tory Higgins, and Paul A. M. Van Lange. London: Sage P, 2011. In Press. Print.

Greenberg, Jeff, Spee Koslof, Sheldon Solomon, Florette Cohen, and Mark J. Landau. "Toward Understanding the Fame Game: The Effect of Mortality Salience on the Appeal of Fame." *Self and Identity* 9.1 (2010): 1–18. Print.

Greenberg, Jeff, Sheldon Solomon, and Jamie Arndt. "A Basic, but Uniquely Human Motivation: Terror Management." *Handbook of Motivation Science*. Eds. James Y. Shaw and Wendi L. Gardner. New York: Guilford, 2008. 114–34. Print.

Hanson, Clare. "Reproduction, Genetics, and Eugenics in the Fiction of Doris Lessing." *Contemporary Women's Writing* 1.1/2 (2007): 171–84. Print.

Hayes, Joseph, Jeff Schimel, Jamie Arndt, and Erik H. Faucher. "A Theoretical and Empirical Review of the Death-Thought Accessibility Concept in Terror Management Research." *Psychological Bulletin* 136.5 (2010): 699–739. Print.

Huet, Marie Hélène. *Monstrous Imagination*. Cambridge: Harvard UP, 1993. Print.

Jenks, Chris. *Childhood*. New York: Routledge, 1996. Print.

Knapp, Mona. "*The Golden Notebook*: A Feminist Context for the Classroom." *Approaches to Teaching Lessing's* The Golden Notebook. Ed. Carey Kaplan and Ellen Cronan Rose. New York: MLA, 1989. 108–14. Print.

Kristeva, Julia. *Powers of Horror: An Essay on Abjection*. New York: Columbia University Press, 1982. Print.

Lessing, Doris. *The Fifth Child*. London: Jonathan Cape, 1988. Print.

———. *The Four-Gated City*. New York: Alfred A. Knopf, 1969. Print.

———. *The Golden Notebook*. London: Grafton Books, 1973. Print.

———. *The Memoirs of a Survivor*. New York: Bantam, 1976. Print.

———. *In Pursuit of the English*. New York: Simon and Schuster, 1961. Print.

Lifton, Robert Jay. *Revolutionary Immortality: Mao Tse-tung and the Chinese Cultural Revolution*. New York: Random House, 1968. Print.

Mohan, John. "Restructuring, Privatization, and the Geography of Health Care Provision in England, 1983–1987." *Transactions of the Institute of British Geographers* 13.4 (1988): 449–65. Print.

Oates, Joyce Carol. "Killer Kids." *The New York Review* 6 Nov. 1997: 17–20. Print.

Rank, Otto. *Beyond Psychology*. New York: Dover, 1958. Print.

———. *Psychology and the Soul*. Trans. Gregory C. Richter and E. James Lieberman. Baltimore: Johns Hopkins UP, 1998. Print.

———. *The Trauma of Birth*. Mineola, NY: Dover, 1993. Print.

Robbins, Ruth. "(Not Such) Great Expectations: Unmaking Maternal Ideals in *The Fifth Child* and *We Need to Talk about Kevin*." *Doris Lessing: Border Crossings*. Eds. Alice Ridout and Susan Watkins. New York: Continuum, 2009. 92–106. Print.

Rousseau, Jean-Jacques. *Émile*. New York: Dutton, 1943. Print.

Rubenstein, Roberta. "Doris Lessing's Fantastic Children." *Doris Lessing: Border Crossings*. Eds. Alice Ridout and Susan Watkins. New York: Continuum, 2009. 61–74. Print.

Stearns, Peter N. *Childhood in World History*. New York: Routledge, 2006. Print.

Sullivan, Daniel, Jeff Greenberg, and Mark J. Landau. "Toward a New Understanding of Two Films from the Dark Side: Applying Terror Management Theory to *Rosemary's Baby* and *Straw Dogs*." *Journal of Popular Film and Television* 37.4 (2009): 189–98. Print.

Ussher, Jane M. *Managing the Monstrous Feminine: Regulating the Reproductive Body*. New York: Routledge, 2006. Print.

Watkins, Susan. "Writing in a Minor Key: Doris Lessing's Late-Twentieth-Century Fiction." *Doris Lessing: Interrogating the Times*. Eds. Debrah Raschke, Phyllis Sternberg Perrakis, and Sandra Singer. Columbus: Ohio State UP, 2010. 149–64. Print.

Watson, Peter. *Ideas: A History of Thought and Invention, From Fire to Freud*. New York: Harper Collins, 2005. Print.

Yelin, Louise. *From the Margins of Empire: Christina Stead, Doris Lessing, Nadine Gordimer*. Ithaca, NY: Cornell UP, 1998. Print.

Ziolkowski, Eric. *Evil Children in Religion, Literature, and Art*. New York: Palgrave, 2001. Print.

Spoil the Child: Unsettling Ethics and the Representation of Evil

WILLIAM WANDLESS

For the seasoned viewer, horror tends to be a commonsensical genre. One does not need many screenings to grasp conventional prohibitions (good things seldom come, for example, to those who enter the woods or the basement), and contemporary fare like *Scream* (1996) and its sequels have nudged formulae to the fore, where they may be subjected to ironic vivisection. Evil routinely appears in recognizable guises, and in some cases the primary responsibility of the audience is to flinch on cue. When one presses past clichés and commonplaces, however, one is apt to discern a second set of indications and intimations that require thoughtful response. *The Exorcist* (1973), for instance, shocks and appalls as a sacrilegious spectacle, yet it also confronts viewers with a weightier obligation, calling for circumspect evaluation of the dynamics depicted and choices made. As Cynthia A. Freeland notes, representations of horror engage viewers in robust interpretive activity: "We are *thinking* as we follow features of the film that guide our emotional response: We make judgments and evaluations as we watch, react, and listen. We may experience standard or predictable emotions...but then we also reflect on why and whether it is right to do so" (3). At its most challenging, cinematic horror appeals to the full array of spectatorial faculties as it raises disquieting questions about the world in which we live. Depictions of evil children dependably number among such provocative offerings, as they implicate viewers in an unsettling analytical, essentially ethical, exchange from which they cannot turn away.

A film like *The Exorcist*, centered on the possession of a twelve-year-old girl, spares the audience certain kinds of interpretive effort by turning explanatory emphasis away from the child and toward the presence inhabiting her. Offerings like *The Ring* (2002), *Godsend* (2004), and *Grace* (2009) likewise shift evaluative emphasis away from children and toward the paranormal abilities, congenital conditions, or unearthly entities they incarnate.

When horror productions involve evil enacted by children with their own methods and motives, however, they task viewers with appraising iniquity of a different order. If supernatural reckonings are tabled, if the behavior of wicked children originates in their volition and abilities, then viewers must account for evils derived, at least in part, from families, institutions, and circumstances not unlike their own. The representation of such children in credible domestic contexts accordingly elicits an uneasy explanatory effort, one that seeks to remedy an agitation inspired by recognition of situational similarities. Depictions of developmental difference may offer conditional relief, but if the maturational arc appears indeterminate, the audience is obliged to look elsewhere for an impetus that could explain the child's malevolence. Characterological analysis of the child also may expose oddities associated with iniquity, as may a survey of siblings, parents, and influential authority figures. Some films nevertheless frustrate the search for catalysts even then, denying viewers recourse to unambiguous environmental triggers that would explain the child's deviltry. Such productions, devoid of diegetic cues that might easily explicate evil, spoil the child for the audience, fouling the comforts that come with interpretive certainty. As I will demonstrate, however, those same offerings afford the audience compensatory consolations, the findings of a critical gaze turned back upon itself.

That I might address these prospects in detail, I will focus on four films: *Halloween* (2007), *Joshua* (2007), *Home Movie* (2008), and, by way of conclusion, *Orphan* (2009). These films epitomize a constellation of concerns about the slippery status of the child, and they brace these matters in analogous terms. *Joshua* and *Orphan* examine evil in the shape of precocious nine-year-olds; *Halloween* and *Home Movie* represent the unrest caused by ten-year-old terrors. All four films feature children who possess an uncanny aptitude for malice, yet that uncanniness speaks not to superhuman endowment but rather to the contrapuntal quality of the evil child: the coexistence of the sweet and the subversive in a play of surfaces and depths. Psychoanalytic criticism offers one valuable means of wrangling with this correlation, yet the extent to which pop psychology pervades the orthodoxies of the genre and our diagnostic parlance suggests the need for an alternative, less deterministic approach to the discrepancy between seeming and being, one that accounts for the fraught relationship of cinematic representation and audience response. To connect the indexical and the ethical—to account for the way depictions of evil children attest to essentially unknowable depths that nevertheless call for characterological explication—I propose a dialectic that addresses the discomfiting incongruity embodied by such children and the interpretive enterprise required to appraise their strangeness, an anxious effort that implicates children, their parents, and the audience.

In children, we find much to be nurtured, much to be feared. The idea of the child elicits a response that, according to Emmanuel Levinas, exceeds love and assumes a transcendent form in fecundity, the self-perpetuating "goodness of goodness" (*Totality* 267–69). At the same time, the sign of the child comprises an antisocial egotism and implacability, a distillation of difference that occurs as "crude otherness, hard otherness" and that belongs to "childhood, lunacy, [and] death," as Jean Baudrillard suggests (124, 128). Cinematic representations of children regularly balance these forces in suspension, their magnetism and meanness capable of inciting tenderness or trepidation. A variety of films depend on this representational fluidity, yoking innocence and affecting vulnerability to recalcitrance and a propensity for lashing out. Such eruptions, of course, do not a monster make. A tantrum is not commensurate to malice aforethought, and even sophisticated ideation might be mitigated by a childlike sense of outcomes. The attribution of elemental evil obliges viewers to proceed warily. When dealing with the handiwork of a seemingly evil child, the viewer must ascertain the competence of the culprit. As Claire Elise Katz implies in her Levinasian appraisal of Cain, the audience must weigh matters of responsibility, situational awareness, and moral education in light of a desire to assign guilt (220–22); if a child is "not yet a fully developed ethical subject," evaluative emphasis changes (223). In horror films we often witness unequivocal iniquity, the work of seasoned ethical agents capable of awful calculation, individuals who grasp the implications of their acts and commit them anyway. The malevolence of such knowing offenders allows for a full array of evaluative options; we may deem them evil and trust the sign has been equitably applied. Wickedness committed by children, however, does not release or relieve the audience so readily. Their acts rouse a hunger for judgment, but questions of consciousness, development, and environment alter the complexion of what may justly be judged.

In the discussion of *Halloween, Joshua, Home Movie,* and *Orphan* that follows, I will demonstrate how depictions of evidently evil children depend on a pattern of indicative interplay, one that exploits, gratifies, and undercuts the desire for evaluative support and interpretive certainty. Reassurance in these films occurs as a superabundance of signs, telling gestures that facilitate the recognition of villainy and the assignment of a loaded label we are at pains to apply to a child. To deem Michael Myers, Joshua Cairn, Jack and Emily Poe, and Esther Coleman *evil*—to find them confirmed in iniquity at the age of nine or ten—the audience requires substantiation sufficient to overcome reservations about their ethical aptitude and to distance these children developmentally and characterologically from ordinary others. More importantly, to yield meaningful relief, the telling gestures must be perceptible and intelligible: comprehensible evidence must correspond to consequent pathology, or else the heightened anxiety that comes with the depiction of wicked children persists undiminished. When behavior seemingly arises from a logical, conventional prompt (the Oedipal complex, for example), the audience may complete the portrait of pathology intuitively, finalizing a diagnosis implied by symptoms in the child or triggers in her environment. A correlation of causes and effects confers comfort, as it implies that developmental deviations might have been avoided and character defects recognized. When the representation of the evil child denies viewers a plausible correlation, however, they must come to terms with increased interpretive pressure. That pressure may be answered with a rational default, the expedient verdict of unmotivated madness, or it may be addressed with an earnest search, a speculative, self-reflexive survey of formative forces that might yield evil. Such scrutiny, conducted when obvious interpretive prospects are exhausted, brings the audience's own ethical sensibilities into focus as they are defined and tried in light of the dynamics onscreen. In the absence of those comforts that come with effortless legibility, this trial of the viewer, this attempt to make ethical sense of the unsettling representation of the evil child, compensates for interpretive uncertainties with conscientious consolations of its own.

HALLOWEEN: DETERMINISTIC DENSITY

Horror films embrace derangement, and the management of the monstrous sometimes requires little more than a glancing allusion to madness. Insanity serves as a formal shorthand, for example, in cases as disparate as those of Rhoda Penmark and Jason Voorhees: her wickedness in *The Bad Seed* (1956) appears as a tendency inherited from a murderous grandmother, while his mayhem in the *Friday the 13th* series (commencing in the second installment of 1981) arises in response to the decapitation of his mother. No further delving is required to grasp what these children will become or why. Such efficient explanations simplify the interpretive efforts of the viewer, who may forego the work of inferring motives. Recent films like *The Cell* (2000), *The Texas Chainsaw Massacre: The Beginning* (2006), and *Hannibal Rising* (2007) elaborate on this explanatory theme, as they epitomize a fascination with the origination of evil in childhood. These films connect popular psychology and pathology explicitly, yet they also disengage the audience to a meaningful degree. In *The Bad Seed* and *Friday the 13th* uncommon causes yield terrible effects; in these new offerings we behold singular, inimitable catalysts (a baptism synchronized with a seizure in *The Cell*, for example, or traumatic witness to cannibalism in the case of young Hannibal Lecter) that give rise to elaborate pathologies and locate evil beyond the pale of all but the most appalling domestic situations. Circumstantial rarities limit the implication of the audience, and while viewers might derive many pleasures from the spectatorial experience, an occasion for self-appraisal is lost. A merger of representational modes—the subjection of less exotic formative moments to more meticulous scrutiny—casts emergent evil in a decidedly different light, a stark illumination that unsettles the viewer but makes available compensatory consolations.

Viewed in this light, the second most comforting film of the new millennium may be Rob Zombie's *Halloween* (2007). It is not, of course, a *comfortable* film. Rendered with the same grittiness emphasized in his earlier directorial efforts, Zombie's update of the John Carpenter classic proceeds as an homage to and radical revision of the 1978 original. The film retraces the steps of Michael Myers, the iconic killer, who escapes from Smith's Grove Sanitarium, returns to Haddonfield, Illinois, on Halloween night, and menaces the heroine, Laurie Strode, slaughtering all who would impede his pursuit. Where the film departs most provocatively from its source, however, is in the depiction of the developmental throes of the ten-year-old Michael. Comfort comes in the form of legibility, of a manifest ethical progression that relieves the viewer of the most fretful, uncertain interpretive work.

The opening of the film features distilled domestic dysfunction, a cluster of cues that builds causal, catalytic momentum. Ronnie, the abusive boyfriend of Deborah Myers, Michael's mother, refers to the boy as "a little bitch" and contends that "he's probably a queer." Michael's sister, Judith, taunts her brother in a similar vein, telling him to "stop jerking off" in the bathroom and simulating masturbation when accusing him of "stroking" his pet rat to death. Against this backdrop, of course, viewers already know that Michael has butchered the rat with a penknife—he is washing blood from his hands at the moment his sister first mocks him—and a later scene will reveal evidence of violence against other animals that even Ronnie reads as a mode of compensatory empowerment. In the midst of this belittlement, Michael's affectionate exchanges with his mother serve as an opposing force and a point of origin from which a rote Oedipal dynamic unfolds. This trajectory becomes overt at school, when Michael confronts a bully named Daryl. He endures Daryl's abuse of Judith in glowering silence, but when his tormentor produces a newspaper clipping featuring a photo of Michael's mother, who dances at a gentlemen's club, and details his plans to exploit her sexually, Michael responds with wild violence. The principal separates the boys and calls Deborah, but by then the stage has been set for an ethical descent viewers can easily anticipate.

It comes as little surprise that Daryl proves to be Michael's first victim. Wearing a clown mask, Michael batters the bully to death, pausing only to claim the clipping from Daryl's pocket. Convinced of the import of Michael's behavior by Dr. Loomis, a consulting psychiatrist, Deborah (unaware of the extent and escalation of his bloodlust) confronts her son but indulgently grants him a night of trick-or-treating while she is at work. The film answers any uncertainties about the orthodox Freudian character of the boy's maternal attachment in the subsequent scene, which crosscuts images of a disconsolate Michael with Deborah's performance. The boy sits sullenly on the curb, ruefully watching passers-by, while his mother dances to the tune of Nazareth's "Love Hurts." Following the parallel sequence, Michael acts on his dejection. He murders his mother's boyfriend in the living room, Judith's boyfriend in the kitchen, and finally Judith herself in her bedroom. He considers her upturned bottom in an unhurried point-of-view shot before trading his childish mask for the expressionless latex face formerly worn by her lover; he then caresses his sister's thigh and, following an altercation, stabs her in the stomach. The change of masks implies an untimely coming of age, a maturation that coincides with Michael's annihilation of all challenges to his sexuality and disposal of all perceived competitors for his mother's attention. The second act of *Halloween* finds Dr. Loomis delving into the boy's troubled psyche, but the first furnishes the viewer with all the gestures necessary to apprehend the essence of his adult character.

Zombie's efforts yield a psychological origin story: the audience, almost certainly familiar with John Carpenter's iconic creation, witnesses incidents that give rise to the mind that inhabits the mask. Michael's ethical destiny serves as the overriding interpretive term, and the 2007 film retrofits the original narrative with a prefatory arc designed to illuminate that characterological consequence. By the time Dr. Loomis closes out his sessions with the boy—"The child christened Michael Myers has become a sort of ghost," he concedes in a voiceover—prevalent Freudian tropes allow viewers to reach the same foregone conclusion about the maladjusted man: an explicit yet unvoiced desire for the mother, a sealed system of Oedipal issues, built pressure in a crucible of abuse and exploded. As Philip Simpson suggests, a double-edged advantage comes with such determined derivation: recourse to "one or two easily identified scapegoats as root causes of the violence" tends to "provoke and reassure" the audience by confirming its deeply held beliefs, even if those beliefs amount to paranoia, prejudice, or oversimplification (18). Armed with a trebled awareness—of what the child seems to be, what he is, and what he will become—viewers may take comfort in the developmental differences that make a Michael Myers possible. If catalysts like Oedipal obsession and abuse generate interpretive confidence yet summon compassion for the boy inside the beast, however, *Halloween* offers brutal reassurance to the audience that the condemnation of the adult Michael is ultimately warranted. Viewers might consider the demise of figures like Daryl and Ronnie as intelligible juvenile retribution, but when Michael in his mid-twenties savages janitors, orderlies, guards, and teens indiscriminately, the audience is absolved of uneasy claims to empathy. Carpenter briskly strips his creation of humanity, while Zombie gradually assimilates the boy into the boogeyman. Both directors supply viewers with a secure interpretive purchase that conceives of the child as a palimpsest, discernible yet scarcely legible beneath the boldfaced text of the murderous man.

In Zombie's *Halloween*, evil has an origin, history, and destiny. The development of Michael Myers can be understood and anticipated as it trends toward a logical, inescapable conclusion. This reasoning depends on representational selectivity and interpretive oversimplification, yet the comfort it confers is no less gratifying. Armed with the requisite psychological supposi-tions, the audience enjoys the illusion of ethical expertise: the origins of evil are made appealingly plain, and cursory self-assessment will find most view-ers innocent enough should they reflect on their own behavior and relation-ships. The familial dynamic that spawns Michael Myers reveals and reassures; it offers viewers a glimpse into a credible domestic situation and sends them away uplifted by a fiction "which produces the deviant subjectivities opposite which the normal, the healthy and the pure can be known" (Halberstam 2). Michael's mature malevolence eclipses those formative moments that might otherwise give the audience pause. In the absence of such forward-looking finality, however, viewers must contend with thornier questions, the likes of which are posed in *Joshua*.

JOSHUA: EVIL AND EXCESS

A temporal shift in *Halloween* lets viewers know that little changes for Michael despite the passage of fifteen years: his character remains determ-ined by the onset of violence. His adulthood echoes his origins, and his pur-suit of Laurie Strode, the baby sister he adored as a boy, emphasizes the rigidity and finitude of his fixation and the limit of the viewer's evaluative responsibility. Even if Michael's mayhem remains a source of interest, charac-ter and motive recede as points of necessary reference. In contrast, the evil child proper—in the midst of ethical development, as a source of interest in his own right—changes the shape and nature of audience response. Resorting to madness as a shorthand explanation for pathological behavior becomes more difficult, as the culpable subject is no longer a finished pro-duct but a work in progress. Psychoanalytical sensibilities may help viewers apprehend developmental events, but the audience cannot perform a facile, finalized diagnosis when faced with inexplicable and inchoate wickedness. The evil child inspires different activity, a search for indicative differences that compensate for comforts lost. *Joshua* offers such solace, but not without undercutting expectations and waking apprehensions of its own.

Joshua originates in a domestic dynamic that instantly solicits sympathy. Although the title implies the centrality of the eponymous nine-year-old, the director, George Ratliff, aligns the progress of the film with the maturation of Joshua's sister, Lily. At "19 Days Old" we find the Cairn family—mother Abby, grandmother Hazel, and grandfather Joe—huddled around the new-born as Brad, the father, records their interactions. Joshua opens the scene playing the piano with his uncle Ned but soon loses his companion to the party fawning over the baby. He continues to play even after his mother requests an intermission, but his disobedience does not strike the assembled Cairns as inordinately willful. Only a subsequent visceral reaction—Joshua vomits as the family serenades Lily—signals the presence of an undefined undercurrent. The scene is strewn with allusions to Abby's depression following Joshua's birth, yet no subtext seems prominent enough to threaten the welfare of the family. In the absence of other indications, initial circumstances in *Joshua* suggest little more than a boy's understandable fear of displacement.

Subsequent scenes, however, introduce a strangeness into the household. Joshua, in a conversation with his father, inaugurates an equivocal distance. "Do you ever feel weird about me, your weird son?" he asks. Brad reassures Joshua every time this line of inquiry recurs, but his reactions reveal increasing uneasiness. Brad acknowledges the call to responsibility elicited by his son, but he struggles to discover a resemblance on which he might found a more settled relation. As Levinas suggests, fatherhood alone does not instate such a correspondence:

> Paternity is the relationship with a stranger who, entirely while being Other, is myself, the relationship of the ego with a myself who is nonetheless a stranger to me .... Then again, the son is not any event whatsoever that happens to me .... The son is an ego, a person. Lastly, the alterity of the son is not that of an alter ego. Paternity is not a sympathy through which I can put myself in the son's place. (*Time* 91)

"We're so different," Brad later concedes to Joshua's teacher, epitomizing the boy's alterity and his own inability to establish empathy. He struggles with his son's extraordinary intellect, his esoteric interests (such as Egyptology), and his idiosyncratic behavior, although he makes regular attempts to find common ground. Brad dramatizes the potential for frustration in the Levinasian "face-to-face relation," a critical enactment of ethical exchange (*Time* 78–79; cf. Hand 63); something about Joshua remains unfathomable to his father, and only Ned seems to possess the intuition needed to appreciate the boy's idiosyncrasies. Joshua's aloofness occurs as a puzzle, but Brad determinedly works to meet his son's perceived emotional needs.

Abby also recognizes Joshua's difference but is more engrossed in the care of Lily, who cries incessantly in a way that recalls Joshua's infantile implacability. Under pressure to pacify Lily, she conveniently converts Joshua's strange behavior into proof of his preternatural maturity. She offhandedly allows him to donate his toys to charity ("I'm starting over," he informs Brad, before preparing a stuffed panda for embalming), and later, when he asks for permission to deliver another donation, she grants it immediately, allowing him to go unattended despite Ned's concerns about his age. "Oh, come on," she sighs, "does he seem like your typical nine-year-old?" At this point viewers already have some sense of how shiftily atypical Joshua is: he is hiding nearby when Abby first responds to Lily's cries, and his screening of a videotape of his own first weeks of life suggests he might be irritating Lily to reestablish his mother's former exasperation. Joshua's motives are obscure, but his willingness to victimize his mother and his sister reveals concerted coldness. In the absence of any clear objective, however, his cruelty exceeds the prompt, a fear of displacement, that ostensibly inspires it. Symptoms of Joshua's difference proliferate, but they resist and defer interpretation.

Despite the persistence with which Joshua executes his plan, Ratliff offers few cues that might illuminate his intentions. While his efforts speak to his tenacity, neither affect nor dialogue suggests that the boy's measures are meant to be punitive, vindictive, or conducive to any end the audience can foresee with certainty. With only two exceptions, in fact, Joshua does not show emotion to any degree that is entirely intelligible. As Lily's cries and Abby's depression take their toll on every facet of the family dynamic, Joshua's absence of affect becomes a telling index of his difference. Viewers cannot determine if he is satisfied or disappointed, or if he finds the plight of his mother delicious or sickening. Like Rhoda Penmark, Joshua exists in what Chuck Jackson calls "an eerie emotional vacuum" (69); even when his mother steps on broken glass and dreamily smears blood on her calf, Joshua simply looks on, expressionless. What seems even more chilling is Joshua's recognition that failure to display emotion might be a liability. Shortly after Abby's accident, the family dog, Buster, dies. A heartbroken Brad searches for a cause (Buster's demise suggestively recalls the fate that befell animals tended by Joshua's class), yet none can be discovered. Distraught, Brad drops to his knees, hugs Buster, and chokes down tears to offer words of parting to his beloved pet. In the midst of this spontaneous grieving, Joshua falls to his own knees, embraces the body, and delivers the same lines with the same intonation. Brad recoils, and his reaction suggests that he has reached a new understanding of Joshua's stilted performance of childishness (cf. Jackson 70–72). While he hesitates to think ill of his son, whose "weirdness" suffices as an explanation for most behavior, the scene carries the viewer to increasingly unambiguous indices of Joshua's monstrous oddity.

A decisive shift occurs when a panhandler approaches Joshua at the park. In response to his solicitation, Joshua makes an offer: "I'll give you five dollars if I can throw a rock at you." The viewer alone witnesses the disclosure of this straightforwardly sadistic dimension of his character, and the scene anticipates an escalation. Shortly thereafter, Joshua persuades Abby to join him in a game of hide-and-seek. She thoroughly searches the house on crutches, only stopping when she discovers Lily is gone from her crib. Her foot bleeding freely, Abby climbs to the penthouse above the Cairns' apartment and collapses; Brad later carries her home, showing her that Lily is safely asleep with Joshua watching over her. With mock petulance, Joshua whines, "Did you even look for me, Mommy?" and Abby's appreciation of his malice sends her into a frenzy. Within the milieu of the film, she alone understands that Joshua spirited Lily away; the ferocity of her reaction implies her realization that he has conducted a siege against her sanity. Brad, who has witnessed only Abby's behavioral unevenness, commends her to psychiatric care. The audience, however, knows that Lily's disappearance was not a product of addled imagination. Although they enjoy the advantage of knowing she searched earnestly, viewers have no way of determining if the removal of Abby represents a means or an end. Joshua's cruelty remains illegible, leaving the audience to grapple with questions of intent.

Fuller revelation of Joshua's ambitions emerges, albeit unclearly. Brad quits his job to mind the children, and he returns home to learn that Hazel has taken Joshua to the museum. Feeling nostalgic, he plays the video of Lily's arrival, only to discover the recording has been taped over. At the close of the new sequence, the camera hovers over Lily's face and a voice whispers, "Nobody will ever love you." The baby cries, and a final shot reveals Joshua hiding in the nursery closet, his expression illegible as ever. Disturbed by the footage and aware of the provocation that produced his daughter's misery and his wife's breakdown, Brad races to the museum. He seemingly arrives just in time: Joshua stands with Lily's carriage at the edge of a flight of stairs, and Brad's presence prompts the boy to linger long enough for Hazel to catch up with her grandson. Brad bears the stroller to safety, but moments later Hazel—after taking Joshua's hand—tumbles after Brad. When he looks up to Joshua, the son impassively considers the father before feigning concern and hastening down. The scene is perplexing: what seems like a scheme thwarted, a plan to end competition with Lily by engineering her demise, gives way to what appears to be the impulsive murder of Hazel, and this assumes the audience, like Brad, believes Joshua pushed his grandmother. The seeming ease with which Joshua shifts between equally eligible atrocities further frustrates the search for an intelligible motive.

Given recent experience, Brad surmises that Joshua plans to dispose of Lily and takes steps to protect her. He concedes the limits of his understanding—"I know what you're doing, Josh," he maintains, "I don't know why you're doing it, but I'm on to you"—and Joshua claims not to understand, although he finds the apartment Joshua-proofed. This impasse continues until a psychologist visits at Brad's behest. Brad loves his son despite his suspicions, and he hopes diagnosis will show him a way Joshua might be recovered. Those hopes, however, are dashed when Joshua produces a drawing that strikes the psychologist as textbook evidence of abuse. Disconcerted by the doctor's insinuation, Brad announces plans to send Joshua to boarding school. Joshua runs away and reappears with a huge bruise, convincing Brad he really has suffered abuse at unknown hands. The boy's entreaties earn him entry into his parents' bedroom, a space Brad had denied him. Joshua turns his father's affection against him, using the subtlety Baudrillard describes as the special province of the child, a strategy by which "children . . . *let* adults believe that they, the children, are children" and exploit the assumption to infiltrate and effect "the eventual destruction of the superior—adult—world that surrounds them" (168–69). A second subterfuge occurs the following morning, when

Brad finds Joshua and Lily missing. His relief at discovering them safe, the brother tenderly feeding his sister, saps Brad's resistance, and he submits when Joshua requests a trip to the park. As a result, Brad ventures unwittingly onto a stage Joshua has prepared, the site of an endgame he apparently had in mind all along. That endgame begets an unsettling act of unmasking—of the father, the son, and the audience as well.

The machinery of the decisive scene is appallingly mundane. Joshua fiddles with Lily's carriage and runs away; Lily wails, and Brad discovers that her pacifier is missing. Convinced that Joshua has taken it, he commands the boy to return. Joshua mimics him instead, refusing to come back and obliging his father to catch him, acting very much like a nine-year-old. The mockery continues even then, and at last Brad slaps his son. The blow elicits a feral grin from Joshua, who hisses the words he whispered to Lily: "Nobody will ever love you." The taunt incenses Brad, and he assails Joshua with such fury that two nearby fathers must pull him away. Brad is arrested, and Joshua claims a history of abuse to the police. The lie delivers him into the custody of Ned, and Joshua unselfconsciously reveals his feelings about the new arrangement: "Ned, I'm glad you're here. I mean you, me—this feels right, doesn't it?" Seated at the piano, Joshua sings an impromptu in which he implies that his parents "should've saved themselves." During the last bars of the song, the film cuts back and forth between the piano and Joshua's room, where movers encounter evidence even viewers have not yet seen: a rubber glove, drawings that reveal Joshua's bloody sensibilities, and a dead gerbil with its belly sewn shut. Back at the bench, Joshua beams at his new guardian, finishing his song with the line "I only ever really wanted to be with you." Judging by his expression, Ned seems to appreciate the mendacious nature of his nephew, and though it affords them little relief, viewers do as well.

Joshua offers a modicum of closural comfort: intentions are revealed, and the sinister son is delivered to a more knowledgeable guardian. The viewer's position at the conclusion of the film, however, begs a battery of retrospective, self-reflexive questions. The completion of Joshua's design reveals deep premeditation; his methods are sophisticated, involving a perfect understanding of domestic and societal dynamics. As an awful prodigy who orchestrates his liberation by manipulating the adults around him, Joshua belongs to an order of conniving creatures viewers will find reassuringly rare. Nevertheless, his machinations raise troubling questions about ethical maturity, as the reconstitution of the family with himself at the center occurs as an objective fit for a nine-year-old boy. Moreover, disclosure of this motive obliges viewers to abandon a viable hypothesis, an account of behavior that proposes the punishment of the mother and destruction of the rival as understandable ambitions. Such a shift erodes interpretive confidence, and a surplus of evidence (the scene with the panhandler, the deaths of Buster and the classroom animals, and the eviscerated gerbil) urges viewers to press further, to conceive of pathologies darker than the central scheme implies.

The emergence of an intelligible motive allays some anxieties, but Joshua embodies an evil that exceeds inclusive explication.

That such excess might arise in an unremarkable, even healthy, family confronts the audience with a second source of discomfort. While most viewers have neither suffered nor perpetrated the abuses featured in *Halloween*, they are likely to reflect on Abby's understandable distraction with mingled censure and sympathy and on Brad's thrashing of Joshua with a distress leavened by cathartic satisfaction. However, Joshua's plot lays bare the manipulative tactics in which most children are versed and, given the consequences that attend intimations of abuse, the asymmetry of the parent-child relationship in the eyes of ethics and the law. *Joshua* offers a disquieting reminder of a lopsidedness that places adults at the mercy of subversive children, and it confronts viewers with the terrible dependency at the heart of the family. The film features a discomfiting disclosure, what Philip J. Nickel calls "a sudden tearing-away of the intellectual trust that stands behind our actions," a rending that exposes "our vulnerabilities in relying on the world and on other people" (28). Viewers may feel some pleasure in being thus undeceived, but the film unkindly reminds us how much we depend on deception.

Nickel approaches such revelation in sanguine terms: the tearing-away viewers experience reminds them of the "epistemological choice" on which the illusion of security depends (17), and he reassures them that such comforting constructions are indispensable (28–30). As I have suggested, however, the suspension of soothing convictions, especially as a result of the encounter with the evil child, yields ethical repercussions that persist after threats have been disclosed or dispelled. The representational strategies used in *Joshua* speed the resumption of trust, but they do not leave the viewer's universe undisturbed. In addition to exposing the motives and machinations of the young and reminding adults of their vulnerability, horrific depictions of children call into question efforts to realize positive, predictable developmental outcomes that correlate to responsible parenting. We may find ways to manage or mitigate the risks that come with the existence of children, helpless as we are to evade them. We may also try to foster creativity, model morality, and cultivate virtue. As Brad's example implies, however, the dangers we pose to ourselves and to others as a result of our impulses, assumptions, and attitudes cannot be so easily exhumed and forgotten. The extent of our knowledge and imagination, the faith we repose in our institutions and relationships, and our reliance on the tools we use to identify and remedy illness and iniquity may also be challenged and ultimately shaken. These are the matters *Home Movie* explores.

HOME MOVIE: ACCIDENTAL DRAGONS

Home Movie unfolds as a faux documentary, a chronicle of life in the Poe family. David, the father, is a pastor, one who hams it up before the camera and jokes impishly behind it. Clare, the mother, is a child psychiatrist who treats the camera as a professional tool but indulgently yields to her husband's cinematic caprices. They are the parents of twins, Jack and Emily, and the narrative proper begins with footage of their tenth birthday party on Halloween night. David and Clare caper around the dining room in high spirits; Jack and Emily, however, sit silent and unmoving, wearing stylized dragon masks. As with *Joshua*, conflict emerges immediately, if enigmatically: when the children realize their father decorated their cake with inextinguishable novelty candles, Jack douses it with water. The film cuts to the family playing hide-and-seek in a basement maze; at the rear of the cellar, the children find a dragon puppet. At the close of the scene, as the camera fixes on the exit at the end of the darkened hallway, Clare exclaims, "Did you just bite me?" The addressee is never identified, yet themes introduced in the sequence—dragons, masks, and biting—eventually resurface and offer unsettling responses to the unanswered question.

Despite their participation in the game of hide-and-seek, the children seem reluctant to engage with their parents. Their sullenness contrasts starkly with the exuberance of David and Clare, who tirelessly exert themselves to engage Jack and Emily. The director, Christopher Denham, tasks the audience with reconciling the dispositions of the elder and younger Poes, but the morbid sensibilities of the children resist assimilation to the parental dynamic. As Colette Balmain suggests, "in the contemporary monstrous-child horror film, the family unit itself is figured as innocent," and the children occur as products of "another irreducibly different world" (136). For the majority of the film, the children inhabit that world; they do not speak to their parents at all. Strategic editing omits the dialogue of Jack and Emily whenever it would occur; missing footage and scrolling videotape yields uncanny silence broken only by gibberish exchanged between the twins in the middle of the film. "It's like their own language," Clare complains, and she scolds the children for keeping secrets though David encourages them to do so. Those secrets, however, become inflected with menace as a result of the children's rebellious behavior. While malice emerges gradually in *Joshua*, leaving viewers to guess the extent of Joshua's implication in the anguish of the family, Jack and Emily express mutinous animosity in every gesture. Their malevolence is legible, even though their intentions are not.

The gulf widens after the birthday party, as a session of batting practice ends with Jack hurling a rock at his father. Clare, in search of a lost baseball, encounters her daughter drawing outside the children's playhouse. A sign outside reads "Jack and Emily's Clubhouse—No Parents Allowed," and Emily denies her mother entry before grudgingly consenting to be wheeled to the backyard in a wagon, eyes closed and arms folded. David punishes Jack with yard work, but the boy finds a dead insect that engrosses his attention. His father urges him to throw the bug away ("Dead things go in trash bags," he explains), but the scene ends before Jack complies. Almost every attempt at bonding, discipline, or dialogue ends in some failure to connect, disrupting a dynamic characterized primarily by parental attentiveness. Only the telling of a bedtime story, "the most vastly inappropriate fairy tale I've ever heard," according to Clare, yields some semblance of togetherness, although the composition of the shot, featuring all four Poes huddled in bed, seems like a parental contrivance. The story describes the trickery employed by a two-headed dragon to earn the trust of children; he dons a paper-bag mask, impersonates a child, and then devours his new peers. Jack and Emily find the story riveting, and the viewer soon learns that the tale anticipates their own growing appetites.

The earliest manifestation of this hunger occurs when Clare allows Jack to make his own lunch. She tries to guess what he has concocted, yet the key ingredient proves to be a goldfish. What might initially be understood as ghastly error, however, soon yields to blatant cruelty. Emily crushes a frog in a vise, and on Christmas morning David finds the family cat crucified. For interpretive purposes the crucifixion is pivotal: that callousness cannot be dismissed as accidental, and it occurs to Clare as a symptom with an unknown cause. "My children need help," she concedes, and many viewers will recognize the abuse of animals (as was the case with Michael Myers, an age-mate of the twins) as a token of additional pathological prospects. As their indifference to animals implies, something is lacking in Jack and Emily. In Levinasian terms, as Katz explains, that lack occurs as an incipient evil, "the inability to be attuned to the other" (215). Clare balks at the recognition of such coldness, yet she sets out in search of a source and finds an eligible origin instantly: her husband's drinking. The connection between David's dependency and the insensitivity of the children at first seems tenuous; the notion gains traction, however, when Clare discovers an inebriated David in bed with both children, their bodies gouged with bites. The children blame "the man in the closet," but the film allows the viewer to entertain the possibility that David is guilty. Clare reveals that David was abused as a child, and her account is cross-cut with shots of him swilling whiskey. "There's a lot I don't know about my husband," she admits, but by the end of the scene she turns to bedrock fact: "The man in the closet is not real. The bite marks are." The audience likewise has evidence from which a hypothesis might be derived, reference to the familiar trope that links pathological practice explicitly to a precedent catalyst. The inclinations of Jack and Emily accordingly might be explained away by David's drunken transgressions.

Circumstances soon reveal the culprits, but not before marital tensions complicate the viewer's interpretive work. On Valentine's Day, Clare prepares to take Jack and Emily to her mother's house, away from David. In response, David fumes, "Our kids are not normal," and he indicates that Clare's normalizing design, "to move into the middle of nowhere and raise them in a Norman Rockwell home," simply "didn't work." He rehearses their misconduct and concludes with new information: "I saw them eating raw meat." The film juxtaposes that surprise with a later recording made by Clare. She reveals that the children have been expelled for cornering and biting a boy named Christian; David then discovers a drawing that indicates they planned the attack. In an effort to understand the incident, Clare administers a Rorschach test to Jack, while David has a tête-à-tête with Emily. Counseling and confession, however, prove ineffectual, and their inability to fathom the intentions of their children prompts Clare and David to counter radical otherness with radical measures: Clare medicates Jack and Emily, and David attempts an ersatz exorcism. The sequence ends with all four Poes whimpering and spent. When the footage resumes, however, Clare declares victory: "Two months have passed. I'm happy to report that since my last report Jack and Emily's antisocial behavior has surceased." As David hides Easter eggs, Clare offers a self-satisfied statement of faith: "There is no good child; there is no bad child. There is only diagnosis, and with the diagnosis, treatment. I have treated my children." The viewer, of course, has good reason to doubt her success, since Clare has silenced symptoms without addressing underlying causes. The third episode of biting, intimations of an unspecified trouble that spurred the family to relocate, the abuse of animals, and the disquieting appetites of the twins reveal the insufficiency of prior efforts to explain away their behavior vis-à-vis David's drinking. Clare's conviction provides a momentary respite, yet generic expectations brace the viewer for an upending of that confidence.

Prior to the egg hunt, Jack and Emily are giggly and loving. They speak intelligibly for the first time and express affection openly. They have also befriended Christian, which Clare takes as proof of the virtues of her treatment. That certainty, however, is short-lived, and panic ensues when the parents discover that all three children have slipped from the bedroom. In a frenetic scene shot by David as he sprints to the clubhouse, the viewer learns that Jack and Emily have butchered the family dog (his head is mounted on a stake); have rejected their parents altogether (the camera pans across a photo with the faces of Clare and David scratched out); have resumed their cruelty (their walls are adorned with gutted frogs); and have stuffed Christian in a trash bag, tied him to a table, and—as evidenced by the utensils Jack brandishes—turned to cannibalism. The script then takes advantage of a narrative contrivance to keep the children at home (Jack and Emily are remanded to the custody of their parents due to the holiday), and their detention yields a confrontation that shatters any illusion of a cure. "The Jack and Emily Show" follows, with Emily manning the camera as brother and sister prepare snares for their parents. The trap is sprung, incapacitating both mother and father, and the recording eventually concludes with David and Clare stuffed in plastic bags themselves, tied to the dining room table, flanked by their children in paper-bag masks, forks and knives in hand. The ending transforms the viewing experience, as it implies that the children produced the final cut of the faux documentary. The staging of those closing scenes further complicates the work of interpretation, as it imbues the iniquity of the children over the course of the entire production with a measure of performative self-awareness. Moreover, the months-long "surcease" of symptoms and consequent simulation of childishness is exposed as a preternatural pretense. Such a conclusion sets viewers adrift, leaving them with provocative yet partial explanations of pathology and fresh sources of distress.

In response to Clare's claim that the tale of the dragon and the paper-bag mask was dreadfully inappropriate, David alleges that the story has an obvious moral: "Don't trust strangers." That those strangers might assume such an innocuous guise yet express such an appalling pathology is the greatest of the ironies *Home Movie* entertains. The prospect that the children have turned to cannibalism—an appetite inspired by birthday masks, a puppet, and a bedtime story—alters the complexion of the viewer's interpretive work as well. While Joshua's machinations might be understood as products of a deep design hatched in an atmosphere of parental inattention, the games of Jack and Emily encourage the audience to find the care of David and Clare itself blameworthy. The alternative is to locate blame beyond the pale of the family, to account for the malevolence of such children via madness, inherency, or the influence of diabolical forces (cf. Hantke 9, Jackson 66, and Sobchack 150). The genre makes such prospects possible, yet resorting to them represents an abdication of the viewer's most significant responsive opportunity. As Martin F. Norden suggests, horror filmmakers routinely employ the image of the Other as a figure that viewers can inscribe with intolerable content (xxviii; cf. Halberstam 85, Santilli 176); in the case of evil children (the masked Michael, the expressionless Joshua, the unfathomable Jack and Emily), viewers find especially eligible opacities, surfaces on which they can imprint a variety of motives, appetites, and inclinations. Such inscription, however, represents only half the input that filmmakers spur viewers to contribute. If the children wear masks, literally and figuratively, on which viewers must write desire, formulating explanations that speak to inscrutable iniquity, the adults around those children serve as screens on which viewers must project themselves. The self-reflexive ethical assessment that attends the consideration of bare and masquerading faces—what Levinas describes as the way the face of the Other "summons me . . . recalls my responsibility, and calls me into question" ("Ethics" 83)—asks the audience to appraise methods and intentions, attitudes and practices, and frailties and failings in an effort to make sense of what might seem senseless. That occasion for observation and critical self-articulation is the principal positive term that the depiction of the evil child makes available to the audience.

Even a cursory appraisal of the collapses that occur in the midst of such creative ethical engagement is sobering. As my earlier reference to Nickel hints, encounters with evil children rob viewers of the illusion of safety—"there is no resolution to our fears," he contends, "except to go on" (20). Going on, I would argue, is irrevocably altered by that face-to-face exchange. In *Joshua* and *Home Movie*, husbands learn to doubt wives, wives to mistrust their husbands; psychology fails, and faith founders; the law stands idly by or villainizes victims. Adults reliably underestimate what Baudrillard calls "the intelligence of evil" (86); they lack the imagination to contend with that against which there is no acceptable defense. If the child-as-monster serves a cultural function by policing normative borders, making audiences mindful of what dwells beyond the preserve of the permissible (cf. Cohen 12–16, Creed 10–11), it also insists there are traitors among us, outsiders hiding in plain sight. If the image of the killer, as Stephen Hantke proposes, promotes a proliferation of efforts by which we might grasp and answer evil (11), evil children stifle such efforts, calling the authority, integrity, and sanity of their accusers into question. If viewers are perpetually threatened by the return of evils ostensibly vanquished (cf. Kristeva 4, Santilli 185), the persistence of the evil child reminds us that these monsters are often homegrown. The invitation to inscription, which prompts the audience to appraise the childlike faces of evil and spurs viewers to turn the same critical, ethical gaze on themselves, offers a kind of consolation for our otherwise insupportable condition, the inescapable anxiety that attends the ubiquity of children.

ORPHAN: SOOTHING CONCLUSIONS

In light of that anxiety, the most comforting film of the new millennium may be Jaume Collet-Serra's *Orphan*, which improves on the representational relief provided by *Halloween*. The narrative presents viewers with telling incongruities that make Esther, the titular orphan, reassuringly singular. From the beginning, when prospective parents Kate and John Coleman discover the lonely girl, evidence of her eccentricity occurs unremittingly. Esther is Russian and dresses exclusively in frocks. According to Sister Abigail, director of the orphanage, Esther is "very mature for her age"; she wears ribbons around her wrists and neck, and attempts to remove them (per the nun) have met with vehement resistance. When asked why she is not playing with her peers, Esther remarks, "I guess I'm different." Difference surfaces in increasingly obvious ways when Esther enters her new environment. She locks the bathroom door when she bathes despite guarantees of privacy; she shrieks when a classmate snatches at the ribbon around her neck; she coolly crushes a dove her brother, Daniel, has wounded with a paintball gun. Kate and John, obliged to reckon strangeness along with the audience, account for their new daughter's behavior via the "discourse of difference," and they approach her as an innocent alien, one who must be "understood, liberated, coddled, and recognized" (Baudrillard 125, 128). Intimations of Esther's otherness become comprehensible, even quaint, when attuned to their expectations of a precocious nine-year-old.

What seems explicable given Esther's origin and the pressures of adjustment, however, quickly becomes sinister. When she shoves the offending classmate from a slide, the audience must sit in judgment: can the incident be understood as impulsive retribution, or is it an index of an inward condition? Although her new sister, Max, proclaims Esther's innocence, the film supports the second prospect, hewing close to stock Freudian logic. While Esther cultivates an affectionate rapport with her father, she resists her mother's attempts to connect. Kate soon becomes suspicious of Esther's performance: "She's always on her best behavior with you," she complains to John; "she's completely different with me." Sister Abigail later seconds Kate's opinion, and Esther confirms all suspicions soon thereafter, bashing the nun with a hammer. Unaware of the murder, Kate nevertheless delves into the mystery of Esther, while John remains willfully benighted. The audience, in contrast, bears witness to a clandestine escalation. Esther, who suspects that Daniel might have witnessed the assault, accosts him with a knife; she throws a tantrum in secret, releasing rage she concealed when meeting with Kate's therapist; she switches the black light in her aquarium on and off, revealing a ghastly gallery of fluorescent images superimposed over her cheery paintings. In keeping with the theme of analytical insufficiency, Kate's therapist finds nothing wrong with Esther. Kate ironically performs a more incisive diagnosis via the Internet, but John rejects her findings and questions her motives. After an affront that recalls Joshua's mockery of Brad, Kate's authority is undone in an altercation with the conniving child: she grabs the girl by the arm, and Esther, exhibiting uncanny resolve, later snaps the limb in a vise. A confrontation follows, and Esther, fully aware of her power over her "abusive" mother, razes the illusion of innocence. Kate asserts her parental prerogative and tries to send the girl to bed, to which Esther replies "Honestly, we're past that now, aren't we?" And Kate, in a manner that mirrors the viewer's inability to account for the duplicity and audacity of this wicked little girl, helplessly concedes.

The filmmakers heighten anxiety in subsequent scenes, exposing the potential for evil that abides in every child. Threatened by Daniel's attempt to recover evidence of the murder, Esther sets his tree house ablaze with him inside. Later, at the hospital, she cunningly manages to smother him, only to see him resuscitated by the medical staff. Kate, enraged, strikes the girl, and orderlies sedate Kate just as she receives a call from the Saarne Institute, a hospital she contacted in an earlier effort to unearth Esther's past. As she drifts into unconsciousness, an exasperated John announces plans to take the children home. The following scene concludes the narrative trajectory the audience has been encouraged to anticipate, an attempted consummation of the Electra complex: in a dress stolen from her mother, Esther mingles childlike and adult gestures in an unnerving effort to seduce her father. Her forwardness prompts him to recoil and rebuff her, and only then is the audience relieved of the evaluative anxieties inspired by Esther's unsettling presence.

In the hospital, Kate connects with the Saarne Institute and learns that Esther is not a nine-year-old Russian girl: she is Leena Klammer, a 33-year-old Estonian whose hypopituitarism has allowed her to pass as a child. Cutting back and forth between the hospital and Esther's bedroom, the viewer learns that the ribbons she wears hide scars from the straitjacket she once wore, that wrappings conceal the curvature of her body, and that she killed seven people prior to her flight to the United States. Kate calls the police and races home, but she arrives too late to save John; Leena springs from the shadows and savages the man who spurned her advances. Using his gun, Leena shoots Kate, but despite her wound Kate incapacitates Leena and escapes. A second skirmish finds the pair fallen through the ice at a nearby pond; Kate clutches the edge of the broken surface, and Leena clings to her. With a knife behind her back, Leena, assuming the guise of Esther once more, pleads with Kate: "Please don't let me die, Mommy!" she cries. Kate, fully aware of the nature of her "daughter," responds with an imprecation—"I'm not your fucking Mommy!"—and delivers a vicious kick that breaks Leena's neck. With that muscular denunciation, Kate exorcizes the deceptions and dependencies embodied by the figure of the evil child on behalf of the viewer.

The anxious interpretive work that attends the evaluation and condemnation of an immature ethical agent and her hateful behavior yields to the effortless indictment of Leena Klammer, a mature murderess. She replicates the strangeness of a boy like Joshua, yet her physical difference, seemingly prodigious intellect, and behavioral idiosyncrasies are readily explicable. Her performance of childishness surpasses that of Jack and Emily, yet the film deepens the gulf between the player and her persona, endows the actress with a lifetime of practice, and treats the role of "Esther" as a consummate act of passing. Her discomfiting desire for possession of the father, a mirror image of the formative forces that drive the monstrosity of Michael Myers, becomes a legible expression of frustrated adult lust. In addition, vivid symptoms like her shocking self-injury smack of settled insanity, a madness that predates the events of the film and absolves viewers of interpretive accountability. Hers is not an equivocal iniquity, not an "insipid simulation," as Baudrillard might say (124), but a species of unqualified evil that completely answers the ambivalence of the audience, the reluctance to condemn the child and thereby scrutinize our idea of childhood, our families, our institutions, and our own ethical selves. With clean consciences, with a certainty and righteousness denied to us in our dealings with representations of legitimate children, evil and otherwise, the audience, like Kate, can send the threat that Esther represents drifting down into the dark.

WORK CITED

Balmain, Colette. "The Enemy Within: The Child as Terrorist in the Contemporary American Horror Film." *Monsters and the Monstrous: Myths and Metaphors of Enduring Evil*. Ed. Niall Scott. New York: Rodopi, 2007. 133–47. Print.

Baudrillard, Jean. *The Transparency of Evil: Essays on Extreme Phenomena*. New York: Verso, 1993. Print.

Cohen, Jeffrey Jerome. "Monster Culture (Seven Theses)." *Monster Theory: Reading Culture*. Ed. Cohen. Minneapolis: U of Minnesota P, 1996. 3–25. Print.

Creed, Barbara. *The Monstrous-Feminine: Film, Feminism, Psychoanalysis*. New York: Routledge, 1993. Print.

Freeland, Cynthia A. *The Naked and the Undead: Evil and the Appeal of Horror*. Boulder, CO: Westview P, 2000. Print.

Halberstam, Judith. *Skin Shows: Gothic Horror and the Technology of Monsters*. Durham, NC: Duke UP, 1995. Print.

Halloween. Dir. John Carpenter. Perf. Donald Pleasance and Jamie Lee Curtis. Starz/Anchor Bay, 2001. DVD.

Halloween. Dir. Rob Zombie. Perf. Malcolm McDowell and Tyler Mane. Weinstein Company, 2007. DVD.

Hand, Seán. "Shadowing Ethics: Levinas's View of Art and Aesthetics." *Facing the Other: The Ethics of Emmanuel Levinas*. Ed. Hand. Richmond, Surrey: Curzon P, 1996. 63–89. Print.

Hantke, Stephen. "Monstrosity without a Body: Representational Strategies in the Popular Serial Killer Film." *Post Script* 22.2 (Winter-Spring 2003). Web. 16 August 2010.

Home Movie. Dir. Christopher Denham. Perf. Adrian Pasdar and Cady McClain. MPI Home Video, 2009. DVD.

Jackson, Chuck. "Little, Violent, White: The Bad Seed and the Matter of Children." *The Journal of Popular Film and Television* 28.2 (Summer 2000): 64–73. Print.

Joshua. Dir. George Ratliff. Perf. Sam Rockwell and Vera Farmiga. 20th Century Fox, 2008. DVD.

Katz, Claire Elise. "Raising Cain: The Problem of Evil and the Question of Responsibility." *Cross Currents* 55.2 (Summer 2005): 215–33. Print.

Kristeva, Julia. *Powers of Horror: An Essay on Abjection*. Trans. Leon S. Roudiez. New York: Columbia UP, 1982. Print.

Levinas, Emmanuel. "Ethics as First Philosophy." *The Levinas Reader*. Eds. Seán Hand. Trans. Hand and Michael Temple. Malden, MA: Blackwell, 1989. 75–87. Print.

———. *Time and the Other and Additional Essays*. Trans. Richard A. Cohen. Pittsburgh, PA: Duquesne UP, 2008. Print.

———. *Totality and Infinity: An Essay on Exteriority*. Trans. Alphonso Lingis. Pittsburgh, PA: Duquesne UP, 1969. Print.

Nickel, Philip J. "Horror and the Idea of Everyday Life: On Skeptical Threats in *Psycho* and *The Birds*." *The Philosophy of Horror*. Ed. Thomas Fahy. Lexington: UP of Kentucky, 2010. 14–32. Print.

Norden, Martin F. Introduction. *The Changing Face of Evil in Film and Television*. Ed. Norden. New York: Rodopi, 2007. xi–xxi. Print.

Orphan. Dir. Jaume Collet-Serra. Perf. Vera Farmiga and Isabelle Fuhrman. Warner Home Video, 2009. DVD.

Santilli, Paul. "Culture, Evil, and Horror." *American Journal of Economics and Sociology* 66.1 (2007): 173–93. Print.

Simpson, Philip L. *Psycho Paths: Tracking the Serial Killer Through Contemporary American Film and Fiction*. Carbondale: Southern Illinois UP, 2000. Print.

Sobchack, Vivian. "Bringing It All Back Home: Family Economy and Generic Exchange." *The Dread of Difference: Gender and the Horror Film*. Ed. Barry Keith Grant. Austin: U of Texas P, 1996. 143–63. Print.

Private Lessons from Dumbledore's "Chamber of Secrets": The Riddle of the Evil Child in *Harry Potter and the Half-Blood Prince*

HOLLY BLACKFORD

> "No book would have given [Tom Riddle] that information."
> —Dumbledore, *Half-Blood Prince*

The penultimate novel in J. K. Rowling's *Harry Potter* series, *Harry Potter and the Half-Blood Prince* grapples with the fundamental challenge of uncovering the conditions under which a child can be understood as evil. By "evil," I mean not a simple binary of good versus evil, as charged by critic Jennifer Sattaur, but a complicated, motivated evil arising from the deepest unmet longings of childhood. In *Half-Blood Prince*, Dumbledore gives Harry private lessons in which he pieces together a history of Lord Voldemort's deprived childhood and development as the orphan Tom Riddle, effectively acting the part of a Freudian analyst who seeks an explanatory reminiscence to account for and *ultimately erase* his institution's—and his own— culpability in fostering the dark lord's education. Looking at Tom's past through the Pensieve, a container of people's memories in liquid form, Dumbledore identifies disturbing elements in Tom's character that, he asserts, were present from their first meeting. Dumbledore thus parses out nature from environmental training, particularly the complex role that the school might have played in Tom's development. This is very much what adults do when a delinquent is brought to trial, sorting out blame and looking at one another to determine responsibility, reifying the governing assumption of John Locke's *tabula rasa*.[1] In particular, Dumbledore, who first admitted Tom to Hogwarts, seeks to avoid sole culpability. By initiating

Harry into his memories, Dumbledore seems to wish for verification of his analysis of Tom's inherently evil nature. Dumbledore's private lessons with Harry display an educator's need to deflect responsibility for the deprived child who embarks on a life of crime.

Dumbledore declares that his memories at least are completely and satisfyingly "accurate," but this is ironic because if the Pensieve teaches anything, it teaches that memory is at worst a product of tampering and at best a product of a particular point of view. The owner of the memory clearly affects the telling, and, as Karin Westman notes, some of the memories are the result of persuasion and therefore dubious, just as the Pensieve violates privacy and boundaries. However, throughout *Half-Blood Prince*, Harry takes an opposing view to Dumbledore's, viewing his own childhood as all too similar to Tom's. Harry thus provides us with an alternative interpretation to the illuminating Pensieve, revealing that the very qualities Dumbledore blindly attributes to early deprivations and flaws in Tom Riddle's nature and family are embedded in the curriculum of Hogwarts. For example, Dumbledore focuses on Tom's early need for trophies and valuable objects without recognizing how the school's culture places value on such trophies and objects. Additionally, Dumbledore points out Tom's "'obvious instincts for cruelty, secrecy, and domination'" (*Half-Blood Prince* 276) and distaste for commonness without recognizing how the school inculcates competition and the drive for dominance in the students through houses, sports, point systems, hierarchies, and favoritism of particular students, not to mention the overriding division between "a socially superior and elite caste of wizards and witches, against the socially inferior and less important muggles" (Sattaur 2–3). The school places special value on students who possess important lineage and who achieve high status such as Prefect, Head Boy, Outstanding O.W.L. or N.E.W.T. status, and Quidditch player. Yet the internalization of the desire for prestige is viewed, in Tom, as evil.

Half-Blood Prince is a rewriting of *Chamber of Secrets* in that both concern the discovery of old, unauthorized books that corrupt the "innocent" children who find and use them—and who, like Dumbledore, ultimately erase their own blame, conveniently externalizing "the nature" of evil as "other." In *Chamber*, Tom Riddle "comes out" of his old diary, which Ginny Weasley, the younger sister of Harry's best friend, Ron, has come to possess. By writing her own discontents in the margins of Tom's childhood diary, Ginny unknowingly opens the school's "chamber of secrets" and brings Tom Riddle back to life. Her re-birthing of sixteen-year-old Tom unleashes horrors upon the school, but in *Half-Blood Prince* the uncovering of the child Tom Riddle is a means to knowledge for Harry. In *Half-Blood Prince*, Harry similarly finds an old book which conveys knowledge in hand-written margins, knowledge that allows him to succeed by reading "between the lines" of the official curriculum. Rowling encourages us to consider the two novels together, emphasizing that the potions book is fifty years old, just as the chamber of secrets was last opened fifty years before Harry's second year. Comparing the stories is instructive because it clarifies the double-voiced discourse about what it takes to succeed at Hogwarts—one authorized and one unauthorized but nevertheless implicit in school culture. As a rewriting of *Chamber, Half-Blood Prince* asks us to read Tom as the unacknowledged child in the margins of Hogwarts education. The child who internalizes unauthorized school lessons—about needing pedigree, winning, and dominating—is symbolically the "secret" chamber embedded in the very walls and chambers of the school. Tom is a monstrous creation of school culture that, in the paradigm of Frankenstein's monster, Dumbledore does not wish to acknowledge.

Dumbledore's need to mentor Harry implies a subtle recognition of his guilt in contributing to Tom's path by denying him a way to voice his own shame, a guilt he wishes to rectify by nurturing Harry's development. I say "nurturing" with a critical eye, for nurturing involves modeling domination, a quality so feared in Tom. I will investigate the imagery of penetration in Dumbledore's lessons and how those lessons make Harry feel obedient but invaded, along with how the final scene in the cave reverses the power structure of the lessons by figuring the cave as a replication of Dumbledore's office. In the cave scene, Harry forces Dumbledore to drink Tom's poison; in doing so, Harry experiences the pleasure of dominance that Dumbledore's intimate lessons have modeled. The queer imagery surrounding Harry, Tom, and Dumbledore, all of whom seek to dominate and penetrate one another in various ways, ultimately speaks to the embedded violence of a classically based educational system in which select boys are equated with nobility and penetrated by wise older men.

I interpret Harry's similarity to Tom Riddle in light of other critics, such as Michael Bronski, Tison Pugh and David Wallace, and Catherine Tosenberger, who have noted analogies between Harry's "coming out" as a wizard to the queer child's experience. This understanding allows us, in turn, to regard the story of Tom Riddle in *Half-Blood Prince* as an unsuccessful coming-out story. If Harry's story in the series follows the paradigm of the coming-out story, and if Harry recognizes the similarities between his story and Tom's, then we have to ask *why* Tom's story is an aborted coming-out story in which a child is cast as a closeted monster that the school cannot exorcise. Tom's story is that of a neglected child aware of his "difference" and left with little guidance for negotiating inherent messages in the school about who and what are valuable. A discourse of shame, analogous to the shame of sexual difference, surrounds Tom's feelings about his background—lack of purity, family, belonging, and accouterments—and this shame sets in motion Tom's intense absorption of many Hogwarts lessons that school officials prefer not to acknowledge. This seems to be why it is Tom's poison that Dumbledore must drink in the end. This poison embodies an educator's failure and individualist perspective, the poison of seeing Tom as a flawed individual and refusing a broader structural or cultural lens on "the capitalist and consumerist culture" (Sattaur 1) of school. *Half-Blood Prince* ultimately shows how a school prefers potters to riddles for their malleability, but inevitably creates monstrous riddles.

THE IMPENETRABLE RIDDLE: THE HIDDEN CURRICULUM AT HOGWARTS

In *Half-Blood Prince*, Dumbledore presents the memory of Tom hoarding the possessions of other orphans and analyzes this as part of Tom's character: "'the young Tom Riddle liked to collect trophies. You saw the box of stolen articles he had hidden in his room. These were taken from victims of his bullying behavior, souvenirs, if you will, of particularly unpleasant bits of magic. Bear in mind his magpie-like tendency, for this, particularly, will be important later'" (277). However, readers familiar with the series might well feel that what Dumbledore views as a "magpie-like tendency" is a pervasive aspect of wizard culture, with its numerous trophies and cups, its hierarchies and conspicuous consumption, its investment in magical objects (such as the power given to the Sorting Hat, which magically determines to which house a student should be assigned), and the value it places on high-quality broomsticks like the Nimbus Two Thousand or Firebolt.[2] Furthermore, it is evident that students and faculty notice when people sport shabby robes and secondhand books,[3] and riches and prestigious titles—not to mention broomsticks—command respect, for Harry's money immediately earns him status in the first novel, and his expenditures somewhat compensate for his lack of knowledge about Hogwarts, wizards, and family. The very fact that the school founders have special, valuable objects and heirlooms—so coveted by Tom—conveys the founding structure of capital and rare objects to the school. Dumbledore analyzes Tom's attachment to material possessions as unique to Tom's desires, yet the novel conveys the value of those objects to everyone.

In many ways, the child who covets trophies and the prestige they convey only heightens the general atmosphere of the capitalistic display pervasive in the school's culture, which *Half-Blood Prince* particularly acknowledges when Harry stumbles upon the Room of Requirement and its massive stash of tokens and objects:

> [H]e could not help but be overawed by what he was looking at. He was standing in a room the size of a large cathedral, whose high windows were sending shafts of light down upon what looked like a city with towering walls, built of what Harry knew must be objects hidden by generations of Hogwarts inhabitants. There were alleyways and roads bordered by teetering piles of broken and damaged furniture, stowed away, perhaps, to hide evidence of mishandled magic, or else hidden

by castle-proud house-elves. There were thousands and thousands of books, no doubt banned or graffitied or stolen. There were winged catapults and Fanged Frisbees, some still with enough life in them to hover halfheartedly over the mountains of other forbidden items; there were chipped bottles of congealed potions, hats, jewels, cloaks; there were what looked like dragon eggshells, corked battles whose contents still shimmered evilly.... Harry hurried forward into one of the many alleyways between all this hidden treasure. (526)

It is no accident that this room of stashed objects becomes the very room through which Voldemort's minions, the Death Eaters, invade Hogwarts. It contains the Vanishing Cabinet that is the twin of one found in Borgin and Burkes, the sleazy shop that sells dark objects. The school's propensity to clutch and invest in objects is symbolically a match to the designs of the commercial store. This room of objects is the seat of entry between school and broader capitalism, with all its attendant waste and wreckage. The room is described as a vanished city, akin to an Atlantis, a non-navigable heap of cultural refuse. It is not a place that exists for school officials. In other words, Hogwarts pretends to be, but is not, sheltered from the broader capitalism of the world. Dumbledore would have Harry believe that a magpie-like tendency was a unique element of Tom Riddle, but the Room of Requirement reveals a consumer wasteland, a mirror of the "chamber of secrets" that the school wishes to repress or deny.[4] The analogy to a "large cathedral" conveys the sacred quality of consumed goods to those who have made a pilgrimage to this room.[5]

The portrait that Dumbledore paints of Tom Riddle is of a child deprived early in life of security and stability, who then sought compensation through the desperate accumulation of valuable objects. Quite literally, these objects are acquired to support the soul, which seems to have been diminished by Tom's very conditions at birth. Dumbledore spends time conveying memories of Merope's (Tom's mother's) abusive and dilapidated household, as if these deprivations explain the depraved tendencies of Tom. However, it is Harry, who, in the memory of the orphanage, seems to be the focalizer in the line, "there was no denying that this was a grim place in which to grow up" (*Half-Blood Prince* 268), an observation that a sparse, impoverished environment might well result in an insatiable desire for things. The desire for trophies and collections is, of course, not foreign to childhood in general, as shown earlier in the series when the impoverished Ron introduces Harry to wizard trading cards (comparable to celebrity baseball cards that children collect and trade), which tellingly bear the face of Dumbledore upon them, acknowledging his celebrity status in mass-produced objects. And clearly Tom is not the only student who becomes attached to things that increase prestige. The book of potions that Harry discovers allows him to outshine even Hermione in potions class, and because of its tip that bezoar can act as antidote to poison, he rescues Ron and achieves yet another feather in his cap for saving members of the Weasley family, a family in which he enjoys honorary membership. Harry begins to sleep with this book, hoarding it and seeking it out as a friend, mentor, or parent. Strikingly, the "official" directions of the old potions book set the children up to fail at the concoctions (telling them, for example, to cut an ingredient when it cannot be cut). To make an assigned potion, Harry must follow the owner's handwritten changes. The book is a corrupting force insofar as it makes Harry's achievements dishonest and fuels his ability to impress potions-master Slughorn, yet seems like fair play in a curriculum that refuses to provide the students with all the information they need.

Similarly, Dumbledore analyzes Tom's ability to gather around him a group of peers as a negative and suspicious trait and views them as forerunners to the Death Eaters. However, the formation of consistent peer groups is of great value to the school and explicitly encouraged by the division of students into houses and classes that define their primary friendships. As Professor McGonagall explains in *Sorcerer's Stone*, the houses are to be regarded as a student's family. Allegiances to houses do indeed run in families, and the organizational principle of houses reigns until the very end of *Deathly Hallows* when, for a brief moment, everyone sits together rather than in houses. However, in the postscript we find that the next generation of students is equally concerned with house admission. It is only the uniting of "misfits" and "loners" that scares the teachers. Harry's private and isolating lessons enable Dumbledore's strategic control, for Dumbledore continually emphasizes secrecy about the lessons but authorizes Harry to tell only Hermione and Ron, hand-selecting and reifying a manageable peer group in a way he wishes he had for Tom.

Furthermore, in the memory Dumbledore presents of Tom acquiring objects for Borgin and Burkes, the sinister and sleazy store that specializes in dangerous objects, Dumbledore highlights Tom's sly and wily ways, but readers of the series know that all the characters in the wizarding world are masters of these skills. In a similar manner, Westman argues, wizards manipulate Muggle minds for their own convenience (157–58), but skilled Legilimens Voldemort, Snape, and Dumbledore "don't broadcast this talent" (159) because of the incredible power and unethical manipulation inherent in such skills. As a container of people's memories, the Pensieve, housed in Dumbledore's office, symbolizes the headmaster's power to collect, assemble, shape, and present the minds of others at will. Furthermore, Dumbledore uses Harry to ensnare Slughorn into accepting the position of potions master so that Dumbledore can extract memories of Tom from him. The implicit lesson of how to "play" people—especially teachers against one another—is symbolized also by Harry's newly acquired potions book, which teaches that success is dependent not on following established rules but exploring possibilities in the margins. In fact, not only does the potions book give Harry unauthorized knowledge, but Dumbledore also commands him to "play" Slughorn for the retrieval of the true memory of what *exactly* unfolded between Slughorn and Tom when Tom sought instruction on how to make Horcruxes (the memory in the Pensieve has been altered to hide Slughorn's true answer). When Harry finally obtains the memory, he appreciates Tom's ability to manipulate Slughorn because Harry, too, knows how to play people: "It was very well done, thought Harry, the hesitancy, the casual tone, the careful flattery, none of it overdone. He, Harry, had had too much experience of trying to wheedle information out of reluctant people not to recognize a master at work" (496–97). Playing a social game is as much a part of the Hogwarts' curriculum as anything else, yet somehow it is seen exclusively as the province of the evil Tom Riddle. If recipes for success are embedded in the margins of official curricula and in secret chambers, then Tom Riddle is simply the hidden curricula that schools do not acknowledge. Perhaps this is why we first meet Tom in *Secret Chamber*, in which the very existence of the secret chamber has been denied by Hogwarts staff for fifty years.

Dumbledore also describes Tom's supposed obsession with his parentage and his desperate search to find evidence of his father's wizardry as desires that slide into depravity once the fruitlessness of the search becomes apparent. The reader cannot help thinking of Harry's desire to learn more about his wizard parents, a parallel Tom draws in *Chamber of Secrets* as well. But implicit observations of lineage and connection occur all the time at Hogwarts. Snape, the Head of Slytherin, a house whose founder prized blood above all else, continually attributes Harry's (irritating) audacity and rule-breaking to the influence of James Potter, the father Harry has never known. Similarly, Professor Slughorn, the newly reinstated potions master who taught not only Tom but the generation including Harry's parents, is convinced Harry has the gift of his mother's nature because Harry, like his mother before him, seems to excel at the subject. Slughorn's privileging of nature is a telling instance of the ways in which the school certainly does value lineage even though it officially frowns upon discriminatory practices favored by the original Slytherin, the founder who felt that only pure-blood wizards were worthy of Hogwarts admission. Slytherin's prejudice is distasteful to the school even though this "blood will out" interpretation of a child is an operative theme in many personal interactions with teachers.

It is not surprising that a child like Tom, who lacks family, should want to embed his soul in founder objects as Horcruxes. Horcruxes are objects into which wizards can embed their souls and thereby earn immortality, but they can only do so by murdering another person. While Tom's desire to make Horcruxes is thus seen as one of the most damning pieces of evidence of Tom's evil nature, *Half-Blood Prince* offers another interpretation. Although it turns out that Tom does have a bloodline to Slytherin and a "specialness" (difference from children in the orphanage) that has a name (wizard) and purpose (command of magic), he does not initially know this. But from the moment he arrives, he sees Hogwarts as a pseudo-family and thus has a particular desire to insinuate himself in the four families or lineages of the school and adopt the founders as his own parents. Tom's need to turn founder objects into his Horcruxes is an attempt at adoption by not one but four families, a "magpie" desire to hoard family and its special heirlooms.

Fearing that the lines between good and evil are not all that distinct, Harry repeatedly compares himself to Tom Riddle throughout the series, but in *Half-Blood Prince* he notes detailed similarities in their feelings and backgrounds. For example, when Harry learns that Merope (Tom's mother) died because she gave up rather than protect a son that needed her, Harry immediately compares and contrasts his own mother and similar loss (262), even though Dumbledore sources Merope's failure to an innate flaw in her character, claiming she never had the courage of Harry's mother. Further, Dumbledore shows Harry memories of rejecting Tom's application for teaching at Hogwarts, without considering the impact of such an action, even though Dumbledore himself has analyzed Hogwarts as the only place to which Tom feels a sense of belonging. When Dumbledore admits, "'Hogwarts was where [Tom] had been happiest; the first and only place he had felt at home,'" "Harry felt slightly uncomfortable at these words, for this was exactly how he felt about Hogwarts too" (*Half-Blood Prince* 431). This discomfort suggests not only Harry's uneasiness at the psychic similarity between him and Tom, but also—more subtly—his anxiety that early conditioning, rather than free choice, might lead him into darkness as well. Harry's worries about becoming more like Tom seem well founded. Harry has felt and feared his connection to the dark lord throughout the series, but in *Half-Blood Prince* the connections between their childhoods make his fears particularly intimate because childhood is imagined as the core of adult personality, a theory of self evident in Dumbledore's lessons.

Harry's perception of his similarity to Tom is nothing new; indeed, he has been taught to view himself that way. Teachers compare the two based on their natural wizarding gifts and disrespect of the rules; even in the first book, the wand-seller Ollivander equates the two wizards when he sells Harry a wand with a Phoenix feather that has only one twin in Voldemort's wand. In the second book, Tom himself draws parallels between him and Harry, which are, at that point, a little jarring, because the dashing, brilliant Tom hardly seems to resemble Harry. Dumbledore implicitly furthers the comparative exercise by explaining in *Half-Blood Prince* that Tom was Harry's age when he began making himself immortal. Yet Harry's tendency to compare himself to Tom and to give credence to the prophecy that Harry is "the chosen one" who will defeat the dark lord or die ultimately frustrates Dumbledore because Dumbledore believes that one makes one's destiny: "'It is our choices, Harry, that show what we truly are, far more than our abilities'" (*Sorcerer's Stone* 333); in *Half-Blood Prince*, he makes an impassioned plea that Harry understand his choices rather than obsess about the prophecy, which, to Dumbledore, means nothing. In some sense, this is what Dumbledore, whom Rowling presents as an admirable educator, must believe; educators stand for the Enlightenment mind that governs itself with the rational choices of a free agent. However, in championing free will, Dumbledore transfers responsibility for Harry's present and future choices squarely onto Harry rather than on the institution molding him, even though in prior books, actions Dumbledore took that were beyond Harry's control had grave consequences for Harry.[6]

Dumbledore's firm belief in free agency makes it all the more ironic that Dumbledore reads Tom's path as the unfolding of a flawed nature. His belief that Tom's evil nature is innate is symbolized when he observes the potion in Tom's cave. We can understand the potion as representing Tom's childhood since the cave was an important place for the young orphan Tom. Dumbledore says of the potion, "'But how to reach it? This potion cannot be penetrated by hand, Vanished, parted, scooped up, or siphoned away, nor can it be Transfigured, Charmed, or otherwise made to change its nature'" (*Half-Blood Prince* 568). Both literally and symbolically, this passage demonstrates Dumbledore's uncertainty about reaching, understanding, and penetrating Tom's soul. Dumbledore's list of methods for changing natural elements fails in truly *reaching* Tom. Yet *Half-Blood Prince* embeds clues about Dumbledore's blind spots, in preparation for a fuller explanation of the headmaster's complexity in *Deathly Hallows*, when Harry worries that Dumbledore may have groomed Harry to die for the purpose of defeating the dark lord: Harry is revealed to be one of Voldemort's Horcruxes, and these Horcruxes must be destroyed before the dark lord can be defeated. Dumbledore's council on free will and choices, then, seems deeply ironic and suspect, a Foucaultian pretense in which Harry, an orphan who might threaten the state if not assimilated, successfully imbibes national values.[7] Toward the end of the novel, the very gaze of Dumbledore makes Harry feel "the usual sensation that he was being X-rayed" (428), the adjective "usual" demonstrating how successful Hogwarts has been at inculcating Michel Foucault's model of discipline through institutional technologies and internalized surveillance. Harry increasingly wishes to please Dumbledore and feels shame if he does not: "A hot, prickly feeling of shame spread from the top of Harry's head all the way down his body. Dumbledore had not raised his voice, he did not even sound angry, but Harry would have preferred him to yell; this cold disappointment was worse than anything" (428). Tom represents the particularly poignant threat of the unassimilated orphan for whom panoptic techniques have failed, despite Dumbledore's vow to keep an eye upon him.

In *Half-Blood Prince*, Dumbledore appears to read Tom according to a deeply Biblical view that "evil" is the antithesis of everything good and moral. No teaching can redeem this sort of evil. Like the savage (unconscious) childhood that was born again in Freudian theory (as historicized by Carolyn Steedman), Tom's brand of evil can "be kept at bay, though never quite eradicated" (*Half-Blood Prince* 645). Dumbledore's view of evil echoes that of Snape, the sinister teacher and head of Slytherin whom Harry despises and who, in turn, despises Harry. Snape defines the dark arts as a monster that grows new heads every time you cut off one, a speech Harry views as disturbingly sexual and therefore inappropriately affectionate: "Harry stared at Snape. It was surely one thing to respect the Dark Arts as a dangerous enemy, another to speak of them, as Snape was doing, with a loving caress in his voice?" (178).[8] This admiration of evil from a Byronic hero at once suggests the heroic call and futility of the teacher battling the dark arts and resembles Dumbledore's seductive lessons to Harry about the charismatic and Byronic Tom Riddle. Dumbledore is thus not so different from the less virtuous Snape. And Harry, who sees himself as Dumbledore's pupil, is incapable of recognizing that his own admiration of Tom later in the novel also sounds very reminiscent of Snape's affection for darkness.

Dumbledore must pay an extreme price for failing Tom in *Half-Blood Prince*; the novel culminates in what seems to be his murder at the hands of Professor Snape, although later in the series we learn that Snape's actions are not exactly his "choices." As the school learns of Snape's supposed allegiance to the Death Eaters, Professor Slughorn exclaims, "'Snape! I taught him! I thought I knew him!'" (627), a precise echo of Dumbledore's relation to Tom, "'I taught Tom Riddle. I know his style'" (563), thus revealing that teachers' influence on students is of paramount importance in *Half-Blood Prince*. How can a teacher know a student's style but claim not to have shaped that style? How can a teacher claim such intimate knowledge of a student's "evil" and be so astonished at an "evil" turn of events? We are subtly given a message about Dumbledore's ironic position of interpreting Tom in the context of his theory that evil is unteachable. By asserting that no book could have given Tom information on how to split his soul into Horcruxes, Dumbledore ironically exposes the central role of the teacher, which is indeed the major plot revelation, for Slughorn *has* given Tom this illegal information. In turn, Slughorn gives the reader much more information about what teachers prize and what values they inspire, and Harry's courting of Slughorn for the true memory of Tom only reifies the power of "private" lessons at Hogwarts. This power is perversely inscribed by Dumbledore as well and is therefore a lesson that recurs "across the curriculum."

THE PENETRABLE POTTER: HIDDEN CURRICULUM BROUGHT TO LIGHT

It is meaningful that Slughorn's words about knowing Snape echo Dumbledore's about knowing Tom. Hardly a positive character, Slughorn attaches himself to students he believes will prove to be good connections. Slughorn is strongly reminiscent of Gilderoy Lockhart in *Chamber of Secrets*, a professor who falsely purports to have done all the amazing things published in his books. Professor Slughorn is introduced in *Half-Blood Prince* as a foil to the worthy Dumbledore, yet both teachers are major forces in Tom's life. This doubling is a purposeful replication since *Half-Blood Prince* is a conscious rewriting of *Chamber*, both in revisiting the dark lord as a child and in focusing on an old book as a dangerous discovery. These coinciding dangers of corruption by dark lords and old books reveal Rowling's emphasis on what children discover in the "secret chambers" of schools. Even though Harry finds the old potions book at the bottom of Slughorn's cabinet, exposing Slughorn's own hidden agenda, Slughorn's hoarding of truth comprises the Hogwarts curriculum as much as Dumbledore's. Snape, who has finally achieved his desired post of Defense Against the Dark Arts teacher, is the "true" voice or memory embodied by the old potions book (it was his book and the marginalia are his); therefore, both Slughorn and Snape represent the sinister roots of the school's heritage, which children learn only in marginalia and private lessons.

Ginny is understandably concerned in *Half-Blood Prince* about Harry's use of the potions textbook. After all, she herself experienced great trauma in *Chamber of Secrets* due to her discovery of an old book, the dark lord's diary. Ginny claims to have found the diary amongst the old texts given to her by her mother, sourcing unauthorized female activity as well as subtly blaming the grown-ups, just as Harry blames the half-blood Prince for the murderous spell he casts on Malfoy (Snape saves Malfoy, which is only fair since the evil spell was his invention in the first place). And yet the repercussions of the unauthorized texts are far different for Ginny than Harry. Ginny's discovered book causes her to withdraw from peers and face sexual trauma. Ginny's descent into the chamber as she voices her complaints in Tom Riddle's diary is steeped in sexual imagery. The book is dangerous both to her and the school, serving as a symbol of female rage (the complaints in her diary), emotions, and desire (one of her complaints is that her crush on Harry is not returned). Certainly, *Chamber* is concerned with Harry's sexuality as well. Alice Mills makes the case that the secrets of *Chamber of Secrets* concern girls; the chamber is accessed through the girls' bathroom, where a sexually aroused female lives (Moaning Myrtle). However, Mills's reading of "the terrors of the toilet" as anal imagery could equally well imply that other sexual secrets lurk behind the girls' bathroom—secrets fundamental to the tradition of boys boarding-school literature, as argued by Pugh and Wallace. Tom Riddle presents himself as an older, sexually mature Harry, and Myrtle, an older teen, invites Harry to share her toilet. Tom's chamber and Myrtle's toilet represent two possible sexual pathways for Harry. *Chamber* reveals that Harry is not ready for any such notions. However, *Half Blood Prince* is quite preoccupied with the newly born "creature" or monster within Harry, the creature that desires Ginny (286–87, 423, 534), hardly an uncomplicated heterosexuality since these urges can also be understood as his desire for the Weasley family and all its members. Throughout *Half-Blood Prince*, Harry is afraid to express his feelings toward Ginny because he fears losing Ron as his mate.

But while Ginny's book acts like a sexual predator, Harry's book is a male mentor that helps him earn respect. The old potions book embeds knowledge of spells and instructions that initially earn him accolades and a relationship with Snape that Harry cannot enjoy in life because he is so pre-judiced against Snape. As horrific as Snape is, he carries knowledge that Harry needs. Harry's book increases his social stature, whereas Ginny's book isolates her. Likewise, although Dumbledore's weighty lessons in *Half-Blood Prince* isolate Harry, too, they make him feel not victimized but *chosen*. This difference in gender can be understood in the context of Amy Billone's argument about Harry Potter as the privileged male character who, like Peter Pan, can cross worlds and feel at home in fantasyland in a way that female characters, such as Carroll's Alice, cannot. For Ginny to tap into unauthorized Hogwarts lessons about power, social savvy, and capitalism is dangerous; should she catch on, she might challenge the status quo. For Harry this same knowledge is an intentional curriculum on the part of the headmaster, who, after his failure with Tom, perhaps recognizes the necessity for different pedagogical approaches.

In contrast to Ginny's immersion in a diary in *Chamber*, Harry's attach-ment to the old book enables his rise. Yet *Half-Blood Prince* eventually reveals the old potions book as the horror that Ginny and Hermione fear it is when Harry casts the spell that almost kills Malfoy. Although Harry blames the unknown owner for the creation of such a spell, it is apparent that Harry does not recognize how much he himself is responsible for experimenting with the book without reflection. Why might this be? One answer is that while Dumbledore and various teachers have repeatedly insisted that stu-dents follow the rules, they have repeatedly violated their words by reward-ing points for experimentation and action without thought, as observed by Torbjørn Knutsen in "Dumbledore's Pedagogy: Knowledge and Virtue at Hogwarts" (204–05). Indeed the points system itself is a sign of an arbitrary economy based on nothing but the powers and personal sentiments of the faculty; faculty members are free to award or take away five or fifty points for whatever action they feel merits points. There is no written guide to this system that might demystify the equivalence of actions and value.

The penetrations of Harry by Dumbledore's silvery stock of memories in *Half-Blood Prince* are treated as far gentler and benevolent lessons than the violent power struggles he has with Snape in *Order of the Phoenix*, yet *Half-Blood Prince* draws a fascinating parallel between Dumbledore's les-sons and the lessons Harry enthusiastically drinks from Snape's old potions book. Although Tom's pleasure in domination is seen by Dumbledore as something distastefully unique to Tom, the structure of relations between teacher and student in Dumbledore's private lessons involves a similar structure of dominance. Harry's penetrability by various male instructors, among whom Voldemort must be ranked with Snape and Dumbledore, must be analyzed as a queer structure as well as the conveyance of queer curriculum.

It is tempting to read Dumbledore as a homosexual given Rowling's later outing, but, as critics have noted, there is very little indication of Dumbledore's sexual orientation in the novels. In fact, same-sex pairings are *never* discussed in Harry Potter's world, making it resemble a much older novel, oddly in conflict with its wide-ranging cast of characters and types, many of whom experience prejudice for different reasons. John Cloud, for one, declares of Rowling's outing of Dumbledore, "Shouldn't I be happy to learn that he's gay? Yes, except. Why couldn't he tell us himself? The Potter books add up to more than 800,000 words before Dumbledore dies...yet Rowling couldn't spare two of those words to help define a central character's emotional identity: 'I'm gay.' We can only conclude that Dumbledore saw his homosexuality as shameful" (Cloud 2). And yet the fact that children's literature rarely focuses on the emotional complexities of adults may contextualize Dumbledore's closeting, and certainly some clues do exist. From *Half-Blood Prince*'s beginning scene in which Dumbledore appears at the Dursley home to begin private lessons with Harry, he is figured as an odd sort of suitor. The Dursleys are shocked by his appearance, and their discomfort with his presence is strongly reminiscent of their response to the entire wizarding world as "abnormal"—"that sort" they do not wish to be seen around. Critics Bronski, Wallace and Pugh, and Tosenberger have read this as analogous to the unseen, closeted gay world that "normal" Muggles intuit and, in embarrassment, choose not to see or acknowledge. Harry feels "distinctly awkward" being alone with Dumbledore as they first set out (57), and Dumbledore asks Harry to take his arm, rather like an escort. The resulting "apparition" (magical travel) feels "as though [Harry] had just been forced through a very tight rubber tube" (58) and results in dizziness, feelings that could be viewed as analogous to sexual initiations.

In a similarly suggestive manner, the memories in the Pensieve, described as neither liquid nor gas, bear a resemblance to semen, particularly in the way the substance becomes exchanged between the two during a shared intimate experience: "Harry bent forward, took a deep breath, and plunged his face into the silvery substance. He felt his feet leave the office floor; he was falling, falling through whirling darkness and then, quite suddenly, he was blinking in dazzling sunlight. Before his eyes had adjusted, Dumbledore landed beside him" (199). Harry undergoes isolation and alteration from these experiences. Dumbledore subsequently has the power to summon him, and Harry never knows when, where, or how he might be called upon by Dumbledore. Harry begins to obsess about when messages will come: "Where was Dumbledore, and what was he doing?...Had Dumbledore forgotten the lessons he was supposed to be giving

Harry?...Harry had felt bolstered, comforted, and now he felt slightly abandoned" (237). Harry feels selected and made special by these excursions, much as a young teen might obsess over a new love interest. Over time, Harry becomes used to the foreign feeling of "apparating" by touching Dumbledore, and, after practice, his descent into the "swirling, pearly memory" of the Pensieve becomes compulsory: "Harry stepped up to the stone basin and bowed obediently until his face sank through the surface" (363). The relationship takes on the unwritten codes of pederasty, which makes it seem relevant that at the very moment Dumbledore freezes Harry before he dies, Harry first sees Greyback, a werewolf who bites children in order to reproduce his species.

On one level, these scenes of penetration are the conveyance of wisdom into the "vessel" of youth, movement from innocence to experience or knowledge, but on another level, they reveal the deepest desires of educators to reproduce themselves through shaping young men. Harry has been commanded to secrecy about these visits, analogous to the many uncomfortable private lessons or punishments that he has been subjected to before in the series—lessons in which he often passed out. These excursions to Dumbledore's office certainly evoke a queer reading, however disturbingly pederastic, as observed by John Cloud in his article, "Outing Dumbledore" (2). Dumbledore needs Harry as a receiver of his semen-like substances. This need seems to take visible form in Dumbledore's wounded hand; he cannot open the memory vials with his own hands, indicating the passing of his prowess. And while these liquid exchanges can be understood as symbolic penetration of Harry, a theme of mind-penetration that continually emerges throughout the series, it can also be understood as a vision of education, a field in which a word like "seminar" shares roots with semen and knowledge deposited and exchanged by older and younger men through a shared canon to which not everyone is privy.[9] But it is not only the relationship between Harry and Dumbledore that is queerly figured. The triangle of Dumbledore-Harry-Tom is constructed around issues of penetration and dominance, mistrust and unconditional obedience. Harry's dizzying physical experiences with Dumbledore reinvoke Harry's experience of Tom's diary in *Chamber*, in which he descends into the diary only after it (or Tom) asks his consent. And Tom's "coming out" (words used in the novel) of the diary, to meet Harry, implies a queer scene: Tom admits that he used Ginny, so that he could get to Harry. Ginny is literally unconscious in the chamber and therefore merely an object "between men," to use Eve Sedgwick's phrase for how women function as objects between men in the English novel. Further, Tom's many observations about how he and Harry look alike and share similar backgrounds throw Harry into crisis until he pulls the Gryffindor sword from the Sorting Hat (only a true Gryffindor can do so). Tom clearly represents a part of Harry that would question whether he is "true" Gryffindor or whether he is shameful.

All of these issues culminate in the cave. The cave signifies a fantasy inversion of Dumbledore's office and power seat, which has showcased Harry repeatedly "drinking in" liquid memories in intimate experiences throughout *Half-Blood Prince*. It is perhaps no surprise that Harry sees in the cave a vision of the headmaster's power, which enables him to decode a power struggle between Tom and headmaster that he perhaps shares:

> The island was no larger than Dumbledore's office, an expanse of flat dark stone on which stood nothing but the source of that greenish light, which looked much brighter when viewed close to. Harry squinted at it; at first, he thought it was a lamp of some kind, but then he saw that the light was coming from a stone basin rather like the Pensieve, which was set on top of a pedestal.
> Dumbledore approached the basin and Harry followed. Side by side, they looked down into it. (567)

The scene represents the passing of the torch from age to youth, as Dumbledore's prowess gets them there and Harry's strength allows them to leave. Dumbledore's blood opens the door, while Harry's blood allows them exit. The basin of poison, reminiscent of the Pensieve, is first on a "pedestal," signifying the loftiness of the headmaster, but this shifts as Harry and Dumbledore become "side by side." In the past, Dumbledore's stature as a great wizard has been articulated by many and by his supporters, especially Hagrid, but not self-articulated. Throughout *Half-Blood Prince*, Dumbledore's comments about his own amazing brain become crassly and strikingly articulated, far beyond everyday rules of etiquette, as if he is holding onto something others no longer believe. Harry's increasing discomfort with his own unquestioning obedience throughout *Half-Blood Prince* prepares him for subsequent individuation from Dumbledore.[10] Harry becomes increasingly frustrated by what he views as Dumbledore's blind trust and tendency to see the good in everyone; however, it is not so much that Harry is right—in Tom's case, the reverse is true. *Half-Blood Prince* can be regarded as Dumbledore's last stand in shaping the main character, and it is fascinating that this relationship centers on a boy who mirrors Harry and who did not receive the same attention. But then favoritism of a particular student is permissible at Hogwarts, just as earlier books have made the point that professors (especially Snape) favor students in their own houses.

But what also occurs in this rather warped scene is Harry's "obedient" action to force Dumbledore to drink what Dumbledore has identified as a piece of Tom's soul. On the one hand, this scene involves the inevitable outcome of Dumbledore's Freudian philosophy: by interpreting Tom according to both natural and familial deprivations solidified in early infancy and childhood, which no educational means can penetrate, Dumbledore is forced to drink in the unchangeable, unmalleable nature of Tom's evil soul. It is poison that "'I cannot touch...I cannot approach,'" says Dumbledore, poison that cannot be "'made to change its nature'" (568). On the other hand, Dumbledore is forced to drink it on his own command, or perhaps as punishment for his own blind ignorance of how Hogwarts and the culture of the school might have contributed to Tom's lust for power, dominance, and the overvaluation of objects.

Dumbledore's regret about Tom's outcome subtly reveals some guilt about whether he could have done more or facilitated an intimacy as he has with the orphan Harry.[11] Dumbledore claims that Tom was always guarded after their initial meeting. It remains unclear how a child guards himself from a skilled Legilimens, but it is certainly in Dumbledore's interest to claim ignorance of Tom's early darkness. If Dumbledore's claim that Tom was guarded after their initial meeting is accurate, we can ask why Tom might have been wary of the professor. Dumbledore proves to Tom that he is a wizard by making his wardrobe flame, and Dumbledore observes, "'I think there is something trying to get out of your wardrobe'" (272). Although there is understanding, sympathy, and likeness implied, there is also judgment, as Dumbledore constructs him in this scene as a thief. The very moment he admitted Tom to school, Dumbledore warned Tom that thievery is not tolerated at Hogwarts, showing immediate distrust. (Those familiar with the series know that in prior books, especially *Order of the Phoenix*, Dumbledore similarly distanced himself from Harry and that Harry both noticed and felt wounded by this treatment.) This moment between Dumbledore and Tom is the most intimate scene they ever share, and continued support of Tom is trumped by suspicion and alienation. In this case, nondisclosure to students (like Tom) who feel shameful about their backgrounds for various reasons—class, religion, race, sexual orientation, sexual abuse, an alcoholic or violent parent—has serious consequences.

Half-Blood Prince places a scrutinizing gaze upon Tom's nature as "different." Slughorn describes the making of Horcruxes as the product of *unnatural* activity, a buzzword for historical prejudice against homosexuals who choose "improper" love objects. Slughorn says it is an act against nature to split the soul, a reading that could also yield anxiety about those who do not choose monogamy (there are seven Horcruxes). Tom's distaste for "Mudbloods," when he is half-Muggle himself, is a denial of his "half blood" nature, a value judgment stemming from cultural conditioning, which could be read as analogous to a history of gay shame and closeting, as traced and theorized by Eve Sedgwick in *Epistemology of the Closet*. The initial presentation of the dark lord as He-Who-Cannot-Be-Named seems akin to the sin "which dare not speak its name." Assuming this resonance with coming-out is purposeful, we can regard *Half-Blood Prince* as a coming-out story that fails and creates a very closeted monster, traditionally a trope for homosexuals in popular film and literature.[12]

I do not mean to suggest that we limit ourselves to a reading of Tom's evil as tapping into a history of gay shame, but I mean to read this familiar theme of closeting as a way to understand Dumbledore's lessons. They are really lessons in what happens when repressed "monsters," or feelings of shame (whatever the source of shame), are not expressed, shared, and discussed. Rowling uses the language of gay shame not to indicate homosexuality per se, but merely the sort of shame that might create a monster like Tom. The coordination of the two plots—Tom's unsupported, unaired shame and Harry's reticence to completely vilify Tom—suggests flaws in the school's refusal to address the emotional realities of students beyond the classroom.[13] The shame associated with a particular background—whatever the nature of that shame—becomes for Tom a layer on which values of school culture (for prestige, objects) are cemented. In a very broad way, then, Tom is literally the school's closet, its chamber, its soul that cannot be exorcised because it is everywhere. He exemplifies the dangers of refusing children support for all their issues.

CONCLUSION

If we view *Half-Blood Prince* as the story of Harry's preparation in becoming the man who must overcome the dark lord and therefore experiment with penetration and dominance, then we can easily read *Half-Blood Prince* as a transfer of the seed of power to Harry. Harry's own sexual awakening with Ginny is both instrumental to his manhood and an impediment to his queer connection with the dark lord; he must express his desire for Ginny in *Half-Blood Prince* and then channel this energy into tracking Tom's soul (Horcruxes) in *Deathly Hallows*, in which he learns to use and somewhat control mental penetration by Voldemort. However, throughout *Half-Blood Prince*, Harry's views of Tom Riddle provide penetrating insight beyond the Pensieve. Dumbledore makes the same mistake with which cultural critics continually charge Freudians: not taking into account the complexity of culture and looking instead at the individual mind and experiences for formative influences. Tom is evil because his family was evil, violent, and obsessed with the purity of blood rather than values; Tom is evil because his mother was beaten down and lacked the courage to stay alive for him; Tom is evil because he was rejected by his father and landed in an austere, impoverished orphanage that could not support him or his special abilities. He was left to his own streetwise devices, and the school—always *good*— could not change these things. Dumbledore renders memories of Tom applying twice to teach at Hogwarts, admitting that it replaced his sense of family and belonging, but he never questions whether those rejections were formative experiences. It is too convenient to believe that neurons and personalities are solidified in early life. In one memory, Dumbledore says Tom should go into politics, and Tom sarcastically says he does not have the connections. Families and connections are continually important in the series; doors open for Harry because everyone knows his name, not to mention his eyes—his mother's eyes. Slughorn opens his door for this reason and because Harry dishonestly presents himself as a prodigy in the tradition of his mother.

The way in which the "evil" child is a synecdoche for cultural conditioning is too complicated for the analyst or courts to handle; thus he is treated as an individual with pathological tendencies and "instincts." This assessment makes the adults feel better, not only because it erases their culpability but because it protects them from recognizing that they, too, lack power over the broader world and culture of which they are a part. Who wants to admit how much capitalism, reflected in the Room of Requirements, shapes interactions, desires, and goals of students? However much a force he is, Dumbledore did not found the school or its broader class culture. *Half-Blood Prince* emphasizes prior headmasters to make the point that Dumbledore did not create the universe, as much as he is equated with a god. And thus even Dumbledore cannot read Tom as the cultural unconscious that all shared texts represent, as Fredric Jameson claims. Tom Riddle is ultimately a shared text that no one wants to name. That is why Tom's soul is everywhere divided, into objects far and wide. Not all the Horcruxes belong to the school, of course, but a good portion of them do. Rowling has drawn for us a sense of proportion in determining who is responsible for an unsupported child: several objects belong to the school founders, founders no longer alive but nevertheless still shaping the very structure of school culture. Tom is ultimately a riddled text that teachers refuse to read and print for their students. Tom's adoption of Hogwarts as a family that cares deeply about lineage, class, trophies, brilliance, winning, and dominance is both legible and understandable. *Deathly Hallows* further reveals that Dumbledore's reading of Tom in *Half-Blood Prince* is essentially a reading of himself as a youth, for Dumbledore fears the lust for power that he distrusts in himself. Freud would have called this countertransference. In denying Tom as a Hogwarts textbook in *Half-Blood Prince*, Dumbledore has revealed a deeply hidden curriculum, which is the most powerful lesson of all.

NOTES

1. I am not suggesting that the concept of *tabula rasa* governs *Harry Potter*, however. The series' insistence on Harry's natural purity and love, not to mention the overriding battles between good children fighting evil adults in the Ministry and in Lord Voldemort's Death Eaters, is more properly romantic. Even wizarding skill is somewhat in-born; Harry's magical gifts, such as flying, are part of his nature, and wizards can be born to non-wizard parents. Hermione, born to Muggles (non-wizards), however, seizes scholarship as a means to knowledge; the series' uneasy characterization of whether children's gifts are natural or not makes an examination of Tom Riddle all the more pressing, calling into question the

relationship between nature and training and setting up Lord Voldemort's ideas about blood as possibly only a perverse exaggeration of socially accepted ideologies (for example, when Professor McGonagall, head of Gryffindor, selects Harry as Quidditch Seeker for his natural skill, she reassures Harry that his father was a good player as well). I would point out, however, that even Locke's *tabula rasa*, for which he is known, was never absolute; he advised parents to observe the inborn temperament of their children and adjust accordingly.

2. Indeed, an entire book is devoted to the Triwizard Tournament, in which students compete for the Triwizard Cup, which symbolically makes the school vulnerable to penetration by the dark lord.

3. For example, the shabby robes of Professor Lupin in *Azkaban* draw even Harry's judgmental attention. In *Chamber of Secrets*, Ginny, too, is only too aware of the importance of class. She has secondhand books because her family has little money and her brothers need new texts. Ginny complains about her secondhand robes and books in Tom's diary, demonstrating her knowledge of being a second-class citizen.

4. The chamber embarrasses the school not only because a girl (Moaning Myrtle) died when it last opened but because it reveals one of the school founder's (Slytherin's) distaste for wizards who are not descended from pure-blood wizards.

5. The room has opened for Harry so he can hide his precious potions book there. It could be argued that the room is a children's space; however, an earlier scene in which we learn that Madame Trelawny stashes her empty sherry bottles there explains the underground quality of consumption in the entire school, inclusive of pupils and teachers.

6. Throughout *Order of the Phoenix*, Harry experiences in dreams exactly what Voldemort is experiencing; sensing that Harry's and the dark lord's minds are dangerously linked, Dumbledore distances Harry and the Order refuses to include him in information-sharing. This solution only endangers everyone, since Voldemort eventually figures out the link and stages a scene that lures Harry to the Ministry of Magic, where he is attacked. At the end of the novel, Dumbledore realizes his mistake.

7. Critics such as Susan Reynolds and Alicia Willson-Metzger have analyzed the manipulative character of Dumbledore in light of his consequentialism and his role as schoolmaster of a neo-Victorian orphan novel, in which an orphan is typically watched until he has internalized mechanisms of surveillance.

8. John Killinger claims that this view of eternal evil is deeply Biblical and Christian. Alternately, Aida Patient and Kori Street have demonstrated that the *Harry Potter* series taps into the trope of Hitler as the ultimate in monstrous evil, citing the many parallels between Nazi policy of racial cleansing and Voldemort's obsession with racial purity, complete with the attenuated irony that he himself is not pure-blood, just as Hitler was hardly Aryan. While critics such as Thomas Hibbs would disagree, Sattaur charges that the unquestioned division between good and evil throughout *Harry Potter* is a problematic replay of contemporary wars on terrorism, the discourse of which identifies "the evil other" as uncomplicated villain.

9. Dumbledore's pooling of memories and need for Harry to receive them are strongly reminiscent of a novel that most young readers would know and that Rowling might have used: Lois Lowry's 1993 *The Giver*, winner of the 1994 Newberry Award. In it, a boy named Jonas is selected to be the next Receiver of Memory for the community. He must slowly and painfully receive memories from a male mentor (the Giver) to learn about the darker forces of life, which his community has forgotten. In *The Giver*, Jonas's receiving of memories from the alienated wizard-like figure is figured as a loss of virginity and innocence. The translation of the memories has a similar physicality; Jonas must lie down and receive the Giver's bare hands upon him, and although the Giver fears giving Jonas pain, the giving of memories, such as a broken limb or war, is a requirement for Jonas to grow. Young readers of *The Giver* are trained to see the selection of a memory receptacle as a great honor and way to change the future, but they are not trained to read the sub-text of the penetration as a model of educational violence that underscores models of "noble" education as conceived in classical texts.

10. Pugh and Wallace have noted that Harry's reference to himself as "Dumbledore's man" "highlight[s] that Harry is not yet his own man" (275), and Dumbledore's death becomes necessary in the series' paradigm of normative heroic masculinity, an ideology in which only one male character gets to become the hero and individuate. Harry is literally paralyzed by Dumbledore in the ending scene with Malfoy and Death Eaters, and he is only able to move again when Dumbledore has died and the spell—seen symbolically as Dumbledore's mental penetration of him—broken. Even the best-intentioned adults can communicate problematic power structures and paralyze when they mean to empower or protect.

11. The film of *Half-Blood Prince* presses the scene of Tom and Dumbledore's first meeting to draw connections between Dumbledore and Tom that do not occur in the novel. In the film, Dumbledore responds to Tom's line " 'I knew I was different' " with " 'I'm like you, Tom. I'm different.' " This line does not occur in the book; in fact, Dumbledore does not seek connection, and only after Tom asks, upon first

meeting him, whether he is a wizard does Dumbledore say he is, and he insists upon his title as Professor or Sir, drawing distance.

12. See Henry Benshoff's *Monsters in the Closet: Homosexuality and the Horror Film* for discussions of the queer sub-texts of characters perceived as monstrous.

13. In fact, *Half-Blood Prince* draws a newly sympathetic Malfoy, who seems a troubled youth and whom Moaning Myrtle has witnessed crying in bathrooms; drawn as a suicidal (ghost) teen throughout the series, Moaning Myrtle—here paired with Malfoy—attests to the marginalization of troubled or suicidal youth in schools.

WORK CITED

Benshoff, Harry M. *Monsters in the Closet: Homosexuality and the Horror Film.* Manchester: Manchester UP, 1997. Print.

Billone, Amy. "The Boy Who Lived: From Carroll's Alice and Barrie's Peter Pan to Rowling's Harry Potter." *Children's Literature* 32 (2004): 178–202. Print.

Bronski, Michael. "Queering Harry Potter." *Z Magazine* (Sept. 2003): 1–5. Web. 9 Sept. 2010.

Cloud, John. "Outing Dumbledore." *Time* 25 Oct. 2007: 1–4. *Time Magazine Online.* Web. 14 Sept. 2009.

Hibbs, Thomas. "Virtue, Vice, and the Harry Potter Universe." *The Changing Face of Evil in Film and Television.* Ed. Martin F. Norden. New York: Rodopi, 2007. 89–100. Print.

Jameson, Fredric. *The Political Unconscious: Narrative as a Socially Symbolic Act.* New York: Routledge, 2006. Print.

Killinger, John. *The Life, Death, and Resurrection of Harry Potter.* Macon, GA: Mercer UP, 2009. Print.

Knutsen, Torbjørn L. "Dumbledore's Pedagogy: Knowledge and Virtue at Hogwarts." *Harry Potter and International Relations.* Ed. Daniel H. Nexon and Iver B. Neumann. New York: Rowman & Littlefield, 2006. 197–212. Print.

Mills, Alice. "Harry Potter and the Terrors of the Toilet." *Children's Literature in Education* 37.1 (March 2006): 1–13. Print.

Patient, Aida, and Kori Street. "Holocaust History Amongst the Hallows— Understanding Evil in *Harry Potter.*" *Harry Potter's World Wide Influence.* Ed. Diana Patterson. Newcastle: Cambridge Scholars, 2009. 201–28. Print.

Pugh, Tison, and David Wallace. "Heteronormative Heroism and Queering the School Story in J. K. Rowling's Harry Potter Series." *Children's Literature Association Quarterly* 31.3 (2006): 260–81. Print.

Reynolds, Susan. "Dumbledore in the Watchtower: Harry Potter as a Neo-Victorian Narrative." *Harry Potter's World Wide Influence.* Ed. Diana Patterson. Newcastle: Cambridge Scholars, 2009. 271–92. Print.

Rowling, J. K. *Harry Potter and the Chamber of Secrets.* New York: Scholastic, 2000. Print.

———. *Harry Potter and the Half-Blood Prince.* New York: Scholastic, 2005. Print.

Sattaur, Jennifer. "Harry Potter: A World of Fear." *Journal of Children's Literature Studies* 3.1 (March 2006): 1–14. Print.

Sedgwick, Eve. *Between Men: English Literature and Male Homosocial Desire.* New York: Columbia UP, 1985. Print.

———. *Epistemology of the Closet.* Berkeley: U of California P, 2008. Print.

Steedman, Carolyn. *Strange Dislocations: Childhood and the Idea of Human Interiority, 1780–1930.* Cambridge: Harvard UP, 1995. Print.

Tosenberger, Catherine. "Homosexuality at the Online Hogwarts: Harry Potter Slash Fanfiction." *Children's Literature* 36 (2008): 185–207. Print.

Westman, Karin E. "Perspective, Memory, and Moral Authority: The Legacy of Jane Austen in J. K. Rowling's *Harry Potter*." *Children's Literature* 35 (2007): 145–65. Print.

Willson-Metzger, Alicia. "*The Life and Lies of Albus Dumbledore*: The Ethics of Information Sharing and Concealment in the Harry Potter Novels." *Harry Potter's World Wide Influence*. Ed. Diana Patterson. Newcastle: Cambridge Scholars, 2009. 293–304. Print.

Terrifying Tots and Hapless Homes: Undoing Modernity in Recent Bollywood Cinema

MEHELI SEN

> Compared with western children, an Indian child is encouraged to continue to live in a mythical, magical world for a long time. In this world, objects, events and other persons do not have an existence of their own, but are intimately related to the self and its mysterious moods. Thus, objective everyday realities loom or disappear, are good or bad, threatening or rewarding, helpful or cruel, depending on the child's affective state.... Animistic and magical thinking persists, somewhat diluted, among many Indians well into adulthood.
> —Sudhir Kakar, *The Inner World: A Psycho-Analytic*
> *Study of Childhood and Society in India*

Since the mid-1990s, following the liberalization of the Indian economy and the prodigious expansion of the South Asian diaspora, Bollywood cinema has come to be a ubiquitous formation in the global market, incorporating not just cinema but an entire culture industry.[1] Ashish Rajadhyaksha has persuasively argued that what is today understood as Bollywood includes much more than just the filmic output of India: "Bollywood admittedly occupies a space analogous to the film industry but might best be seen as a more diffuse cultural conglomeration involving a range of distribution and consumption activities from websites to music cassettes, from cable to radio" (116). Although hydra-headed Bollywood continues to grow and absorb myriad creative and commercial attractions, the scholarship on Indian cinema has the challenging task of playing catch-up.

I will approach the Bollywood conglomerate through a rarely studied genre—horror. Here, I interrogate Bollywood's recent romance with the horror genre especially in terms of the figuration of nuclear families, children, and teenagers. Globally, horror has generated intense debates about morality—public and private, aesthetics, the politics of taste, and the effects of violence and sensationalism. In regard to Hindi film, these debates have been largely absent; horror is not discussed very often, either in academic circles or in journalistic ones—a measure of its marginal, low-brow status.

Hindi cinema's most sustained engagement with horror began in the 1970s when the rambunctious Ramsay brothers—seven siblings, each of whom handled a distinct aspect of the production process—produced a series of low-budget hits, including *Do Gaz Zameen Ke Neeche* (1972), *Purana Mandir* (1984), *Veerana* (1988), and *Bandh Darwaza* (1990). Bordering on pornography in their tacky exploitation of female bodies and featuring low-brow stars and threadbare plots, these films came to be identified with the smuttiness of the genre in this era. In fact, the Ramsay horror film can be understood as a genre unto itself—a hybrid iteration that combines copious quantities of sex, violence, and western motifs, with local idioms and homegrown tales of horror and the supernatural. The divorce between horror and a certain idea of "respectability" thus comes to be firmly entrenched at this time. In the hands of the Ramsay brothers, the screen became awash with lurid fake blood and inhabited by a series of bizarrely monstrous creatures—amorous monster women, predatory werewolves, and lustful male and female vampires. The content was excessive and subversive in its economy of representation as well as its address to a certain kind of spectatorship; the Ramsay film's determined rejection of bourgeois trappings and standards of taste, I would argue, makes it a radical iteration of horror in South Asian cinema.[2] And appropriately, as Kartik Nair points out, the Ramsay film made most of its earnings in semi-urban and rural sectors, an indicator of its marginal—non-metropolitan, non-bourgeois—status.

After a brief hiatus in the 1990s—at least in terms of noteworthy films—horror has staged a recent comeback within the Bollywood framework. Filmmakers like Ram Gopal Varma and Vikram Bhatt have "rescued" the genre, as it were, from its low-brow habitations and circuits of dispersal. Recent horror cinema—especially the films I discuss below—is very much about the bourgeoisie as well as made for metropolitan, bourgeois spectators. This rehabilitation involves relatively bigger budgets and a general glossiness of production values that the Ramsay product never realized or, one might argue, even aspired to.[3] The sanitization of the genre—its embourgeoisement, if you will—has drained the genre of not only the outlandish, excessive components but also of any subversive potential it had in the 1970s and 1980s.

In this essay, I argue that recent Bollywood horror films function as excellent barometers for India's post-economic liberalization anxieties. As trade pundits laud India's spectacular growth rates and the meteoric expansion of the middle class, it is the critically neglected, obscure horror genre that registers most powerfully the less celebratory aspects of the nation's determined efforts to participate as an economic and cultural force on the global market. Bollywood itself has come to be emblematic of a marginal form's obdurate and successful resistance of the Hollywood behemoth, at least within South Asia. Horror, I argue, allows us a point of entry into the underbelly of this much-hyped success story; the genre articulates the undertow of the large transformative processes brought about by globalization via the depiction of fear, resentment, vulnerability, and disempowerment. Not surprisingly, Hindi horror cinema has not become a globally popular genre; nightmarish tales of the undead, dispossessed, and vengeful ghosts and spirits have not garnered audiences beyond the political boundaries of the Indian subcontinent. Having said that, however, some of these films have been commercial successes nationally. Partially, these box-office returns are the result of relatively modest production budgets, but I would argue that, in fact, these horror films inscribe into their plots a backlash against the success story described above. The sheer number of recent horror films and the regularity with which they are made resonates with all that is left by the wayside—un-attended to—in the story of globalization.

But Bollywood's romance with horror must be contextualized within the genre's global dispersal in recent years: from the spectacular success of Hideo Nakata's *Ringu* (1998) which has spawned a series of sequels and Hollywood remakes to Takashi Shimizu's *Ju-on* franchise, horror films from Asia trumped all other contributions to the genre over the last decade or so. Startlingly, and for my purposes, crucially, children, pre-teens, and teenagers occupy the narrative and affective core of recent Asian horror cinema.[4] Bollywood has come to respond to this phenomenal global success not only by often mimicking the styles and technologies of these films, but also by incorporating children and young adults into its own narratives of terror and the supernatural.

For Hollywood, the trend started in earnest in the 1970s and 1980s with films such as *Rosemary's Baby* (1968), *The Exorcist* (1973), *Carrie* (1976), *The Omen* (1976), *Amityville Horror* (1979), and *The Shining* (1980), all of which focus on terrifying tots or monstrous adolescents. Slasher films of the 1980s and beyond continued to feature imperiled teens and young adults. Scholars such as Vivian Sobchak and Lucy Fischer have persuasively argued that these films articulate the anxieties that beset post-Vietnam and post-Women's Movement America, resonating with the shifting roles of women and the changing structure of families in U.S. culture. Are similar fears now plaguing Asian cinemas? Most scholars of recent Japanese cinema, such as Jay McRoy and Lindsey Nelson, seem to think so and read the predominance of children in films like *Ringu, Dark Water* (2002), and *Ju-on* (2002), among many others, to the shifting economic and social landscape in Japan and its impact on gender roles and the institution of the family. Interestingly, most of the Japanese texts feature fractured families and single parents, an indication of the foundational upheavals that have transformed both social and cinematic terrains.

I argue that recent Hindi horror films resonate with not only the current obsession with children in East and South East Asian films but also Hollywood's 1970s concerns with families under siege. However, as Ashis Nandy has pointed out, children and childhood do not harness the same meanings in every culture: "Childhood is culturally defined and created.... There are as many childhoods as there are families and cultures, and the consciousness of childhood is as much a cultural datum as patterns of child-rearing and the social role of the child" (56). Thus, having noted Bollywood's indebtedness to global cinemas, it is important to underscore the fact that a range of meanings gather around children and childhood that are specific to the Indian sub-continent, both within cinema and without.

GLOBALIZATION AND ITS DISCONTENTS: HAUNTED CHILDREN, HAUNTED FAMILIES

Children in the subcontinent bear markers of caste and community in their names.[5] For the massive number of children who live amidst poverty in the subcontinent, public discourses echo welfare policies undertaken by the state, involving basic health, care-giving, and education. Although infant mortality rates have decreased dramatically in recent decades, they are nowhere near the standards demanded by organizations such as UNICEF (Infant Mortality Rate). In India, child labor laws are openly flouted, and a large number of these children also participate in unorganized sectors such as domestic labor and in hotels, spas, small-scale restaurants, tea-shops, and so on (Gathia, Pandey). Children of middle and affluent classes are burdened in a different sense: as India pursues its global economic policies aggressively, children come to be seen as baton bearers for the nation's shining future. This fervent ambition translates into brutal school curriculums and sadistically demanding institutions of higher education. Academic expectations from children of the middle classes are so excessive that almost every year thousands of children commit suicide under parental and social pressure for scholastic excellence ("Growing Trend").

Hindi popular cinema, for the most part, has remained indifferent to these predicaments.[6] Children feature as symbols of happy families as well as unhappy, incomplete, dismembered ones.[7] Siblings get separated by cruel circumstances in childhood and are united miraculously as adults. Scores of films take refuge in the melodramatic modality of coincidence in order to enable this re-union at the dénouement. Most often, children fall victims to corrupt villains and cruel gangsters who bring them up as criminals like themselves—the worst blow to befall any upright, virtuous family within Hindi cinema's moral economy. However, apart from the horror genre, Bollywood has rarely represented children as malevolent forces; thus, the representational idiom I am engaging with here is something of a novelty.

Hindi film's primary generic modality is melodrama; thus, families and familial relations form the narrative and ideological crux of this cinema. As noted by film theorists such as Thomas Elsaesser and Christine Gledhill, the melodramatic mode understands, inscribes, and inflects all large socio-political and economic conflicts into the realm of the familial. Indeed, this is perhaps the most important ideological task performed by the melo-dramatic mode—a relentless translation of all questions into the language of the personal. The relationship between the horror genre and its familial allegiances has also been theorized: Robin Wood's now classic essay "An Introduction to the American Horror Film" identifies the modern family as horror's "true milieu." Given Bollywood's textual hybridity, the horror film remains unconcerned with the incursion of the melodramatic mode; in fact, melodrama's favorite stomping ground—the family—becomes, almost exclusively, the site for the eruption and elaboration of the horrific. The three films I analyze at length here, *Vaastu Shastra* (2004), *Phoonk* (2008), and *Gauri* (2007), were all made after the liberalization of the Indian economy in the early 1990s. As such, all of these texts feature the modern nuclear fam-ily unit and the upper-middle class consumer ethos that liberalization not only brought into being but also made visible and viable in the last two dec-ades.[8] This is the class that is at the vanguard of the "progress" that is bandied about endlessly in the global media vis-à-vis India's coming of age as an emergent powerhouse in the global arena. The films under discussion offer intermittent glimpses into the fissures that rupture—at least sporadically—the deceptive plenitude of that story.

All three films under discussion here can be grouped under the rubric of "multiplex cinema," films made for affluent audiences and smaller theatres that have mushroomed across cities in India in recent years.[9] Apart from offering the spectator an immersion in variegated spaces of consumption and entertainment—many of these theatres are housed within swanky, up-market shopping malls—the films in question also target the spectators *as metropolitan consumers*.[10] In other words, a new kind of cinema is being crafted to appeal to a new kind of spectator—the upwardly mobile, confi-dently bourgeois subject described above. Multiplex films, in popular par-lance, typically feature tight scripts, shorter durations, and often abjure song and dance sequences that Hindi films have traditionally included. When songs are present—as is the case with *Gauri*—they are more snugly inte-grated into narrative situations, rather than functioning as spectacular inter-ruptions.[11] Themes, too, have come to be more varied and "off-beat," as the middle-class audience is understood to have become savvier in its cine-matic tastes. The recent visibility of horror, I would argue, should be situated within this new context of industry-audience relations and the perceived desire for novelty.

Vaastu, Phoonk, and *Gauri* all fulfill the criteria for multiplex films, especially because all of them, at least at first glance, appear to affirm a determinedly modern, metropolitan ethos. However, in the following discussion, I argue that all three films, in distinct ways, elaborate a dismantling of what might be understood as the multiplex dispensation—discourses that attend to modern subjectivities and formations in a globalized world. The figure of the child enables this dissolution of modernity in each of the three films discussed below. The children in question are not "evil" in a traditional sense; however, the films situate pernicious energies within children, rather instrumentally, in order to mount critiques of the larger ideological terrains they inhabit.

VAASTU SHASTRA: I MISSED YOU, MOMMY!

Vaastu Shastra was not a commercial success in India, which is hardly surprising as this was Saurabh Narang's first directorial venture; moreover, the film does not boast any of the A-list stars considered necessary for boosting box-office earnings. The fact that it was clearly marketed as a horror film may not have helped matters either, because the audience for this sort of cinema was unevenly emerging at the time. *Vaastu Shastra* features an urban nuclear family: Dr. Jhilmil Rao and her husband, Viraag, a professional writer, purchase a sprawling bungalow away from the city of Pune in order to escape the chaos and vicissitudes of metropolitan existence. Soon after they move into their new home with Jhil's teenage sister, Radz, the couple's little son, Rohan, starts displaying strange behavior and claiming to have invisible friends, two in particular, whom he refers to as Manish and Jyoti. Meanwhile, a madman pursues Jhil everyday and attempts to tell her something about her new home, episodes that make her understandably nervous. The negative energies that plague the new home seem connected to a dead banyan tree in the yard, to which Rohan develops an unhealthy attachment. Since Viraag, the child's primary caregiver, is unable to juggle childcare duties with his writing, the family employs a maid, Rukma, to keep Rohan company. Rohan, however, dislikes Rukma and accuses her of being a thief; in turn, Rukma traumatizes the child and threatens to kill him. Soon after, Rukma is mysteriously killed in what appears to be a hit-and-run incident, and the police confirm Rohan's version of the woman's dishonesty. Initially amused by the child's imaginative potential, the parents get anxious when Rohan's visions of a "bad man" and some other angry spirits living in their home become more strident. Since none of the adults are able to see the ghosts yet, Rohan is diagnosed with a psychological disorder accompanied by visual and aural hallucinations. However, once Radz is brutally and inexplicably murdered, the madman is finally able to communicate to Jhil the truth of the evil tree that kills everyone who inhabits its home, but not in time to save Radz and Viraag, who fall victim to these evil forces as well. After a protracted struggle with the malevolent undead that now includes both Viraag and

Radz, the tree is destroyed, and Jhil is able to save her son. The evil force, however, continues to live within the child.

Vaastu expends considerable time and narrative energy establishing the modern worldviews of the couple and their family. Although they move away from the city, the couple brings their modern metropolitan ideologies to the wilderness. The family's non-traditional living arrangements are underscored by the presence of Radz, Jhil's sister, who is included in the family unit and the fact that Jhil is the professional breadwinner while Viraag stays at home writing and serving as the primary caregiver to Rohan. Soon after the family moves into the new home, spectators witness the unorthodox domestic arrangements when Jhil and Radz leave for the hospital and college respectively, while Viraag is left at home to cook, clean, and look after the child. We are expected to note the liberal and liberated politics of the family via these expository sequences.

I argue that in *Vaastu*, the child Rohan is used strategically in order to mount a stringent critique of the discourses of neo-liberal modernity that the couple embodies, for the film makes apparent Viraag's inability to provide the child with the company he clearly craves. In a key sequence, Rohan unsuccessfully tries to draw Viraag's attention to his ball that mysteriously gets suspended in mid-air. The mise-en-scene, particularly the blocking of actors, alerts the spectator to Rohan's plight, since for much of the scene he remains in the foreground trying to make sense of the haunted ball while Viraag is placed in the deep background, with his back facing his son and the audience. In other words, the placement of actors in space demonstrates Viraag's inattention, as his child encounters supernatural forces in plain sight. After being gently shepherded away by his father, Rohan ventures into the shed in their backyard where he meets his new "friends" (presumably for the first time). While Viraag seems oblivious to his son's loneliness, Jhil's guilt over abandoning her child for her profession is immediately apparent—an early indication of the film's rhetorical allegiances—as she frantically searches for Rohan as soon as she comes home from work and eventually locates him in the ramshackle shed. It is instructive to note the length of time the adults in the film spend hunting for an elusive Rohan; the implication is that the child would not be missing in the first place, if properly looked after.

Rohan's behavior becomes increasingly more bizarre as he insists on the real-ness of his new friends. The very next day, Viraag finds him gone once again and finally sees him talking to his invisible friends, Manish and Jyoti, under the banyan tree that is the repository of malefic forces in the film. Initially amused by Rohan's imaginative explorations, his parents become understandably alarmed when they find him missing from his bed at night and perched on top of the banyan tree, after yet another protracted panicky search. As Rohan continues to try to convince his parents unsuccessfully of the existence of his new friends, Jhil and Viraag speculate that the child is perhaps not able to handle the new space and his new environs.

Rohan is the narrative fulcrum of *Vaastu*, and while the child does not embody evil on his own, the spiteful supernatural forces in the film use him as a conduit for terror. The film deploys a cornucopia of stylistic techniques to alert viewers to the evil that resides in the new home.[12] One of the most effective devices used are crane shots that simulate the point-of-view of the dead/dreadful tree; the audience is optically aligned with the tree during these "looks" at the hapless abode, via birds-eye-view shots that dwarf the home and render it vulnerable. The cinematography, more generally, is absolutely crucial in generating terror in *Vaastu*: a restless, mobile camera constantly "stalks" the characters, while weird, canted frames render spaces and people out of kilter. The sound track combines ominous music with a plethora of disturbing noises, including, inexplicably, the loud buzzing of insects and high-pitched sounds of children giggling. All of these sonic components coalesce to create the disturbing aural universe of the film, a perfect foil for the unsettling visuals.

It is the absence of family members—extended family members—that propels the family into crisis; the film implies, I would argue, that it is the non-traditional familial situation to which Rohan falls victim. *Vaastu* subtly criticizes not only Viraag's care-giving skills but also Jhil's professional commitments which keep her away from home and child. It comes to be a critique of modernity—of the modern nuclear family, of the modern companionate couple, modern professional femininity, and even modern parenting. Again, I would argue that Rohan—and by extension the rest of the family—is haunted by big empty spaces; there is so much space between characters in their new home that Manish, Jyoti, and the other undead are easily able to inhabit it. The uncanny, the unhomely, very easily erupts into domestic space that is left empty and unattended. It is the lack of "real" people that forces Rohan to befriend the spectral children; the film wants us to believe that his far-too-modern parents create the situation that imperils him.

The crisis reaches a fever pitch when Jhil and Viraag employ Rukma, an ersatz parental figure to look after Rohan and provide him companionship. Again, we are made aware of the lack of genuine familial care. Rukma's "care" for Rohan turns out to be not just inadequate but, in fact, pernicious. In a disturbing take on class and domestic labor, Rukma is portrayed as a deceitful thief and a verbally and physically abusive person who threatens to throw Rohan under a speeding truck. When Rohan complains to his parents about Rukma having pinched items from their home, they— in typical, liberal employer fashion—not only dismiss his tale, but also wonder if the child's disturbed psyche demands psychiatric intervention. *Vaastu's* ideological propensities congeal around this event. Meanwhile Manish, Jyoti, and other ghostly inhabitants murder Rukma, and Rohan's version of events is vindicated once the police come to report her death and return the stolen items. The police inspector also reports that a truck driver had witnessed Rukma threatening to toss Rohan under its wheels, a horrible revelation that sends Jhil into paroxysms of remorse for having doubted her son.

The unearthly undead grow increasingly more assertive after Rukma's death; Rohan is able to see not only the dead children but also the malefic adult ghosts who walk about freely through the home. Until this point in the film, we had only seen the ghostly inhabitants fleetingly, but now they appear to us as solid, corporeal beings that wander about unafraid and even gaze silently at the family members as they sleep. Physically, they look more or less human, except for their unusual pallor and darkly shadowed eyes.[13] In Rukma's absence, the spaces between the other characters seem to grow and expand, filling up with the angry undead. Rohan clearly articulates this to Radz, telling her that Manish and Jyoti are no longer his friends because the ghosts are now very angry with the family. The cause of their anger, however, remains unclear.

The climax of the film involves Radz's steamy tryst with her boyfriend, Murli, which eventually leads to her brutal death. Echoing countless American slasher films, Radz seems to be punished for her promiscuity, but we do not see exactly how she is killed. After Murli disappears in the middle of their sexual encounter, Radz walks downstairs to look for him in what she perceives to be a game of erotic hide-and-seek. Something horrific accosts her soon after, but her terrified look off-screen is all we are privy to. An abrupt, disjointed cut transitions us into the next sequence, as Jhil, Viraag, and Rohan return home after an evening out. Jhil—to her abject horror—discovers Murli's mutilated corpse on Radz's bed and her sister's body strung up on the banyan tree. On the final day, a distraught Jhil leaves Rohan at home with Viraag, creating the necessary conditions for the climactic series of attacks. She will become the target of ghostly assault upon her return.

The madman who had been uttering garbled warnings from the very beginning manages to draw Jhil's attention at her hospital on this day, but his explanation of the haunted home and murderous tree and their wicked inhabitants remains as incomplete and incoherent as Rohan's understanding of the ghosts' angry energy. I would argue that this incoherence at the very heart of *Vaastu* lays bare its political propensities—we never quite find out what transpired in the site of the home. Our knowledge of past events and past violence—arguably crucial to our understanding of any horror film that invokes past events—remain vague intimations and inchoate ramblings from a madman and a terrified child. In other words, the foundational reason for the hauntings remains unarticulated, decidedly unclear, indeed, incomprehensible. Likewise, the attack on Viraag is implied by his horrified look at something off-screen, but like Radz's death, the specifics of the violence remain unseen by spectators. I would argue that it is this silence that enables us to unravel the specters that plague the family; it is in resonance with this informational vacuum that Viraag's final attack on Jhil comes to be meaningful. When Jhil rushes back to the house, terrified for her husband and child, she is finally confronted by the monumental canker that has been slowly but surely eating away at her home—a crowd of silent, angry undead including Rukma, Radz, and, worse, her now (un)dead husband, Viraag. Finally the empty spaces of the home are full of bodies and energies that it has seemed to have lacked from the beginning.

Viraag's attack on Jhil is immediate, horrific, and inexplicable. He throttles her repeatedly and flings her across the room in a show of immense strength and profound rage. The audience does not echo Jhil's astonishment at this instance because we realize that the film has come full circle—the dénouement is a decisive blow to the discourses of modernity that Jhil has so confidently inhabited so far. Viraag's feelings of inadequacy and impotence finally boil over—he is not, after all, as comfortable assuming the feminizing role of homemaker/caregiver as he had deluded himself into believing. The non-traditional family unit, the lack of patriarchal/feudal supervision, the unorthodox organization of professional and domestic duties, finally prove too much for Viraag. He is emasculated, rendered obsolete in this much too modern household.

Vaastu finally makes its ideological allegiances obvious: it is a cautionary tale about being or becoming modern. Wealth, education, and bourgeois discourses of consumption and coupledom can be endorsed only up to a point: when traditional gender roles are subverted, the family taps into a fountainhead of rage that requires no naming or explanation. At the closure, Jhil—the confident, articulate professional woman—is rendered completely silent and on the verge of psychological implosion. She finally realizes the sheer fragility of her modern existence and the extent of her self-deception. It is moreover no accident that Rohan—the male heir—remains the bearer of the last look and the last laugh. The last look, which Rohan casts over Jhil's shoulder as she holds him, situates the source of evil within Rohan via his now hypnotically gleaming eyes. Somehow, unseen by us, the evil energy has been transferred to the child.[14] The malevolent force that has destroyed his family lives on in him, a warning of things to come.

PHOONK: THE RE-ENCHANTMENT OF RATIONALISTS

Phoonk was a significant box-office success India, alerting us to the horror genre's newfound popularity in the subcontinent. This success was undoubtedly buttressed by director Ram Gopal Varma's reputation as a horror *auteur*, who has delivered remarkable horror films in the past, such as *Raat* (1992), *Bhoot* (2003), and *Darna Mana Hai* (2006). *Phoonk* is both similar to and distinct from *Vaastu* in that here, the disassembling of modernity is channeled through the re-education of a rational technocratic ethos. *Phoonk* revolves around Rajiv, Arati, and their daughter, Raksha, who becomes the victim of black magic unleashed by Madhu, Rajiv's female business associate, who is fired for embezzlement early in the film. Madhu is accompanied by her husband, Anshuman, on her quest for revenge. The family also includes their young son, Rohan, Rajiv's mother, Amma, and a bevy of help. Rajeev works on a construction site, and part of the film's action also takes place in this non-domestic space peopled by urban laborers. It is here that a rock bearing the features of Lord Ganesha, the god of luck and prosperity, appears, and the laborers demand a shrine for it. Rajiv, however, refuses to pander to what he considers an irrational request until the very end. Meanwhile, psychiatrist Seema Walke diagnoses Raksha's condition—seemingly uncontrollable fits—as the psychological malaise Dissociative Personality Disorder and orders a series of tests. As Raksha's affliction worsens and doctors and medical science remain largely ineffectual, Rajiv capitulates and approaches a blind seer, Manja, for help. Manja apprehends the culprit, removes the curse, and kills Madhu, thereby ensuring a happy ending. Initially unable or unwilling to accept the "superstitious" and fantastic notion of black magic, Rajiv finally comes to accept the limits of his knowledge as a rational, modern subject. In this film, the figure of the child is deployed in order to stage a process of "re-enchantment" for its male protagonist, Rajiv. Raksha, the child who unwittingly becomes the victim of adult machinations, is not evil per se. However, as the embodiment and conduit of Madhu's malevolent, enraged curse, she functions as the cause for the instability and terror experienced by the family.

The film's affective universe is divided between the rational and the irrational along strictly gendered lines: Rajiv is the bearer of an absolute, obdurate, technocratic rationality, accompanied by the doctors. On the other side—the realm of the credulous, the imaginative, the irrational, the hysteric and, crucially, the childlike—are the women, the children, and the witch doctors: Amma, Arati, Madhu, Manja, and, of course, Raksha who becomes a victim of demonic possession. The laborers at the construction site belong to the second group, infantilized by their obstinate faith in the deity of Ganesha, as I explain below. *Phoonk* carefully arranges the principal characters on either side of the divide before bringing them into conflict.[15]

The fact that Madhu chooses Raksha as the instrument of her revenge against Rajiv is not accidental; she is clearly delineated as Rajiv's favorite offspring. The connections between Madhu and the child are established early on—as Raksha's rudeness toward the woman is returned by Madhu's apparent affection.[16] Rajiv, too, understands Madhu's strangeness, but he views it as a result of her "childishness," evidenced by her high-pitched giggle and generally odd behavior. Madhu singles Raksha out as the object of her vindictive rage not simply because she is Rajiv's favorite but also, I would argue, because she recognizes in the little girl her own mirror image. Madhu seeks revenge for the humiliation she undergoes at the hands of Rajiv after he discovers the couples' embezzlement; however, the extent of her rage comes to be incomprehensible in the light of the fact that Rajiv's feelings of betrayal are *entirely justified.* In other words, Madhu's desire for revenge remains meaningful only if we engage with her as a willful, irrational, hysterical, malevolent child—and the film underscores these qualities repeatedly.[17] Rajiv's professional decision to fire Anshuman and Madhu is also, of course, personal—we learn, early on, that the trio not only collaborate professionally but have been close friends. In the light of their personal relationship, Madhu's attack on Rajiv's life via his favorite child makes sense. In this sense, the home and the construction site—the private and the public spaces— come to be co-extensive, both equally vulnerable to Madhu's monumental wrath.

Phoonk is not only about adults and children, the rational and the irrational, but also about transforming the former into the latter—the narrative is one of re-educating Rajiv via his induction into the realm of the irrational. For the purposes of my argument here, *Phoonk* is foundationally a text of re-enchantment and, if you will, one of infantilization—of transforming adult disbelief into childlike faith. Rajiv's rational skepticism is harnessed not only to masculinity, but also to his identity as a technocrat, a class that the economic liberalization of India has made immensely vocal. Secure in his faith in the realm of reason, Rajiv initially gently refuses and later angrily dismisses the workers' request for a shrine on the construction site. In fact, he refuses to comply with this simple demand on at least three different occasions, despite entreaties from friends, colleagues, and even Arati. The construction site—Rajiv's favorite terrain for the exercise of his faith in reason—thus remains unsanctified.

Interestingly, the film does not rest on this evidence: *Phoonk* continues to expend considerable narrative energy in buttressing Ravi's pigheaded, intractable—almost irredeemably masculinist—rationality. When cursed fetish objects—animal bones, lemons, vermilion, etc.—are found in the yard, Rajiv ignores the entire family's requests and tosses them out with the trash. Predictably, he turns a deaf ear to all of Amma's warnings and Arati's concerns regarding the possibility of black magic afflicting their home. Preceding this material evidence of things going awry, Raksha mysteriously disappears from home and is finally located in the vicinity of a park seemingly unaware of her surroundings. Arati, who locates her, is relieved to note that the child seems physically unharmed; however, she is puzzled at her daughter's inability to explain how she arrived at that location. Also disquieting is Raksha's interest in a crow; insistent shot reverse shot editing shows her apparently in deep communion with the bird. Crows function as bearers of evil in *Phoonk*; each time Raksha is attacked or possessed by the evil spirit, she is shown exchanging looks with a crow, usually perched on a tree in the vicinity.

Following the disappearance, Raksha complains of hearing strange noises and also claims that someone has cut off some of her hair, complaints that are brushed aside by Rajiv. Raksha's first major "episode" occurs when she is at school. Soon after she enters the school, the steadycam performs the role of the predatory spirit in pursuit, circling and following Raksha into the building. Once again, just before she enters her classroom—where she eventually will laugh maniacally, frightening her teacher and classmates before passing out—she exchanges a series of glances with a crow. In this sequence, close-ups of the crow alternate with extreme close-ups of Raksha's chillingly expressionless face and eyes. In the series of these attacks that follow the initial episode, she speaks in a guttural, manly voice and becomes violent. The violence is primarily directed at adults who try to attend to her, especially at a distraught Rajiv. The child also acquires enormous physical strength during the fits of possession and is able to shove adults away from her bedside, a fact that astonishes the family doctor. In one particularly terrifying instance, Raksha recites nursery rhymes in this alien voice, in a seemingly catatonic state. Amidst all of these disturbances, a crow maintains a stubborn vigil outside Raksha's bedroom window, casting a watchful eye on proceedings; the soundtrack also incorporates the cawing of the birds. Once again Amma tries to intervene, only to be lectured about her superstitious television programs. Rajiv's response to the crisis is to summon doctors and rush Raksha to the hospital.

The entry of psychiatrist Seema Walke is important, not only because she diagnoses Raksha with Dissociative Personality Disorder—medicalese that Rajiv gratefully hangs his rationality on—but also because the film stages one of the most crucial battles between the realm of the scientific and the terrain of faith via a conversation between the doctor and Amma. Desperate to help the suffering child, the elderly woman eventually brings her request to Seema. The latter's response is more generous than Rajiv's—she concedes that what plagues Raksha can indeed be called a ghost or an evil spirit but remains adamant about the psychological nature of the problem. Crucially, Seema finally blames Amma's homespun wisdom—i.e., her superstitious nature—and her "fantastic stories" of ghosts and demons for Raksha's "deep psychological trauma"; according to her medical expertise, it is the effect of being exposed to these, in conjunction with objects in the yard, that push the child into a state of fear and distress.

Meanwhile, Amma summons a Shaman to exorcize the evil spirit that she believes is haunting their home and her grandchild. Predictably, when Rajiv discovers the shaman performing the rites of purification, he flies into a rage and evicts the mystic from the house. Following this altercation, Raksha's situation worsens—she actually begins to levitate close to the ceiling in absolute defiance of the rules of gravity. As Raksha shrieks and flails about uncontrollably, the terrified parents rush her back to the hospital. The medical personnel promptly restrain the child and begin their scientific ministrations. It is this final attack and a confrontation with the truly incredible that finally bring about Rajiv's transformation. Raksha's immense suffering forces him to capitulate to the suggestion of his friend and self-proclaimed religious opportunist, Vinay, that they find an "alternative solution."

Vinay takes Rajiv to Manja, a blind mystic who immediately seems to have knowledge of Rajiv's plight. It is Manja's wisdom that brings about the foundational changes in Rajiv's belief system. Unable to scoff at Manja's methods of investigation—which involve divination with iron spikes—he witnesses, instead, the mystic's superior powers. Manja bluntly tells Rajiv that his daughter will die unless the couple casting the black spells is stopped immediately. On the way to Anshuman and Madhu's, Rajiv gives the order for the Ganesha shrine to be built on the construction site—the final evidence of Manja's transformative powers. What follows is the climactic struggle between good and evil—polarities that are now both firmly grounded in the realm of the irrational. Madhu is dismembered and destroyed, as are her evil designs on Raksha. Ironically, when Rajiv embraces his now healed daughter, Arati is convinced that it is the doctors and medical science that have saved the child's life. This ironic reversal of roles between believers and skeptics closes *Phoonk*.

Phoonk remains a typical melodramatic conflict between opposing forces; the film neatly arranges the rational and irrational on either side of its central battle between good and evil. What makes the film especially interesting, as mentioned above, is that the final apocalyptic clash of bipolar ideologies are aligned to the realm of the modern, rational, scientific on the one end and the supernatural, the non-rational, and the child-like on the other. When Rajiv sheds his skepticism, he also sheds his rationality and, in a sense, his masculine obduracy; he enters the realm of the women and the children, the realm of the irrational and the magical. *Phoonk* gives us a glimpse of the re-enchantment that not only saves Rajiv's family but also by extension, redeems his soul. *Phoonk* allows for the voices of the marginalized to be heard above the din of a ruthlessly commonsensical technocratic rationality that has accompanied India's love-story with globalization; Manja's victory is, above all, an affirmation of an "unofficial" spiritual domain, one that is not aligned to any dominant religious formation in the subcontinent. Rajiv's final capitulation is the film's endorsement of these universes—of faith, spiritualism, child-like belief, and magic—that have fallen by the wayside in recent decades.

GAURI: THE REVENGE OF THE FETUS

Gauri, like *Vaastu*, was not a commercial success and for similar reasons. Director Aku Akbar is primarily a Malayalam-language filmmaker, and *Gauri* was his first foray into the Hindi-language industry. The lack of stars and its relatively low budget ensured that the film went largely unnoticed by mainstream audiences. However, reviewers commented on the film's innovative visual effects as well as its "socially relevant message."[18]

When married couple Sudeep and Roshni decide to go on vacation, their young daughter, Shivani, insists that the family return to their old home in the wilds of Neelgiri. Initially resistant, the parents eventually capitulate, and the family travels back to the place where Sudeep and Roshni had spent the early years of their marriage. Soon after returning to this old home, the couple realizes that some terrifying force is haunting their house and also Shivani. This ghost turns out to be Gauri, the spirit of a female fetus they had aborted early on in their marriage. Gauri, now inhabiting Shivani's body, delivers a dreadful ultimatum: she declares that after three days of subjecting the couple to acute terror and suffering, she will kill Shivani to avenge the termination of her own life. Sudeep and Roshni plead with Gauri but to no avail. However, the ghost frees Shivani at the end of the stipulated period once she realizes that the parents are genuinely regretful of her "murder." The family in turn embraces Gauri as a spirit-daughter to assuage her pain and their guilt.

Gauri is a frightening film in many respects—not the least of which is an unrelenting sentimentalization of the hugely important issue of reproductive rights which so many women are still struggling for. Interestingly, the film makes no distinction between the appearances of Gauri and Shivani which would enable us as well as the parents to tell them apart; we encounter Gauri only in Shivani's body, rendering the victimized child monstrous as well. I read *Gauri* as an especially troubling text, which deftly blurs the lines between the selective abortion of female fetuses with the larger issue of reproductive rights and freedoms; in doing so, the film disavows the very notions of modern coupledom and conjugality by prohibiting them from deciding if and when to have a child.

The issue of abortion is a hugely contested one in India, with implications that are considerably different from controversies in the West. Given the bugbear of population explosion in the subcontinent, the right to abortion is a given; it is legally available to all citizens as the state's intervention into population control. However, this "progressive" right continues to be widely deployed all over the country for the selective abortion of female fetuses after sex determination tests, thus raising vexed issues for feminist activists who support the right of women to keep control over their bodies but simultaneously oppose the termination of female fetuses on ethical grounds (Menon). While *Gauri* does not invoke the public or policy debates surrounding abortion, I would argue that the specter of female feticide does haunt the margins of the text; the film simply relocates this rhetoric within the private ambit of the family. In other words, the fact that the aborted fetus is female remains consequential in the larger discourses with which the film resonates.[19]

Sudeep, Roshni, and Shivani present a perfect picture of the modern, affluent nuclear family in the opening sequences of *Gauri*. The couple is also liberal in parenting techniques, as witnessed in their indulgence of Shivani's every wish and the relative absence of disciplining measures. It is Shivani who insists that they vacation in the family's old home, instead of Mauritius, the more suitable holiday destination that Roshni suggests. The child—presumably already possessed by the spirit of Gauri—brings the couple back to the scene of the crime, where Gauri had been conceived and the couple had made the decision to terminate the pregnancy. Once Sudeep and Roshni realize that Gauri has returned to exact revenge—Shivani gives them details of the abortion that she cannot possibly know—the film takes an ominous turn.

Via flashbacks, we learn of the early days of their marriage and of Roshni's desire to name their future child Gauri—a mythic name for the goddess Durga or Shakti, the symbol of female power within the Hindu pantheon.[20] We also learn that while Sudeep had been firm in his opinion about terminating the pregnancy (he felt unprepared to be a parent at the particular stage in life and career), Roshni vacillated widely in her decision about the pregnancy, and it had caused her considerable distress. Finally, however, she relented to Sudeep's wish, and the couple moved on with their lives. It was Sudeep's elderly father (unnamed) who struck a crucial note of dissonance in the midst of all this: once informed of the decision, he delivered a lengthy diatribe against the present generation's "selfishness and irresponsibility" and shunned the couple thereafter. His speech included, among other quasi-religious discourses, a description of the "magical moment of conception when a life miraculously takes birth in the womb," which echoes exactly the rhetoric of right-wing, conservative, pro-life groups everywhere.

Once Sudeep and Roshni discover the horrific nature of their predicament, Gauri delivers her ultimatum to the hapless parents via Shivani: just as she had awaited in dread the moment of her death in the womb, she will now terrorize the couple for three days after which she will kill Shivani as retribution for her own "murder." The terrified couple initially tries to escape with their child and then pleads in desperation, but to no avail. Gauri gleefully executes a series of attacks on the terrified, cowering parents, which range from spectral knives thrown at Roshni to an unbearable medley of weeping infants who keep the couple awake at night.

Gauri is essentially a neo-traditionalist, pro-life text that disregards the entire discourse of free will and individual rights. It does so particularly effectively by sentimentalizing the trope of home. As mentioned above, the demonic fetus not only brings the parents back home but also brings home to them the implications of their decision to undergo the abortion. In the process of attributing blame and culpability, the very topos of their house comes to be haunted and terrifying, since Gauri stubbornly claims it as her own home and continues to assert that the family belongs there. Beyond this hostile takeover of domestic space, Gauri also relentlessly lectures the parents on the womb as a metaphoric home: it is the womb in which a "baby" is supposed to feel most secure and loved, and yet she was brutally murdered in the very space of supposed sanctuary. We read Roshni's pregnant body retrospectively as colonized terrain in a sense, while Gauri's sermons simultaneously imbue the fetus with vindictive consciousness.

On the final night of their three-day period of terror, the film takes us into a virtuoso display of Computer Generated Imagery (CGI) to drive home the monumental nature of Gauri's wrath: luminous, ghostly fetuses descend from the night sky and literally besiege Sudeep and Roshni's home. Another horrific scene follows when glass shards rain on the unprotected Shivani, and the helpless parents cower in abject terror.[21] This attack presumably re-creates Gauri's experience of the termination of her life with sharp instruments. Thus, the latter half of the film is a long-drawn phase of epiphany for the couple, as they are driven to paroxysms of guilt and suffering and finally to the dreadful realization that their only child will be murdered by vengeful the ghost-fetus, Gauri. Gauri finally relinquishes her rage but not until she extracts a crucial promise from her "parents" that she will find solace in their home and family whenever she feels alone, insecure or threatened. The final images show a vastly chastened Roshni making room on their bed for the spectral form of Gauri, now rendered as luminous orbs of light, and finally lavishing on her the love that the film tries to convince us she deserves.

Needless to say, as the ageist counterpart to Gauri's rhetoric, Sudeep's father returns to the scene in a key moment in the latter half of the film. As the unheeded patriarch whose homespun wisdom was spurned by the much too modern couple, the dénouement is as much his vindication as it is Gauri's. The fetus/ghost tells him that she has missed him, and he holds her in his arms in affection and regret for the life lost; clearly, for him, Gauri is not simply a vindictive ghost but a child who could/should have been. The obscenity of the moment when grandpa and Gauri embrace in profound communion is unmistakable: the unborn fetus and the feudal patriarch reserve the right to pass judgment on the irrelevance of reproductive rights and, by extension, comment on the ethics of companionate coupledom, conjugality, and procreation.

Gauri is a horrifying text in many ways, not least because it conflates the issue of abortion with the selective termination of female fetuses, which continues to plague a rapidly globalizing India. In referring to Gauri as "she," my analysis, too, risks bestowing personhood/gender on the fetus; in embodying the fetus as a little girl, the film manages this canny sleight of hand whereby we can no longer refer Gauri as "it." *Gauri* systematically and horrifically dismantles the very notion of the modern couple in allowing not only the feudal patriarch—Sudeep's father—but also the unborn zygote to articulate their opinions on the matter of reproductive rights and planning parenthood. Finally, it affirms their rhetoric—a rhetoric of miraculous birth that brings the past (grandpa) and the potential future (Gauri) together in a curious but efficacious indictment of modernity. The overdetermined terrain of parental love and nurture is deployed, I would argue, in a dissolution of modernity itself.

CONCLUSION

As demonstrated in my readings of recent films, the horror genre in Bollywood offers us a valuable optic into the dissonant, disruptive, and disturbing aspects of the triumphant narrative of globalization. As mainstream Bombay cinema participates wholeheartedly in the rhetoric of progress, globality, and consumption that supposedly accompanies India's entry into late modernity, it falls on the much-derided horror genre to register the voices of discontent and dissent.

We can engage this dissonance in several ways, some of which are more sobering than others. As foundational transformations attend to the Indian socio-cultural and economic fabric, chasms yawn between classes, women contribute in increasing numbers to urban workforce, divorce rates skyrocket, and families come to be imperiled more than ever before. The horror film responds to these changes in several ways: first, the genre imbibes the rhetoric of backlash, a reactionary, conservative discourse that holds late modernity, especially modern women and couples, culpable for all the ills plaguing Indian society. In this respect, the horror film abets and indeed resonates the neo-traditionalist rhetoric of Hindu nationalists and other right-wing formations. Most troubling perhaps is the instrumental use of the figure of the child—innocent, vulnerable, in need of nurture—in buttressing this regressive ideological terrain. *Vaastu Shastra* and *Gauri* remain exemplary films in this context.

Phoonk intervenes into this tug and pull of the modern and the non-modern in a way that remains, I suggest, more compelling. It calls for a re-enchantment of private and public domains that have come to be entirely disenchanted in the wake of industrial and post-industrial modernity. In this reading, *Phoonk*, and other films of its ilk generate a desire for a re-inscription of the magical, the mystical, the feminine, the childlike, and the irrational into a world that has relentlessly marginalized these nodes of experience. The figure of the child, however privileged, then serves as a stand-in for an abject subaltern; the child articulates all that is lacking and is ruthlessly marginalized and silenced in the story of India's triumphant and celebrated romance with globalization.

NOTES

1. For a discussion of the implications and valences of the label "Bollywood," see Prasad.

2. The Ramsay films are finally receiving much-deserved critical attention from cult cinema fans as well as film scholars. See, for example, Tombs.

3. Although this newer crop of films were certainly made and circulated in a transformed industrial environment, filmmakers, especially Varma, continue to cite and pay homage to the Ramsay films through mise-en-scene and iconography.

4. Examples abound and including *Dark Water* (2002), *Whispering Corridors* (2003), *A Tale of Two Sisters* (2003), and *Acacia* (2003).

5. First and especially last names in South Asia clearly indicate what caste, community, and religion an individual belongs to. It is virtually impossible to disguise these markers of social belonging once a person has been officially named.

6. Exceptions to the rule: Mrinal Sen's *Kharij* (1983) represented the exploitation of young rural children as domestic workers and Aamir Khan's *Taare Zameen Par* (2007) invokes a different kind of child labor—the enormous burden put on children by the arguably harsh scholastic systems in India.

7. Although male children are most often represented, curiously, many of the actors playing little boys are actually girls—a tendency that has fallen somewhat out of vogue in recent years.

8. Much scholarly work has recently focused on the emerging middle classes in pre- and post-liberalization India. See, for example, Fernandes.

9. For a discussion of the Multiplex boom and attendant transformations in distribution and exhibition of films, see Sharma.

10. This immersion within a larger space of consumption is so crucial to understanding the spectatorial experience of the viewer that Amit Rai has coined the term "Malltiplex" to describe the textured and sensate world of the urban multiplex.

11. For a theorization of Indian cinema through the trope of interruptions, see Gopalan.

12. Style in *Vaastu*—and the other films discussed here—remains highly self-conscious. The filmmakers clearly speak to an audience that is competent in reading, or is at least relatively familiar with, formal conventions typically deployed by the horror genre in Hollywood and beyond. It is this "knowing" spectatorship that Philip Brophy gestured towards when he wrote, "The contemporary Horror film knows that you've seen it before; it knows that you know what is about to happen; and it knows that you know it knows you know. And none of it means a thing, as the cheapest trick in the book will still tense your muscles, quicken your heart and jangle your nerves."

13. The undead in *Vaastu* look very similar to those in Takashi Shimizu's global hit *Ju-on*; the children in particular seem to have been modeled on those in the earlier film. The emphasis on a cursed home where inhabitants die mysteriously is also resonant with the plot of the Japanese film.

14. One possible explanation for *Vaastu's* open-ended closure is that the producers may have had plans for future sequels. The director's untimely death in 2010, however, makes this possibility unlikely.

15. This division—and particularly Rajiv's claim to adult rationality in the film—is resonant with Nandy's reading of modern childhood, in that it resonates powerfully with the adult anxiety of regression: "childhood has become a major dystopia for the modern world. The fear of being childish dogs the steps of every psychologically insecure adult and of every culture that uses the metaphor of childhood to define mental illness, primitivism, abnormality, underdevelopment, non-creativity and traditionalism" (65).

16. When Anshuman and Madhu visit the family, Raksha clearly states, "I don't like her," prompting an immediate demand for an apology from an embarrassed Rajiv. At the fateful party, Madhu pinches Raksha's cheek cooing, "She doesn't like me. But I love her!" Madhu's sinister energy is signposted most clearly in her interactions with the little girl.

17. Especially in the party sequence, Madhu's defiant screaming even after having been discovered—her lack of remorse and her aggression—alert us to the insane, irrational child within. Her reaction to their humiliation is a childish covering of her eyes and wailing—hardly, I would suggest, the response of an adult. What I would like to emphasize here is that Madhu's baroque anger is linked to her child-likeness, which eventually becomes pathologically vindictive.

18. See Taran Adarsh's review.

19. Even user reviews on IMDB mention female feticide in relation to the film's take on abortion.

20. Interestingly, the name "Shivani" also refers to the same goddess, another technique by which the film equates the child and the fetus.

21. As an aside, it is interesting to note that in many of these films CGI—a modern technological innovation that has irrevocably transformed the cinema in recent years—is deployed in aid of elaborating and often buttressing a non-modern, traditionalist ideology.

WORKS CITED

Adarsh, Taran. Rev. of *Gauri, The Unborn. One India Entertainment.* Greynium Information Technologies, n.d. Web.17 Apr. 2011.

Brophy, Philip. "Horrality: The Textuality of Contemporary Horror Films." 1983. *Philip Brophy.com*. Web. 21 May 2011.

Elsaesser, Thomas. "Tales of Sound and Fury: Observations on the Family Melodrama." *Film Genre Reader II*. Ed. Barry Keith Grant. Austin: U of Texas P, 1995. 350–80. Print.

Fernandes, Leela. *India's New Middle Class: Democratic Politics in an Era of Economic Reform*. Minneapolis: U of Minnesota P, 2006. Print.

Fischer, Lucy. "Birth Traumas: Parturition and Horror in Rosemary's Baby." *The Dread of Difference: Gender and the Horror Film*. Ed. Barry Keith Grant. Austin: U of Texas P, 1996. 412–31. Print.

Gathia, Joseph. "Child Labour in India." *Merinews.com*. Bizsol Advisors, 19 June 2008. Web. 9 Oct. 2010.

Gauri. Dir. Aku Akbar. Adlabs, 2007. DVD.

Gledhill, Christine. "The Melodramatic Field: An Investigation." *Home is Where the Heart Is: Studies in Melodrama and the Woman's Film*. Ed. Christine Gledhill. London: BFI, 1987. 5–69. Print.

Gopalan, Lalitha. *Cinema of Interruptions: Action Genres in Contemporary Indian Cinema*. London: BFI, 2008. Print.

"Growing Trend in Child and Student Suicides in India." PRLog. 24 Jan. 2010. Web. 10 Oct. 2010.

"Infant Mortality Rate." *World Bank, World Development Indicators*. Google Public Data. Google, 2009. Web. 10 Oct. 2010.

Kakar, Sudhir. *The Inner World: A Psycho-Analytic Study of Childhood and Society in India*. Oxford: Oxford UP, 2009. Print.

McRoy, Jay. "Ghosts of the Present, Specters of the Past: The *kaidan* and the Haunted Family in the Cinema of Nakata Hideo and Shimizu Takashi." *Nightmare Japan: Contemporary Japanese Horror Cinema*. Amsterdam: Rodopi, 2007. 75–102. Print.

Menon, Nivedita. "Abortion and the Law: Questions for Feminism." *Canadian Journal of Women and the Law* 6 (1993): 103–18. Print.

Nair, Kartik. "Run For Your Lives: Remembering the Ramsay Brothers." *The Many Forms of Fear, Horror and Terror*. Ed. Leanne Franklin and Ravenel Richardson. Oxford: Interdisciplinary P, 2009. PDF File.

Nandy, Ashis. "Reconstructing Childhood: A Critique of the Ideology of Adulthood." *Traditions, Tyranny and Utopias: Essays in the Politics of Awareness*. New Delhi: Oxford UP, 1987. 56–76. Print.

Nelson, Lindsey. "Ghosts of the Past, Ghosts of the Future: Monsters, Children and Cotemporary Japanese Horror Cinema." *Cinemascope: Independent Film Journal* 5.13 (2009): 1–14. Print.

Pandey, Geeta. "India Tightens Child Labour Laws." *BBC News*. BBC, 10 Oct. 2006. Web. 9 Oct. 2010.

Phoonk. Dir. Ram Gopal Varma. Junglee Music, 2008.

Prasad, Madhava. "This Thing Called Bollywood." *Unsettling Cinema: A Symposium on the Place of Cinema in India* 525 (May 2003): n. pag. Web. 17 Apr. 2011.

Rai, Amit S. *Untimely Bollywood: Globalization and India's New Media Assemblage*. Durham: Duke UP, 2009. Print.

Rajadhyaksha, Ashish. "The 'Bollywoodization' of Indian Cinema: Cultural National-ism in the Global Arena." *City Flicks: Indian Cinema and the Urban Experience.* Ed. Preben Kaarsholm. Calcutta: Seagull P, 2004. 113–39. Print.

Sharma, Aparna. "India's Experience with the Multiplex." *Seminar* 525 (May 2003): n. pag. Web. 17 Apr. 2011.

Sobchak, Vivian. "Bringing it All Back Home: Family Economy and Generic Exchange." *The Dread of Difference: Gender and the Horror Film.* Ed. Barry Keith Grant. Austin: U of Texas P, 1996. 143–63. Print.

Tombs, Pete. "The Beast from Bollywood: A History of the Indian Horror Film." *Fear Without Frontiers: Horror Cinema Across the Globe.* Ed. Steven Jay Schneider. Surrey Place: Fab P, 2003. 243–53. Print.

Vaastu Shastra. Dir. Saurab Narang. Spark, 2004.

Wood, Robin. "An Introduction to the American Horror Film." *Movies and Methods: An Anthology. Volume 2.* Ed. Bill Nichols. Calcutta: Seagull Books, 1993. 195–220. Print.

"The Power of Christ Compels You": Holy Water, Hysteria, and the Oedipal Psychodrama in *The Exorcist*

SARA WILLIAMS

Though made forty years ago, William Friedkin's *The Exorcist* (1971) remains a shocking film, as scenes of Regan's bodily contortions and convulsions, explicit acts of masturbation, and sexual abuse of her mother destroys the construct of the innocent child society holds dear. The film, however, restores some sense of innocence through its interpretation of the novel as an incontestable narrative of possession: Regan cannot be held responsible for the murders of Dennings, Merrick, and Karras because it is not she who kills them but rather the demon using her body as a vessel in the material realm. Regan emerges from the ordeal an innocent victim, with little recollection of what she has experienced or indeed what she has done. The scenes in which she performs physically impossible movements—scuttling down the stairs in a spider-walk, levitating, moving furniture telekinetically, and most infamously twisting her head around 360°—become empirical proof of her body's possession and confirm *The Exorcist* as unambiguously supernatural.

Even though William Peter Blatty penned the original novel upon which the film was based as well as the screenplay, the two differ considerably. While the film opts for a supernatural explanation—Regan is possessed by the Babylonian devil Pazuzu—Blatty's novel consistently questions the authenticity of Regan's possession by providing an alternate explanation for her behavior: hysteria. As Marsha Kinder and Beverle Houston have discussed, it is the abandonment of the text's psychological realism that makes Friedkin's film a deeply conservative one which "presents us with data for a psychological interpretation . . . then rejects it in favor of a phenomenological Devil" (45). This article will show how the original text presents a psychological diagnosis of hysteria that precedes and challenges the metaphysical explanation of

Regan's behavior which has been accepted culturally due to the enduring popularity and notoriety of the film.

Based loosely on the reported exorcism of a young boy known as "Robbie Manheim" in 1949 (Kermode 11–22), Blatty's novel articulates the tensions between the scientific and superstitious Catholic discourses which both desire to "save" the child through the characterization of Father Damien Karras, a priest and a psychiatrist struggling with his faith who has researched the occult "from the psychiatric side" (77). As Ann Douglas comments, the novel inaugurates the "family horror" genre which articulated late twentieth-century middle-class anxieties about the "splitting of the atom of the nuclear family," with Regan, Chris and the absent father Howard "constitut[ing] the postmodern familiar cluster in fission" (294). For Douglas, family horror novels are "post-Freudian case studies" which "narrate a crisis, a moment of traumatic disturbance in the external and internal life of a single character or cluster of characters, member[s] of a nuclear or self-involved, self consti-tuted family" (304). Within this context, Douglas reads Regan's possession as "an extreme version of Bertha Pappenheim's acute hysteria of a century earlier, which Freud and Josef Breuer immortalized as the illness and recov-ery of Anna O." (ibid.). Expanding on Douglas's contention that Regan finds a precursor in Anna O., I will demonstrate how the novel can be read as a specifically Oedipal hysteria narrative through which Regan-as-demon expresses both sexual desire for the absent father and a violent rejection of the mother.

Although Freud's thinking on the Oedipus conflict was complex and changeable,[1] throughout my argument I use the terminology "Oedipal" to refer to the process of ego formation wherein the child desires the parent of the opposite sex and so rejects the parent of the same sex, with whom they eventually identify in order to disavow their unconscious incestuous desires and become a socialized subject. In earlier articulations, Freud considered the Oedipus complex in girls to be analogous to that of boys, but in its final stage he reformulated a female Oedipus complex which has a "prehistory," where the girl's first love object is her mother ("Psychical Consequences" 675). This pre-Oedipal stage ends when the girl, having come to understand that she and her mother lack a penis, blames her mother for this lack, and rejects her in favor of the father, for whom she wishes to provide a child as a penis-substitute; thus, the Oedipal phase commences (675–76). How-ever, while boys destroy the Oedipus complex in the face of the threat of castration presented by the mother's body and the vengeful father, as Freud explains, "[i]n girls the motive for the demolition of the Oedipus complex is lacking" (677). It is this persistence of the female Oedipus complex which I see as articulated by Regan's hysterical "possession." Juliet Mitchell seminally remarked that "hysteria was, and is . . . the daughter's disease: a child's fantasy about her parents" (*Women* 308), and recent feminist scholarship has recast hysteria as symptomatic of the yearning for the pre-Oedipal maternal dyad.

Barbara Creed understands the film version of *The Exorcist*, in which the close relationship between Regan and Chris is visualized and emphasized, as a violent reconciliation with the abject pre-Oedipal maternal. While these interpretations necessarily challenge the phallocentricism of Freud's model, this article reads the original novel in its socio-cultural context of post-Freud, but not yet pre-Oedipal, conservative, bourgeois America. I argue that Regan's fixation on her father and failure to resolve her Oedipal conflict can be just as damaging to patriarchy as the reunion with the pre-Oedipal mother which Creeds contends is performed through possession in the film.

Freud developed his psychoanalytical theories on unconscious and repressed desires through his early work in the 1890s with female hysterics.[2] The Oedipus complex thus originated from the psychodramas of Freud and Breuer's female patients, and Blatty's text appeared when the cultural construction of the Oedipal concept of hysteria remained embedded in this Freudian precedent. This is evidenced frequently by the text, such as when Chris notices how Regan's abnormal behavior first emerges after not hearing from her father on her birthday, a recognition that establishes the Oedipal context of the desired but unattainable father:

> Beginning on the day after Regan's birthday—and following Howard's failure to call—[Chris] had noticed a sudden and dramatic change in her daughter's behavior and disposition. Insomnia. Quarrelsome. Fits of temper. Kicked things. Threw things. Screamed. Wouldn't eat. In addition, her energy seemed abnormal. She was constantly moving, touching and turning; tapping; running and jumping about. Doing poorly with schoolwork. Fantasy playmate. Eccentric attention tactics. (57)

The narrative follows the diagnostic history of hysteria as Dr. Klein,[3] Regan's psychiatrist, first offers the neurological possibility of a scar on Regan's temporal lobe, echoing the nineteenth-century neurologist Jean-Martin Charcot's diagnosis of demonic possession as the psychosomatic result of a trauma to the brain (101). Indeed, Freud and Jung are name-dropped periodically throughout the text by both Klein and Karras, and Freud's theories of unconscious desires are offered as an explanation for Regan's behavior. For example, Klein explains to Chris that "hysteria . . . is a form of neurosis in which emotional disturbances are converted into bodily disorders" and suggests that Regan could be suffering from "what Freud used to call the 'conversion' form of hysteria," that "grows from unconscious guilt and the need to be punished. Dissociation is the paramount feature here, even multiple personality. And the syndrome might also include epileptoid-like convulsions; hallucinations; abnormal motor excitement" (127, 128). Klein further suggests that her parents' divorce would produce unconscious feelings of guilt and stress in Regan which could manifest bodily as "rage and intense frustration" (128), and a "noted neuropsychiatrist" is called in, in the tradition of Charcot and Freud, to question Regan under hypnosis (120). This session ends abruptly when Regan objects to the interrogation by "squeezing his scrotum with a hand that had gripped him like an iron talon" (125), a sexually aggressive response which signals the violent intensity of her Oedipal desire, as provoked by male psychiatric probing.

Within this context then, descriptions of Regan "shrieking hysterically" or "hysterical[ly] screaming" (83, 108) explicitly connote her neurosis. The text is well versed in the epistemology of hysteria and clearly provides a psychiatric explanation for Regan's condition. Somatizing her libidinal outrage at being separated from her father by the divorce, the text implies that she converts the unconscious trauma of paternal loss into a demon which occupies her body and compels its deterioration. Yet, while the diagnosis of hysteria continues to be implied throughout the text, the deepest and most disturbing cause of her neurosis is left unidentified, that is, her Oedipal desire for her father. Regan's possession continues, and the psychiatric explanation is dismissed in favor of more desperate religious measures. Reading the novel in this way exposes the film as a reductive and conservative interpretation which, in assuming the metaphysical explanation over the psychological, re-establishes and asserts the patriarchal Christian moral order as Regan's savior.

"MY DEAR, THERE ARE LUNATIC ASYLUMS ALL OVER THE WORLD FILLED WITH PEOPLE WHO DABBLED IN THE OCCULT": THE HYSTERICAL PRECEDENT AND THE DEMONIC OEDIPAL PRECEDENT

The concept of hysteria has a long history dating back to Plato,[4] but it was Charcot who understood the condition as a visual performance and at his hospital *la Salpêtrière* he exhibited patients for a hungry audience. A favorite subject was Augustine, an icon of hysteria who was admitted to the asylum in 1875 at the age of fifteen for " 'paralysis of sensation in the right arm' and for contractures or anaesthesias which affected the organs on the right side of her body" (Didi-Huberman quoting Bournville 100). Charcot had Augustine's convulsions sketched and photographed for the collections *Iconographie photographique de la Salpêtrière* (1876–1880) and *Les Démoniaques dans l'art* (1887), and in response she played the part of hysteric, in return for his attention (Showalter 154). Prefiguring Freud and Breuer's hysteria case studies, Augustine was the daughter/patient to Charcot's masterful father/doctor. Consequently, hysteria was established simultaneously as a medical condition and the performance of one—a result of, and a response to, paternal authority. Freud later developed Charcot's idea of physical trauma into a psychodynamic one, and his phallocentric model re-inscribed the disease as a neurosis centered on the daughter's Oedipal desire for the father.

In 1895, Freud and Josef Breuer co-authored *Studies on Hysteria*, which documented the analysis and treatment of their hysterical subjects through the "talking cure," a term coined by Breuer's most famous patient "Anna O." to describe the cathartic process (34). As will be discussed, it is this absence of catharsis which proves most problematic for Regan.

Freud and Breuer's cases discuss adolescent girls who had extreme psychosomatic responses to the literal or emotional loss of their father, and thus the Oedipal drama as the etiology of hysteria was established. Breuer treated "Anna O." (Bertha Pappenheim) for symptoms of hysteria including "paralysing contractures, complete paralysis in the upper right and both lower extremities, partial paralysis in the upper left extremity," as well as a squint and disturbances of vision, hearing and speech, hallucinations, split personality, and loss of consciousness which he diagnosed as the somatic response to caring for her ill father "whom she idolized" and who eventually died (Freud and Breuer 26, 29). Similarly, in "Fragment of an Analysis of a Case of Hysteria," Freud diagnosed "Dora" (Ida Bauer) as suffering from hysterical loss of voice in response to her father's affair with "Frau K," for whom she babysat, and her husband "Herr K's" own advances towards her. Both analysts became embroiled in the Oedipal fantasies with which they had diagnosed their patients, as both girls exhibited symptoms of hysterical pregnancy, with the paternity of the phantom babies being attributed to their respective analysts (Mitchell, *Mad Men and Medusas* 67, 68).

Consequently, the advent of the psychoanalytic explanation enabled doctors and historians to diagnose cases of hysteria which were understood at the time to be evidence of demonic possession. In *Les Démoniaques*, Charcot and co-author Richer, through their method of *medicine retrospec-tive*, pathologically bound religiosity to neurosis when they argued that medieval saints, stigmatics, and ecstatics should be classified as hysterical in the same manner as those thought to be demonically possessed (Mazzoni 27; Midelfort 204). In "A Seventeenth-Century Demonological Neurosis" (1922), Freud extrapolated psychoanalytically on Charcot's contention that what was considered evidence of demonic possession in the middle ages was symptomatic of a neurological disorder. He translated the demon in terms of psychiatry, explaining that "the demons are bad and reprehensible wishes, derivatives of instinctual impulses that have been repudiated and repressed" (72). Within this Freudian model, Regan's demonic transformation embodies the eruption of her Oedipal desires, the once repressed "bad and reprehensible wishes" which surfaced following her parents' divorce and her geographical and emotional separation from her father. Despite the melodramatic veneer of demonic possession, Regan's behavior closely echoes the Oedipal etiology of the archetypal case studies of Freudian hysteria, Dora and Anna O., and before them Charcot's Augustine.

Consequently, Regan's sexually aggressive possession becomes a form of rape fantasy wish-fulfillment as she submits to a powerful masculine force, which she unconsciously interprets as having the father-as-Devil physically "inside" her. As such, Regan shares much in common with other historical cases of demonic possession. Lyndal Roper, for example, has shown in her study of medieval witchcraft how women's communion with the Devil fitted the Oedipal theme and discusses the case of Regina Bartholome, who in 1670 confessed to living with the Devil, fantasizing that she fulfilled the Oedipal triad of daughter/lover/wife (227).[5] Like Regina before her, Regan's communion with the Devil enables her to express her forbidden desires towards her father by proxy.[6] Thus, Regan's hysterical manifestation of the Oedipal drama has a precedent in both psychoanalysis and the cultural unconscious, which Karras affirms when he cites Freud's "Demonological Neurosis" which discusses a case of male hysteria-as-demonic possession that makes explicit the symbolic role of the Devil as father-substitute (208).[7] Through her (self-)possession Regan attempts a sexual union with the father; because her body houses both herself and the demon, her acts of masturbation become symbolic paternal penetration.

Furthermore, it appears that Regan herself is well-versed in this history. We learn that she has prior knowledge of demonic possession from clandestinely reading a book leant to her mother called *A Study of Devil Worship and Related Occult Phenomena* that contains a chapter "States of Possession" which mentions "quasi-possession—those cases that are ultimately reducible to fraud, paranoia and hysteria" (166). Thus, Regan is not only aware of the signs of demonic possession, she has also read that the body itself can manifest such signs factitiously. As with Karras's intertextual nods to Freud, this textual self-referentiality reveals the often-overlooked complexity of *The Exorcist* as a novel which engages with the tensions between demonological and medical discourses of possession.

"THERE'S NOTHING SUPERNATURAL ABOUT IT": REGAN AS HYSTERIC

Like the hysterics at *la Salpêtrière*, Regan is subject to numerous diagnostic tests before Chris rejects a medical explanation in favor of possession. The description of these tests and Regan's reactions follow the structure of Charcot's performance-as-diagnosis plot in which the subject would respond to his probing in an extreme manner so as to confirm her hysteria through the act of spectacle (Didi-Huberman 83–279). Regan is uncannily like Augustine in her hysterical attacks: like Regan, Charcot's patient would "vociferate, laugh, and vomit, all at once" (Didi-Huberman 261), and after having X-rays taken, Regan exhibits her most extreme symptoms of hysteria, including the acquisition of a previously unknown language, the uncharacteristic use of obscene language, the performance of bodily convulsions and contractures, and public displays of masturbation. Echoing Augustine's hysterical paroxysms, Regan's demonic Oedipal psychodrama reads as an example of textbook hysteria:

> Shrieking hysterically, [Regan] was flailing her arms as her body seemed to fling itself horizontally into the air above her bed and then slammed down savagely onto the mattress.... She would lift about a foot each time and then fall with a wrenching of her breath, as if unseen hands had picked her up and thrown her down.... The up and down movements ceased abruptly and the girl twisted feverishly from side to side with her eyes rolled upward into their sockets so that only the whites were exposed.... Still twisting and jerking, Regan arched her head back, disclosing a swollen, bulging throat. She began to mutter something incomprehensible in an oddly guttural tone.
>
> "...nowonmai...nowonmai..."
>
> ...A yelping laugh gushed up from her throat, and then she fell on her back as if someone had pushed her. She pulled up her nightgown exposing her genitals. "*Fuck* me! *Fuck* me!" she screamed at the doctors, and with both hands began masturbating frantically. (109–11)

Furthermore, the obstruction in Regan's throat, which she implies is caused by the demon inside her body—"Please, *stop* him! It hurts! Make him *stop*! Make him *stop*! I can't *breathe*!" (110)—echoes the symptom *globus hystericus* from which "Dora" suffered, a sensation of choking which, as Plato suggested, indicated that the empty womb was rising up through the body and suffocating the subject. The symptoms Regan manifests symbolize her Oedipal desire to provide her father with a child, as represented by her lamenting womb wandering around her body. This episode culminates in a violent bodily contortion that evokes the *arc de cercle* (Didi-Huberman Figure 106, 267), a pose which the "possessed" Loudun nuns[8] and many of Charcot's patients, including Augustine, were purported to have made during attacks of *grande hystérie*: "[Regan] started to arch her body upward into an impossible position, bending it backward like a bow until the brow of her head had touched her feet. She was screaming in pain. The doctors eyed each other with questioning surmise. Then Klein gave a signal to the neurologist. But before the consultant could seizer her, Regan fell limp and wet the bed" (110). Regan later repeats the *arc* when she "[glides], spiderlike, rapidly...her body arched backward in a bow with her head almost touching her feet...her tongue flicking quickly in and out of her mouth while she hissed sibilantly like a serpent" (119); here, Regan also echoes the image of Augustine with her tongue stuck out during fits (Didi-Huberman Figure 105, 260). Charcot defined such contractures as *attitudes passionnelles*, poses that re-enacted past incidents of the patient's life and to which in *Iconographies* he gave subtitles such as "amorous supplication," "ecstasy" and "eroticism," which Elaine Showalter points out "suggest Charcot's interpretation of hysteria as linked to female sexuality, despite his disclaimers" (150).

Freud would later make explicit the implication that hysterical subjects were repeating past sexual trauma or desire with his theory of the Oedipal etiology of hysteria. Regan communicates her desire through her bodily manipulations as she lifts her groin up and places it as the highest point of her form, presenting herself, as Freud explained, "in the posture of a body that is suitable for sexual intercourse" ("Hysterical Attacks" 230). Indeed, the entire episode of possession constellates around Regan's bed as the site of her unfulfilled desires. Augustine's *attitudes* were described in a similarly sexual nature and interpreted as the call to an imaginary lover: "She closes her eyes, her physiognomy denoting possession and satisfied desire . . . then then come the little cries, smiles, movements of the pelvis, words of desire or encouragement" (Bournville qtd. in Didi-Huberman 144). If, as Charcot attested, the *attitudes* played out past experiences which contributed to the patient's hysteria, then Augustine's imaginary lover may well be her employer and mother's lover who attempted to rape her and who is associated with her own father in her hysterical flashbacks: "Pig! Pig! I'll tell papa . . . . Pig! How heavy you are!" (qtd. in Didi-Huberman 160). Trapped in the Oedipal dynamic, Augustine is in a state of "possession," at the mercy of the father figure as she replays her trauma in an "incessant deliria of rape" (160). Father is to be desired, revered, and feared, and we see Regan articulating this tension in her own hysterical seizures and contractures.

Regan's *arc* is translated infamously to monstrous effect on screen when, arched over backwards like a spider, she scurries fiendishly down a flight of stairs, hissing and bleeding profusely from her mouth. It is testament to both the special effects and the original description of Regan's contortion that this scene, despite its relative crudeness, remains so viscerally inassimilable, and yet it is not, as deceptively suggested by the text, "an impossible position." During attacks of *grande hystérie*, Charcot's patients would regularly contort and convulse in a tetanic manner which attested to the ability of the hysteric's body to be "*articulated* at will, endowed as it was with an incredible *plastic submission*" (see Figures 46–8 in Didi-Huberman, 192). Charcot's beloved Augustine in her *attitudes* struck the archetypal poses of hysteria and shows that, possessed by hysteria, the adolescent female body was capable of things considered alien and unknown to itself: "The whole *body* became rigid; the *arms* stiffened, sometimes executing more or less perfect circumduction; then they would often approach each other on the median line, the wrists touching each other on the dorsal side" (Didi-Huberman quoting Bournville and Régnard 123). Regan's ability to move her bed from the floor during her seizures (83, 285) also echoes Augustine's attacks, as Didi-Huberman describes how she would be straitjacketed "on a bed that she would have turned upside down if she had not been fettered" (113). Scholars since have identified such seizures as female orgasms (see Maines), and so within the Oedipal framework Regan's fits are the climax to her sexual communion with the Devil-as-father who she believes is literally inside her.

Even the welts on Regan's chest, "bas-relief script rising up in clear letters of blood-red skin. Two words: help me" (262), which appear to have been written from inside her body as though the real Regan is trapped inside herself, find a physiological explanation in the medical condition *dermatographic urticara*, in which the skin becomes raised and inflamed in response to touch. As Janet Beizer has discussed, this was translated as a symptom of hysteria by Charcot and others, evidence of the hysteric's body as impressionable, hypersensitive and hyperexpressive (20). Beizer mentions how doctors "fascinated by dermatographism often used the sign of the Devil in their writing experiments" and reproduces a photograph of a woman's back which has SATAN inscribed in large welts above her shoulder blades (Figure 3, 25). Regan's dermatography thus inscribes hysteria on her body in the same manner as the wounds of Christ do with stigmatics (see Littlewood and Bartocci 598), but at the same time it also evidences her own visceral belief in her possession. The confirmation of Regan's possession as performance comes from her reaction to being doused with unblessed tap water, which Karras tells her is holy water: "Immediately the demon was cringing, writhing, bellowing in terror and in pain: 'It burns it burns! Ahh, stop it! Cease, priest bastard, cease!' Expressionless, Karras stopped sprinkling. *Hysteria. Suggestion. She* did *read the book*" (227). Karras sets up this deceit as a test to expose Regan's possession as a masquerade, and it works, but he ultimately rejects this evidence and instead pursues the possession route to its fatal conclusion in order to reaffirm his faith. Regan's hysteria is a performance in which all actors must take their parts for it to play out successfully, and in this sense the masquerade of demonic possession can never fully be exposed.[9] By omitting the text's Freudian references in the film's adaptations of these episodes, the psychological interpretation, originally emphasized in the novel, is suppressed in the film.

As Charcot and his spectators had invested in the diagnosis of hysteria and desired visual proof in the form of performances and photographs, so did audiences of *The Exorcist* want evidence of Regan's demonic possession. Seeing was believing, and both Augustine's and Regan's bodies were subjected to scrutiny and interpretation, and in Regan's case the translation from text to film is especially reductive. The most shocking scene of the film graphically depicts Regan's head spinning 360° and this scene thus offers empirical evidence of possession, as the special effects show Regan's body contorting into a physiological impossibility. Crucially, however, in Blatty's original text, this contortion is only viewed by Chris, who is deeply emotionally and psychologically disturbed following her oral abuse at the hands of her daughter:

> Chris crumpled to the floor in a daze of horror, in a swirling of images, sounds in the room, as her vision spun madly, blurring, unfocused, her ears ringing loud with chaotic distortions as she tried to raise herself,

was too weak, faltered, then looked toward the still-blurred bed.... Then she cringed, shrinking back in incredulous terror as she thought she saw hazily, in a swimming fog, her daughter's head turning slowly around on a motionless torso, rotating monstrously, inexorably, until at last it seemed facing backward. (184)

The film's literal translation is repeated during the scene of the exorcism, where Linda Blair's head rotates a complete 360°, thus eliminating the ambiguity of the text which is not so explicit. In the novel, by contrast, Regan's contortions can be read as the hysteric's orgasmic seizure, her apparently anatomically impossible head-spinning finding a precursor in Augustine's "fantastic" contractures during which "her neck would suddenly twist so violently that her chin would pass her shoulder and touch her shoulder blade" (Didi-Huberman 122). Furthermore, Chris's reliability as a witness is questionable. Earlier in the text, Chris had mentioned, "I thought I saw someone levitate once. In Bhutan" (68), indicating both a belief in psychokinesis and an implicit doubt in the reality of the spectacle, and her witnessing of the contortion is characterized by the same visual uncertainty; her vision is spinning, blurred, "unfocused" when she "*thought she saw*, hazily, in a swimming fog" Regan's head spin. Chris needs to believe a malevolent influence is making her daughter behave in such a grotesque manner because the alternative, that Regan's own psychosis is responsible, is too much to bear. This is evidenced by Chris's conversation with Karras about Regan killing Dennings, as Karras tries to persuade Chris she imagined the contortion: " 'But the head turned around' said Chris. 'You'd hit your own head pretty hard against the wall' Karras answered. 'You were also in shock. You imagined it.' 'She told me she did it,' Chris intoned without expression" (242). Chris would rather believe that her daughter is possessed and in this state has committed murder, rather than consider the possibility that her daughter might be rejecting her.

"YOUR MOTHER SUCKS COCKS IN HELL": THE OEDIPAL REJECTION OF THE PRE-OEDIPAL MATERNAL

In her discussion of Friedkin's film, Creed argues that Regan's possession expresses the pre-Oedipal bond shared between mother and daughter before the intervention of paternal authority and that her obscene outbursts and brazen excretions "[construct] monstrosity's source as the failure of paternal order to ensure the break, the separation of mother and child" (38). Creed translates this failure of the paternal into "a *refusal* of the mother and child to recognize the paternal order" which rearticulates Regan's possession as a protest that returns her to a pre-Oedipal maternal state, and certainly the film does emphasize the closeness of the mother-daughter relationship (40). Regan's body, in its disgusting carnivalesque display, represents for Creed what mothers would be if not tempered by paternal rule: "The deep bond between mother and daughter is reinforced . . . at a number of different levels: Mother's swearing becomes Regan's obscenities; Mother's sexual frustrations become Regan's lewd suggestions; Mother's anger becomes Regan's power" (39). Thus, for Creed, the Devil inside Regan "may well be female" (32).

Although Creed's argument is rewarding in that it rearticulates the demonic possession narrative into a psychosomatic one, it does not account for the subtleties of Regan's rejection of paternal rule. Although Regan violently abjects herself in front of both priests by vomiting, she also implores them, as Fathers, to have intercourse with her—"Do you want to fuck her? Loose the straps and I will let you go at it!"—while to the male doctors who visit her she commands, "*Fuck* me. *Fuck* me!" and "with both her hands began masturbating frantically" (197, 109). The crucifix masturbation scene further confirms Regan's unconscious desire to have sex with her father, as she uses Christ on the Cross, God's representative on earth, to penetrate herself. This scene does not depict the demon's desire to corrupt the body of an innocent through a sacrilegious act but instead expresses Regan's wish to have sex with the (Holy) Father, whom Freud identified as interchangeable with both the Devil and the biological father ("Demonological Neurosis" 86).

Rather than simply forbidding paternal intervention, as Creed argues, Regan seduces men who desire to cure her into her room, then dispatches them if they prove a threat to the absent father she desires. This is evidenced most acutely through the murder of Chris's friend and director Dennings, whom Regan identifies as possible heir to her father's position crucially *before* she is in the throes of her apparent possession. At one point, she sullenly states, "[Y]ou're going to marry him, Mommy, aren't you?"; when Chris says no, Regan then asks, "[Y]ou don't like him like Daddy?" (47). Clearly, what is important to Regan is not the threat to her own place in her mother's affections but the possibility that her father could be so easily replaced. Dennings's horrendous death—Regan breaks his neck and twists his head round before throwing him out of her window—thus becomes her disavowal of his threat through a symbolic decapitation/castration and his expulsion from the family home.

In the same conversation, Chris asserts, "I *love* your daddy, honey; I'll always love your daddy"; whether a white lie or the truth, Chris has set herself up in opposition to Regan's desire for her father. Their divorce does not void the Oedipal dynamic but instead "reinterprets and rearranges . . . what Freud called the 'family romance' for a post-nuclear family generation" (Douglas 302). Evidently, your parents don't have to be married for you to feel the Oedipal tension. Furthermore, Regan's rejection of male scrutiny can also been understood as her projection of the jealousy she wishes her father would feel in response to other men examining her. Ventriloquizing the father-as-Devil, her warning to Klein to keep his "goddamned fingers away from [my] cunt" (61) and the assault on the neuropsychiatrist are the threats Regan hopes her father-as-lover would make to rivals of his own objectifying gaze. Through her possession, Regan expresses a desire for her absent father's possessiveness.

The Exorcist thus presents an extreme consequence of severing the Oedipal bond before its potential resolution, for Regan solicits then violently rejects all other possible father figures whom she sees as replacing the original father's place in the family unit; tellingly Karl, Chris's handyman, who is married to Willie the housekeeper and embroiled in his own filial drama, is not dispatched as she does not perceive him as a threat.[10] Similarly, the married Lieutenant Kinderman who investigates Dennings's death is safe, as he never enters Regan's room or comes into direct contact with her. So, though Creed does identify that "Regan is 'possessed' with an incestuous longing" (41), she continues to attribute this longing for mother. Yet, though Regan does engage in a sexual act with her mother, the graphic oral rape which leaves Chris covered in the blood of her daughter's lacerated vagina is not an extreme expression of erotic desire to reunite with her but a vicious mockery and rejection of her maternal authority, as symbolized by Regan's literal and violent pushing away of Chris after the act: "'*Lick* me, *lick* me! Aahhhhhh!' Then the hand that was holding Chris's head down jerked it upward while the other arm smashed her a blow across the chest that sent Chris reeling across the room and crashing to a wall with stunning force while Regan laughed with bellowing spite" (183). This scene figures Regan's bleeding as both menstrual and sexual, as her "vagina gushed blood onto sheets with her hymen, the tissues ripped" (183). While her penetration with the crucifix means she has lost her virginity to the symbolic father and locates her body as a site of sexual desire for him, the notion of menstrual blood signifies her womb's desire, and failure, to bear him a child. Just as Augustine's periods started when she entered *la Salpêtrière*, where "under the very eyes and tender concern of her physicians...she 'became a woman'" (Didi-Huberman quoting Bournville 117), so, too, does Regan's menstruation correlate with her hysterical manifestation of the desire to please her father.

This hostility toward the mother is present in the text even before Regan is fully possessed, as evidenced by her refusal to let Chris play with the Ouija board because she is not pretty enough (45–46). This attack is articulated through Regan's imaginary friend Captain Howdy, a figure of patriarchal authority that Chris recognizes is modeled after Regan's father, Howard: "A fantasy playmate. It didn't sound healthy. Why 'Howdy'? For Howard? *Pretty close*" (45). Despite Howard's absence in the text, it is Chris who embodies abandonment. At the height of her exorcism, Regan-as-demon reveals that she blames Chris for the disintegration of her family, the loss of her father, and her own psychosis: "'Ah, yes, come see your handiwork, sow-mother! Come!...See the *puke*! See the murderous bitch!...Are you pleased? It is *you* who have done it! Yes, *you* with your career before *anything*, your career before your *husband*, before *her*, before...your *divorce*!'" (291). Desiring the absent biological father's love, Regan continues to fulfill the Oedipal pattern through her rejection of the mother whom she blames for his departure. As Creed's pre-Oedipal reading demonstrates, psychoanalytical theory has evolved beyond Freud's phallocentric model of the Oedipal conflict, and the psycho-analytical and cultural epistemologies of hysteria are at a distinctly post-Freudian point.[11] However, Blatty's novel, written before the feminist post-structuralist concept of *l'ecriture feminine* re-appropriated the figure of the hysteric, is still bound up in the incestuous father/daughter, doctor/patient dynamic which Charcot established with Augustine and Freud and Breuer continued with Dora and Anna O. Regan repeats this dynamic with her doctors and then her priests, all of whom subject her to scrutiny to which she responds with sexually aggressive hysterical outbursts. That Regan ulti-mately rejects the attention of these men serves to underpin the severity of her originary Oedipal conflict: no one will do but her father. Initially, Chris, versed in pop-Freudianism, is not blind to the possibility of this type of neurosis, for she interprets Captain Howdy as Regan's father Howard, reads Howdy's rejection of her as "unconscious hostility" (46), and anticipates the psychiatric diagnosis of hysteria brought about as a reaction to the trauma of divorce (241). Chris is clearly aware of the psychological possibilities, but it is more comforting to accept that her daughter is possessed and thus maintain an emotional connection with her, albeit a distressing one, rather than accept that her daughter's anguish is caused by a deep affection for the estranged father which would implicitly devalue her own parental status.

"THAT THING UPSTAIRS ISN'T MY DAUGHTER!": *FOLIE À DEUX*

Because Chris accepts Regan's hysterical performance of demonic possession as reality, she not only encourages the psychosis but perpetuates it. This dynamic is symptomatic of Shared Psychotic Disorder, or *Folie à Deux*, first reported in 1877 by Ernest-Charles Lasègue and Jean-Pierre Falret, which the Diagnostic and Statistical Manual of Mental Disorders defines as "a delusion that develops in an individual who is involved in a close relationship with another person (sometimes termed the 'inducer' or 'the primary case') who already has a Psychotic Disorder with prominent delusions" (305). Karras overtly diagnoses the mother as herself hysterical, *"that's just what it is: hys-terical imagining"* (243), and so there is implicitly a lingering sense of her-edity surrounding Regan's condition which echoes the nineteenth-century belief that hysteria was passed down the maternal line; in the narrative, it is Chris who first hears/hallucinates the rapping sounds which are later asso-ciated with the demon (21). She is described elsewhere as being "on the brim of hysteria" (107) and, as an actress, she fits Charcot's hysterical model of performing a melodramatic part for an audience. Freud argued that the daughter's mimicry of hysterical symptoms "signifies a hostile desire on the girl's part to take the mother's place, and...expresses her object-love towards her father" (*Group Psychology* 38). If Chris is predisposed to hysteria, Regan's condition is a jealous response which replicates and betters it in order to supersede her rival.

S. J. Kiraly discusses a case of *Folie à Deux* between mother and daughter in which both parties were convinced they were being spoken to and influenced by the Devil. Like Regan, the daughter experienced familial tensions: her father (like Anna O.'s) was ill and both she and her mother, who like Chris is described as "very theatrical" and "giving her history with a hysterical flavour," were involved in his convalescence (224). With the father absented through his illness, the mother-daughter dynamic is established, and Kiraly interprets their shared psychosis of possession as the manifestation of the daughter's unconscious guilt towards the father and hostility towards the mother, which the mother identifies with "in order to rescue the relationship" (227). Chris's conviction fulfills the same function; having lost a young son, Jamie, several years ago to the failure of medicine, Chris harbors a "deep distrust of doctors and nurses" (115) and so rejects the logical psychiatric diagnosis that Regan is hysterical, instead pursuing the supernatural explanation of possession in an attempt to re-possess and lay claim to her daughter.

This is confirmed by her refusal to tell Regan's father about his daughter's condition despite Karras's encouragement: "'I've asked you to drive a demon *out, goddammit,* not ask another one *in!*' she cried at Karras in sudden hysteria.... '[W]hat in the hell do I want with *Howard?*...[W]hat the hell good is *Howard* right now? What's the *good?*'" (241). Via his psychiatric background, Karras identifies the source of Regan's illness and starts to suggest to Chris that "there's a strong possibility that [her] disorder is rooted in a guilt over—" but she anticipates his reasoning and cuts him off: "Guilt over what?...Over the divorce? All that psychiatric bullshit?" (241). Regan's separation from her father and the severing of the Oedipal structure that underpinned the family unit, triggered by Chris's rejection of Howard through divorce, is the trauma to which Regan has reacted so violently through her hysterical performance of possession.

Yet Chris refuses to accept that a reunion with the father would help, instead figuring him as a malevolent force just as damaging as the demon inside her daughter, denying that their divorce is the cause of the trauma and so implicitly exonerating herself of any blame. Indeed, Chris would rather believe that Regan is possessed than concede that her father's involvement would be beneficial. The possibility of hysteria as a response to the Oedipal dynamic is unbearable for Chris as it displaces her primacy as mother and instead positions Regan's father at the center of her desire; as Karras identifies, Chris is *"worried that her daughter is* not *possessed!"* (233). Left a single mother by an acrimonious divorce, she would rather lose possession of her daughter to the Devil than to the biological father. In this sense, then, Regan's hysteria becomes an act of self-possession as she establishes a subject position which is not answerable to mother and which allows her to express her taboo unconscious desires. What is problematic, and what remains open and unacknowledged at the end of the text, is that these desires are not sufficiently tempered as Regan is still locked in the Oedipal psychodrama, which Freud prophesized as female destiny: "Girls remain in it for an indeterminate length of time; they demolish it late and even so, incompletely" ("Femininity" 129). Perhaps this is also why both Sharon, Regan's nanny, and Chris find Father Karras so attractive (76, 290).

This *Folie à Deux* proves infectious, evolving into a case of *Folie à Plusieurs* (like the Loudun nuns), as more characters submit to the demonic possession explanation in order to assuage their own anxieties. While Chris must participate in Regan's hysterical charade to reject the possibility that her daughter harbors incestuous desires for the father, Merrin needs to believe it is Pazuzu who inhabits Regan as its defeat has been his *raison d'être*. Similarly, Karras, who initially asserts the psychiatric diagnosis, invests in the Devil inside Regan which he mimics through his own possession in order to triumph over his crisis of faith and atone for the death of his mother who he feels he neglected when she was admitted to a state-run psychiatric hospital. This sense of neurotic contagion continues beyond the text through the film's effect on audiences, who reacted with similar hysterical symptoms of fainting and vomiting, which James C. Bozzuto interestingly argues is related to viewers' own parental loss.[12] Evidently, not diagnosing Regan's Oedipal hysteria within the text has succeeded in perpetuating psychosis beyond it.

"AND, YE FATHERS, PROVOKE NOT YOUR CHILDREN TO WRATH: BUT BRING THEM UP IN THE NURTURE AND ADMONITION OF THE LORD" (EPHESIANS 6:4): REPRESSION AND REBELLION

As Regan's "possession" plays out in Georgetown, Washington, D.C., the center of the Nixon administration, her behavior exposes the fallibility of the traditional conservative emblem of the patriarchal family unit and forecasts the shattering of the American Dream. As Douglas and Hoppenstand have discussed, Regan's adolescent body becomes the battleground on which the fight propriety and rebellion is waged and, in the film, a vessel for the eventual reestablishment of order; like Anna O., she remembers very little. Regan's possession and salvation thus offers comfort to a Western lay-Christian audience, as the existence of the Devil must necessarily confirm that of the ultimately more powerful God.

If read as a supernatural narrative of possession, not despite but because of its demonic content, *The Exorcist* is a profoundly religious tale with a relatively happy ending which reassures its readership by restoring order through the triumph of good over evil.[13] Perhaps this explains why Blatty, "conservatively-inclined" and "deeply Catholic" (Cull 47), omitted the ambiguity from the original screenplay. Colleen McDannell argues that through the film, "Blatty sought to bring to the screen his real theological concerns and answers," and thus "*The Exorcist* then is not merely a horror film; it is a *Catholic* horror film. And, more specifically, it is a *Jesuit* horror film" (198–99). Similarly, Nick Cull writes that in the wake of the Cold War and the threat of Communist opposition both overseas and in America, Blatty "wrote *The Exorcist* and produced it as a motion picture to scare a new generation of Americans back into church. [He] was quite open about this aim. He called his novel 'an apostolic work' " (47). If taken at face-value as an uncomplicated tale of demonic possession, the film's (mis)interpretation of the novel reinforces the hegemony and so ultimately does not undercut, but rather underpins, values of Western conservatism.

However, while Blatty's moral intentions are clear, the text nonetheless supports a psychological reading, and interpreted as a hysteria narrative, it ends with the deaths of three men at the hands of a young girl, whose psychosis has hoodwinked not only those around her but also readers and critics into believing she is an innocent victim. Hoppenstand, for example, reads the text much like McDannell views the film: as a possession narrative which articulates Blatty's concerns about "the efficacy of the Church in the modern, pragmatic world" (36) and which uses the possessed body of "*an innocent* adolescent girl," "the child as *victim*" as a metaphor (36, 37, my emphasis). As a response to the trauma of divorce, the failure of the family unit, and the absent father whom she desires, Regan's hysteria articulates anxieties about the implosion of the traditional nuclear family with the innocent and well-mannered child at its core, yet does not allay these anxieties through the eventual re-establishment of a moral force. If Regan's behavior is read as evidence of repression and psychosis as opposed to possession, *The Exorcist* becomes unsettling for entirely different reasons, for blame cannot be shifted from the child and apportioned to the demon. Thus, all Regan's obscene and sacrilegious actions, the masturbation with the crucifix, the oral rape of her mother, the murders of three men including two priests, are performed not through her but by her, and no one else.

Within the Freudian model of hysteria, the root cause of the neurosis, that is, the Oedipal trauma, must be diagnosed, discussed, and disavowed in order that the patient is cured. It is this act of catharsis which provided Freud and Breuer with their case studies, as Julia Borossa summarizes: "Hysterics' symptoms made sense, inasmuch as they were a response to a psychic (as opposed to physical) trauma . . . . [T]his trauma had to do with libidinal impulses which had been thwarted" and required "a cure, of a cathartic nature, depended on the remembrance and expression of that trauma in narrative form, within the context of a therapeutic relationship" (32). However, because the potential diagnosis of hysteria is rejected in favor of the supernatural explanation of demonic possession, Regan is not given the opportunity to talk through her anxieties surrounding her absent father, and thus her neurosis, undiagnosed and unabated, transforms into psychosis. Regan's true anxiety, her "Ur-text" as Douglas defines it, "alone can validate its authenticity and existence" but remains "forever inaccessible" (304) and at the end of both novel and film she "is lost, latent again, not expressed: the narrative closes over her" (298). Repressed and not possessed, inevitably Regan's hysteria erupts again, this time in the movie sequel *Exorcist II: The Heretic* (1977), in which psychiatrist Dr. Tuskin discovers that "the demon" still lurks within her. Clearly, not diagnosing and curing hysteria has its commercial advantages

The novel *The Exorcist* confirms the Oedipal conflict as the driving force behind Regan's condition. Her father pervades the text by his very absence; his presence echoes around the house through his daughter's longing for him. The very title evokes the Catholic Father and places the figure of the patriarch as the epicenter of the text around which all trauma orbits. Regan is the modern-day Augustine, Dora, Anna O., expressing the Oedipal tensions of the hysteria narrative which has been embedded in the Western cultural (un)conscious since the latter part of the nineteenth century. Her body performs the script of the father/daughter/doctor/patient dynamic in which the female hysteric repeatedly finds herself locked and from which she cannot escape. Regan remains trapped in her hysteria as Chris's unwavering belief in her daughter's possession attempts to remove the psychosomatic possibility that her body is capable of its own grotesque transformation and the murders of three men, while audience responses to the text and its filmic adaptation have concentrated on the supernatural element and so exonerated Regan by rejecting the notion of psychosis. Even Creed's insightful interpretation neglects Oedipal hysteria, the role of the father and the daughter's desire for him. So, it seems, the demonic is more permissible than the neurotic, and *The Exorcist* ultimately demonizes hysteria.

Consequently, *The Exorcist* as a good versus evil tale of demonic possession has become a cultural given, and to offer an alternative reading seems sacrilegious. The demonic possibility is so seductive and possessive that while the novel suggests that our repressed anxieties and desires can potentially have a catastrophic effect on the social and moral order, the film's interpretation of literal demonic possession through the fetishization of Regan's abused body as cipher for such neuroses undoes this suggestion. Although perhaps not as satisfying to post-Freudians as a pre-Oedipal reading, considering *The Exorcist* as a case study of Oedipal hysteria exposes how the phallocentric model can be potentially ruinous for the patriarchal society it underpins. It is precisely because Regan has not sublimated her desire, because it remains so potent beneath her innocent surface that through the masquerade of demonic possession this *"angel"* (24) can murder three men, yet escape blame or punishment.

NOTES

1. See Bennett Simon and Rachel B. Blass (1991) for a concise overview of the evolution of Freud's theories on the Oedipus complex. Jung coined "Electra complex" (which Freud rejected) to define the female Oedipus complex (154), but for reasons of clarity and concision I will not be using the term.

2. Hendrika C. Freud emphasises the causality between the Oedipus complex and hysteria, explaining that "in psychoanalysis, hysteria and the Oedipus complex were for a long time more or less synonymous" (159).

3. Dr. Klein could be a reference to the psychoanalyst Melanie Klein, a contemporary of Freud and pioneer of object relations theory.

4. The classical definition of hysteria, derived from the Greek *hysteron*, womb, fashioned the condition as a female preserve by locating its origins in the reproductive system. The womb was considered a volatile organ which if left empty would migrate around the woman's body in search of a child, blocking the respiratory passages and "by not allowing her to breathe, throws her into extreme emergencies, and visits all sorts of other illnesses upon her" (Plato 87, 91c). The empty womb as mechanism of hysteria was expanded by Freud whose Oedipal model of the neurosis, with the desire to have sex with the father and provide him with a child at its core, located a paternal trauma as the root cause of his patients' symptoms. Freud studied under Charcot, promoter of hystero-epilepsy as a neurological condition, the diagnosis Regan's doctor Klein originally offers before suggesting the Freudian alternative of conversion hysteria.

5. Regina's behavior betrayed her Oedipal desires which she fulfilled vicariously when she signed a diabolical pact where she had "forsworn God and the Trinity, and she had taken the Devil—her lover—as her father in God's stead" (226). As such, Regina enters into a relationship with the Devil in which he takes the place of both fathers, biological and holy, and in her confession she explained how "she had even imagined the possibility of giving him children," which "allowed her to develop the Oedipal narrative yet further so that she might in imagination provide her father with the phallic compensation of children" (234).

6. Regan's condition also finds a precedent in the mass "possessions" of the Ursuline nuns at the French convent of Loudun between 1632 and 1640, where "hysteria was the devil's ventriloquist" (Beizer 47). In the Loudun case, the "young girl" Sister Clara prefigures Regan with her "strange convulsions, blaspheming, rolling on the ground, exposing her person in the most indecent manner...with foul and lascivious expressions and actions" while the collectively "possessed" nuns are an example of *Folie à Plusieurs*, or group hysteria (des Niau 2: 31).

7. In "Demonological Neurosis," Freud discusses how Christoph Haizmann made a pact with the Devil to improve his business and nine years later began to experience terrible seizures. When he signed the pact, Christoph's father had recently died, and as such the Devil becomes a replacement for the absent father. Freud makes this explicit by drawing on the correlation between the Devil and God as the ultimate imago of the "exalted father": "Thus the father, it seems, is the individual prototype of both God and the Devil" (85, 86). As the Oedipal model is predicated on heterosexuality for Freud, he could not explicitly diagnose Christoph as a hysteric but conceded that his delusions are the return of his repressed "feminine attitude to [the father] which culminates in a phantasy of bearing him a child" (90).

8. The nuns performed erotically charged *attitudes passionnelles* similar in description to Augustine's and Regan's head spinning and *arc de cercle*: "[They] struck their chests and backs into their heads, as if they had their necks broken, and with inconceivable rapidity.... They threw themselves back till their heads touched their feet, and walked in this position with wonderful rapidity, and for a long time.... They made use of expressions so indecent as to shame the most debauched of men (des Niau 2: 31, 37–34, 44). Regan's hysterical onslaught of sexual violence thus finds a genealogy in both Augustine and the Loudun nuns, whose repressed desires were also aimed at the Father, the handsome and corrupt priest Urbain Grandier about whom the nuns had purportedly had illicit dreams and who was accused of, and executed for, invoking their possessions (see de Certeau).

9. In "La Foi qui gúerit" ("Faith Healing"), Charcot conceded that the idea of a miraculous cure could be just as potent as a medical one; as such, Regan can be "saved" because her possession-as-hysteria demands it, and within the context of auto-suggestion her belief in the possession requires an equally potent faith—that of Father Merrin in Jesus Christ—to cure her. As Didi-Huberman summarizes, "healing is not a cure but a symptom—*a hysterical symptom*" (242).

10. Karl's drug addict daughter Elvira is an interesting counterpoint to Regan, as while Elvira's rejection of her parents disavows the Oedipal family drama which still traumatizes Regan, she fulfils a

similar function in the text as the rebellious daughter destroying the family unit, and by association society, with her bad behavior (see Hoppenstand 37). Tellingly, this subplot, which services the psychological narrative over the supernatural, is completely omitted from the film.

11. Feminist scholars such as Elisabeth Bronfen (1998) and Hendrika C. Freud (2011) have refigured hysteria engagingly to show how it can be read as the response to the first trauma we all experience, that of separation from the maternal body, while work on shell shock and Post Traumatic Stress Disorder has dispelled the notion that hysteria is a female preserve (Showalter 167–94).

12. Bozzuto cements the notion of Devil-as-parent and suggests that for his subjects the film precipitated a psychotic reaction because it tapped into their own trauma regarding parental loss and "forced them to experience anger and hostility" toward the lost parent which "resulted in these fears of identification with the Devil, or in concerns over possession" (47).

13. The film was commended by Father Kenneth Jadoff in the *Catholic News* as "deeply spiritual" (Kermode 10).

WORKS CITED

American Psychiatric Association. *DSM-IV: Diagnostic and Statistical Manual of Mental Disorders*. 4th ed. Washington, DC: American Psychiatric Association, 1994. Print.

Beizer, Janet. *Ventriloquized Bodies: Narratives of Hysteria in Nineteenth-Century France*. Ithaca: Cornell UP, 1993. Print.

Bernheimer, Charles, and Claire Kahane, Eds. *In Dora's Case: Freud-Hysteria-Feminism*. 2nd ed. New York: Columbia UP, 1990. Print.

Blatty, William Peter. *The Exorcist*. 1971. London: Corgi, 1974. Print.

Borossa, Julia. *Hysteria*. Cambridge: Icon, 2007. Print.

Bozzuto, James C. "Cinematic Neurosis following *The Exorcist*: Report of Four Cases." *The Journal of Nervous and Mental Disease* 161.1 (1975): 43–48. Print.

Bronfen, Elisabeth. *The Knotted Subject: Hysteria and its Discontents*. Princeton: Princeton UP, 1998. Print.

Charcot, Jean-Martin. *"La Foi qui gúerit."* *Revue Hebdomadaire* 3 Dec. 1892: 112–32. Print.

Charcot, Jean-Martin, and Paul Richer. *Les Démoniaques dans l'art*. Paris: Delahaye & Lecrosnier, 1887. Print.

Creed, Barbara. *The Monstrous Feminine: Film, Feminism and Psychoanalysis*. London: Routledge, 1993. Print.

Cull, Nick. "The Exorcist." *History Today* 50.5 (May 2000): 46–51. Print.

de Certeau, Michel. *The Possession at Loudun*. Trans. Michael and B. Smith. Chicago: U of Chicago P, 2000. Print.

des Niau. *The History of the Devils of Loudun: The Alleged Possession of the Ursuline Nuns, and the Trial and Execution of Urbain Grandier, Told by an Eye-Witness*. Trans. Edmund Goldsmid. 3 vols. Edinburgh, 1887. Print.

Didi-Huberman, Georges. *The Invention of Hysteria: Charcot and the Photographic Iconography of the Salpêtrière*. Cambridge: MIT P, 2003. Print.

Douglas, Ann. "The Dream of the Wise Child: Freud's 'Family Romance' Revisited in Contemporary Narratives of Horror." *Prospects: An Annual of American Cultural Studies* 9 (1984): 293–348. Print.

The Exorcist. Dir. William Friedkin. Warner Bros., 1973.

Exorcist II: The Heretic. Dir. John Boorman. Warner Bros., 1977.

Freud, Hendrika C. *Electra vs. Oedipus: The Drama of the Mother-Daughter Relationship*. Trans. Marjolijn de Jager. London: Routledge, 2011. Print.

Freud, Sigmund. "Femininity." *Strachey* 22 (1933): 112–36. Print.

———. "Fragment of an Analysis of a Case of Hysteria ("Dora")." 1905 [1901]. Strachey 7: 3–112. Print.

———. *Group Psychology and the Analysis of the Ego*. 1921. New York: Norton, 1959. Print.

———. "A Seventeenth-Century Demonological Neurosis." 1922. Strachey 19: 69–108. Print.

———. "Some General Remarks on Hysterical Attacks." 1909. Strachey 9: 227–34. Print.

———. "Some Psychical Consequences of the Anatomical Distinction Between the Sexes." 1925. *The Freud Reader*. Ed. Peter Gay. London: Vintage 1989. 670–78. Print.

Freud, Sigmund, and Josef Breuer. *Studies on Hysteria*. Trans. Nicola Luckhurst. Harmondsworth: Penguin, 1974. Print.

Hoppenstand, Gary. "Exorcising Devil Babies: Images of Children and Adolescents in the Best-Selling Horror Novel." *Images of the Child*. Ed. Harry Eiss. Bowling Green, OH: Bowling Green State U Popular P, 1994. 35–58. Print.

Jung, Carl Gustav. *C. G. Jung The Collected Works, Volume Four: Freud and Psychoanalysis*. Ed. Herbert Read, et al. London: Routledge & Keegan Paul, 1961. Print.

Kermode, Mark. *The Exorcist*. Rev. 2nd ed. London: BFI, 2005. Print.

Kinder, Marsha, and Beverle Houston. "Seeing is Believing: *The Exorcist* and *Don't Look Now*." *American Horrors: Essays on the Modern American Horror Film*. Ed. Gregory A. Waller. Urbana: U of Illinois P, 1987. 44–61. Print.

Kiraly, S. J. "Folie à Deux: A Case of 'Demonic Possession' Involving Mother and Daughter." *Canadian Psychiatric Association Journal* 20.3 (April 1975): 223–27. Print.

Littlewood, Ronald, and Goffredo Bartocci. "Religious Stigmata, Magnetic Fluids and Conversion Hysteria: One Survival of 'Vital Force' Theories in Scientific Medicine?" *Transcultural Psychiatry* 42.4 (Dec. 2005): 596–609. Print.

Maines, Rachel P. *The Technology of Orgasm: "Hysteria," the Vibrator, and Women's Sexual Satisfaction*. Baltimore: John Hopkins UP, 1999. Print.

Mazzoni, Cristina. *Saint Hysteria: Neurosis, Mysticism and Gender in European Culture*. Ithaca: Cornell UP, 1996. Print.

McDannell, Colleen. "Catholic Horror: *The Exorcist*." *Catholics in the Movies*. Ed. Colleen McDannell. New York: Oxford UP, 2008. 197–225. Print.

Midelfort, H. C. Erick. "Charcot, Freud, and the Demons." *Werewolves, Witches and Wandering Spirits: Traditional Belief and Folklore in Early Modern Europe*. Ed. Kathryn A. Edwards. Kirksville: Truman State UP, 2003. 199–215. Print.

Mitchell, Juliet. *Mad Men and Medusas: Reclaiming Hysteria*. New York: Basic, 2000. Print.

———. *Women: The Longest Revolution: Essays on Feminism, Literature and Psychoanalysis*. London: Virago, 1984. Print.

Plato. Timaeus. Trans. Donald J. Zeyl. Indianapolis: Hackett, 2000. Print.

Roper, Lyndal. *Oedipus and the Devil: Witchcraft, Sexuality and Religion in Early Modern Europe*. London: Routledge, 1994. Print.

Showalter, Elaine. *The Female Malady: Women, Madness and English Culture, 1830–1980*. 2nd ed. London: Virago, 1998. Print.

Simon, Bennett, and Rachel B. Blass. "The Development and Vicissitudes of Freud's ideas on the Oedipus Complex." *The Cambridge Companion to Freud*. Ed. Jerome Neu. Cambridge: Cambridge UP, 1991. 161–74. Print.

Strachey, James, et al., eds. *The Standard Edition the Complete Psychological Works of Sigmund Freud*. 24 vols. London: Hogarth P, 1943–1974. Print.

How to See the Horror: The Hostile Fetus in *Rosemary's Baby* and *Alien*

A. ROBIN HOFFMAN

Despite the many aspects of style, narrative, and of course chronology that distinguish *Rosemary's Baby* from *Alien*, these films share an interest in humans' potential to incubate, literally, their own destruction. Perhaps more importantly, in both cases curiosity about latent/fetal power manifests itself partly through cinematic interrogation of the limits of human vision. Thus, when at the conclusion of *Rosemary's Baby* (1968) Rosemary cries out at the sight of her eponymous offspring "What have you done to its eyes?" the viewer is not granted access to what Rosemary sees; the camera remains trained on the mother rather than revealing the bassinet's contents. This conspicuous denial results in frustration mixed with relief: we want to see whether her fetus was physiognomically doomed or redeemed, but we also want to avoid the shock of seeing marks of evil in the flesh.[1]

A similarly suspenseful approach to gestation, with corresponding pressure on the visual, also characterizes Ridley Scott's science fiction film *Alien* (1979). However, in *Alien*, we are in unfamiliar territory (even more so than was the case with the ominously labyrinthine New York City apartment building where the drama of *Rosemary's Baby* unfolds) as we are floating in outer space with inhabitants of the future who approach intergalactic errands with casual boredom. Such dislocations allow science fiction to probe the logical limits and potential disasters of ever-more-complex technology. And with its exploration of dark human interiors, both physical and emotional, *Alien* anticipates films like *Innerspace* (1987), which not-so-subtly implied that the human body is the real "final frontier." In this metaphor of outer/inner space, the fetus becomes the potentially hostile new life for humanity to encounter (Cobbs 201). *Alien* simply represents this real-life threat analogically, with a literal alien rather than a pregnant human who might compare her experience to alien invasion.

Stimulated by America's need to confront the fraught effect of visual access on the social power of fetuses in the 1960s and 1970s, these two horror films counter the rhetorical and technological triumphs of medical imaging with warnings about the irrevocable consequences of revealing what lies hidden. Before fiber optics, this human "innerspace" would have been destroyed by the dissection necessary to make it visible, but by the 1960s and 1970s the womb could be illuminated intact by photographers like Lennart Nilsson and by ultrasound. In less than fifteen years, fetuses went from being invisible, both literally and politically, to practically unavoidable.[2] Literal or symbolic fetuses began appearing in horror films, and their shocking appearances—by which I mean both their mere presence and their visual characteristics—register what must have been done to *viewers'* eyes by the process of gaining access to fetuses *in utero*.

Many post-mid-century American horror movies have featured terrifying offspring, and although individual films have attracted a significant amount of attention from scholars, the phenomenon as a whole remains understudied.[3] Furthermore, the films themselves tend to gloss over gestation and forge ahead to the appearance of the demon-child. *The Bad Seed* (1956), *It's Alive!* (1973), *The Omen* (1976), and other films mining the demon-child vein follow this course. However, while films about specifically fetal threats are comparatively rare, those that do exist have achieved high profiles according to both critical and commercial indicators: *Rosemary's Baby* was one of the first of the "evil offspring" films to garner the level of acclaim suggested by its recognition at the Academy Awards, while *Alien*'s staying power was demonstrated by its 2003 theatrical re-release and profitable sequels.[4] Perhaps more importantly, threatening and powerful images of fetuses, along with fetuses in general, have received an impressive amount of attention, especially from feminist critics. The many studies on representations of the human fetus published in recent years—spurred primarily by legal debates over civil rights and the increasingly medicalized experience of pregnancy—describe the ways in which fetal imagery has been used to "humanize" fetuses and grant them subjectivity, often with corollary threats to women's rights. For instance, Rosalind Pollack Petchesky's landmark analysis of "The Power of Visual Culture in the Politics of Reproduction" notes that for antiabortion activists, "a picture of a dead fetus is worth a thousand words" (263). Meanwhile, some feminist critics of film have also noticed the appearance of benign fetal characters in movies like *Look Who's Talking*, released in 1989 (Mehaffy 178).

Uniting film criticism and a feminist view of cultural history, I follow the path suggested by Ernest Larsen, who rightly notes that "Hollywood horror narratives in which women give birth to monsters" would naturally lead to films dealing with the horror of "fetality" itself because "*every fetus*" is "a potential monster" (italics in original, 240–41).[5] It is my contention that both *Rosemary's Baby* and *Alien* are social documents of the growing horror of pregnancy experienced by both women and sympathetic men from the 1960s up to the 1980s, as reproductive technology and legal actions colluded to empower the fetus at the expense of the previously sacrosanct pregnant woman. I thus align myself with film scholars like Paul Wells who claim that we cannot understand what is horrifying about a horror movie without understanding the contemporaneous fears and concerns that penetrated both its production and the viewing public who first screened it, however unconscious the correspondence.[6] The release of *Rosemary's Baby* in 1968, not long after the publication of Nilsson's famous *in vitro* photography series "Drama of Life Before Birth" in *Life* in 1965, obviously coincides with widespread and various forms of social upheaval that dominated the 1960s (including civil rights and women's movements) as well as with the new and increasing availability of ultrasound technology.[7] Likewise, *Roe v. Wade* (1973) and the birth of Louise Brown, the world's first test-tube baby, on July 25, 1978, were closely followed by the release of Ridley Scott's *Alien* in 1979.

It was also at this point in time that the fetus began to separate from the pregnant woman carrying it; in 1970, the state of California first added the word "fetus" to its Penal Code's description of potential murder victims. This paved the way for fetuses to acquire a perhaps disproportionate level of agency, as we have been subject to what Susan Squier describes as "the growing presence of a hypostatized fetal voice, speaking to us from the margins within" (17).[8] At the very least, women's authority over their own pregnancies has been erased in favor of laboratory tests, and physicians "know" that a woman is pregnant before she does (Farquhar 163). It is no coincidence that both of the films I discuss feature representatives of the medical industry who are belatedly exposed as villains, controlling—and thus capable of thwarting—individuals' efforts to monitor their own condition. The "other" side of the legal debates about fetuses naturally revolves around the rights of the pregnant woman/nascent mother, but the physical difficulty of choosing sides in this situation effectively demonstrates the potentially tangled character of social, emotional, and political concerns. Related trends have continued into the 1990s and beyond so that, "increasingly, the maternal, or more precisely the potentially maternal, body is no longer conceived of as a discrete entity under the control of the mother. . . . Rather, it is seen as a being that colonizes another marginal and oppressed being, the fetus" (Squier 17). The name of the National Right to Life Committee, founded in Detroit in 1973, concisely evokes the stance that developed during a time of heightened awareness about the fraught legal status of fetuses. The "Right to Life" perspective has since been adopted by many Americans and remains a potent means of framing political discussion about how to apportion rights to both maternal and fetal bodies.

Different forms of visual access to horrifying fetuses in these two films—suppressed in *Rosemary's Baby* and technologically invasive in *Alien*—suggest that pregnancy offers a particularly visceral way of figuring ambivalent power relationships mediated by the possibility of visual contact. Together, the two films manifest the rising anxiety about fetal personhood generated by fetuses' increasing visibility; independently, each confirms that whether a particular fetus is visible or not at a given moment is ultimately less important (or threatening) than the status *all* fetuses gained in the mid-1960s as *potentially* visible. Even more specifically, these films emphasize the crucial role that the possibility of visual access played in bringing fetal threats into individual and social consciousness. The hostile, monstrous fetus in horror is a powerful figurative backlash against the inundation of purportedly helpless fetuses and the potentially oppressive ripple effects of their "silent screams."[9] As such, it provides viewers with a narrative, lexical, and visual framework in which their fears about physical colonization and the medical industry's invasion of reproductive processes can be articulated.

A PREAMBLE ABOUT CONTEXT: AMERICAN CONCEPTIONS OF FETUSES AND PREGNANT WOMEN IN THE 1960S AND 1970S

In her feminist history of pregnancy, Kathryn Allen Rabuzzi describes the experience as "much like a socially constructed initiation rite," during which women gradually assimilate motherhood into their identities (54). Participants and observers of the American version of that "initiation rite" during the latter half of the twentieth century noted the ways in which women experienced pregnancy as being at times horrifying, even when the child was wanted. In her classic commentary on the experience of motherhood, *Of Woman Born* (first published in 1976), Adrienne Rich admitted that "without doubt, in certain situations the child in one's body can only feel like a foreign body introduced from without: an alien" (64). In a similar rhetorical move made two years later, Sheila Kitzinger compared pregnancy to "possession" or "being taken over by an unknown and even hostile stranger" (78). Myra Leifer's study of the psychology of pregnancy, conducted toward the end of the 1970s, found that many women were cataloguing the possible deformities of their unborn children (47). One mid-1980s pregnancy manual urged women to "be free of fear and full of confidence," presumably because that state may not have come naturally (Curtis and Caroles 4). Feminist accounts of pregnancy in the last quarter of the twentieth century thus countered the insistently upbeat approaches of parent and pregnancy guides by admitting that denial may be a woman's first response, particularly if she does not want to become pregnant (Rabuzzi 55). She may experience ongoing ambivalence about the fetus, granting it subjectivity and withdrawing it as her comfort level permits (Rabuzzi 59). Most important for my purposes is what Rabuzzi describes as "the sometimes terrifying, sometimes exhilarating play of the imagination" during pregnancy, when fears about monstrous and dead fetuses often are expressed as nightmares (62–63). These documented experiences of gestational horror powerfully testify to a real-world resonance embedded in their cinematic representation.

For the women who helped form the original audiences of *Rosemary's Baby* and *Alien*, such visceral fears could be exacerbated by more abstract yet extremely pressing legal concerns. Increasingly sophisticated technologies granted doctors, lawyers, judges, and people in general—although not pregnant women, whose access to their fetuses is presumably already as intimate as possible—greater access to fetuses and a stronger sense of their potential personhood, with sometimes oppressive effects for pregnant women. We may, as Robyn Rowland does, recognize a correlation between the feminist movement of the late 1960s and the increasing pressure on women to hand over care of their fetuses to external agents:

> It is no accident of history that the emphasis on the fetus as a patient with "rights" comes at the time when women are demanding more control over pregnancy and birth, many of them moving outside the Western medical tradition to home birth and to women's health centres. The technologies developed to monitor, save, "improve" or discard the fetus endanger this control. All the technologies affect the mother, yet the fetus is named as the central character. By giving the fetus rights, medicine ends up giving it greater rights than a woman. (122)[10]

In Nilsson's pictures and similar ones disseminated by right-to-life groups, the fetus is most often portrayed as a smaller, redder, and strangely luminescent newborn; in fact, the fetus's resemblance to a fully formed baby often is insisted upon where it may not be apparent (Farquhar 165).[11] In this way, such groups implicitly respond to or undermine pro-abortionists who would pre-empt a fetal claim to civil rights by denying human ones. But in all cases, the fetus's vulnerability and reliance upon external assistance must remain unquestioned in order for there to be a debate about how much power it should be granted. Fetuses actually offer a logical extension or amplification of an affective mechanism described by Sabine Büssing, who suggests that unusual powers of intellect or strength are part of the recipe for "horrific children."[12] If powerful children are horrifying and unnatural because they defy expectations of helplessness and dependency, then fetuses in possession of personal agency would constitute an even more horrifying contrast.

Many critics have relied on a psychoanalytic approach when discussing cinematic representations of horror, including the specific evil fetuses of *Rosemary's Baby* and *Alien*. As, for instance, when Barbara Creed brings Julia Kristeva's abject mother to bear on her exploration of the "monstrous-feminine" in *Alien*, these perspectives are primarily concerned with relationships between mothers and children, and usually in a way that demonizes the mother. The demonization of the mother may be encouraged by the medium of film itself; E. Ann Kaplan suggests that "film is perhaps more guilty than other art forms of literalizing and reducing Freudian motherhood theory" (128). The primary drawback of the psychoanalytic approach is that even the phenomenon of birth trauma fails to recognize the full experience of pregnant women and their relationships with their unborn offspring by focusing on the postpartum human. Kristeva's allusions to the horrors of "a border" (9) or what Creed interprets as "the undifferentiated" (48) thus far have failed to be identified with the fetus's literally undifferentiated cells. I list these shortcomings primarily to bolster my effort, inspired by Kaplan, to keep the "historical" and the "psychic" mother separate (138). I also wish to maintain some distinction, however fuzzy, between a pregnant woman and a mother, as well as between the social and personal experiences of pregnancy and motherhood. Although psychoanalytical approaches undoubtedly tap into the subconscious reactions of a viewing audience, they dismiss more literal readings of the ways in which horror films like *Alien* and *Rosemary's Baby* utilize a highly visual medium in order to explore, enact, and even exploit real fears predicated by visual representations of fetuses circulated widely in contemporary media.

Like Barbara Duden, I favor a historicist reading of the coincidence of reproductive monitoring technologies, civil rights for fetuses, and women's increasing personal autonomy. Duden insists that the fetus "as conceptualized today, is not a creature of God or a natural fact, but an engineered construct of modern society" (4). Technology's gradual absorption of the fetus separates it from its mother, lends it an aura of subjectivity and, in a number of cases, the right to an attorney, and can plunge women into (perhaps unwanted) sensations of motherhood or place the "diagnosis" of motherhood in medically licensed hands (Duden 28). Such technologies offer the promise of early diagnosis, better prenatal care, and even "bonding" between the fetus and the world outside the womb. But Petchesky convincingly has likened the fascination with fetal images to a "fetishization" that eclipses their purported medical functions and almost inevitably fosters women's subjugation to the fetuses they carry (277).[13]

Thus, during a period of heightened anxiety about the corollaries of fetal personhood, we find cinematic representations of fetuses that register their disproportionate—and increasing—power as a form of monstrosity. More importantly, the films share a thematic preoccupation with vision that I will explore in greater detail below and which plays out in what the characters can or cannot see (especially regarding the visual marks of fetal monstrosity) and whether or not they can trust what they do see. These cinematic power struggles dramatize the real-world consequences of visual access. At the moment when fetuses suddenly became visible, politically relevant, and even capable of indirect legal compulsion, they also became candidates for horror villainy. *Rosemary's Baby* and *Alien* cast the hostile fetus in a narrative struggle between good and evil, corralling the audience's unfocused fears into moral parameters that validate them. Indeed, in the case of *Alien,* we encounter a *symbolic* fetus in the form of the titular creature, rather than a literally pregnant human, which allows the filmmakers to more clearly mark hostility through monstrous physiognomy. Ultimately, the fetus's status as a potential threat becomes downright self-evident when translated to contemporary reality by way of such cinematic representations.

ROSEMARY'S BABY AND THE SUSPENSE OF THE HIDDEN

I begin with *Rosemary's Baby,* directed by Roman Polanski, primarily because the hostile fetus is not only central to the plot but—with Rosemary's swelling belly serving as a proxy—frequently in the visual center of each shot as well. The relationship between the camera and audience perspective introduces a significant variable for interrogating the status of the unborn as it relates to visibility. Closely based on the novel of the same title by Ira Levin, the film's basic narrative survives adaptation: through the collusion of her husband Guy and the well-meaning Satanists next door, Minnie and Roman Castevet, Rosemary is apparently raped by Satan during a drug-induced half-dream. When she becomes pregnant, those closest to her conclude that she is bearing Satan's offspring, but Rosemary only gradually becomes aware of her status as the prospective mother of the Antichrist. Her ignorance is overshadowed by both a physically trying pregnancy and a growing sense of betrayal and deception. However, the film differs significantly from the novel in its refusal to confirm or deny the infant's status as the Antichrist. As I suggested at the outset, the ambivalence of the film's concluding scene is anchored in the visual. Although Rosemary herself must spend the film untangling the truth of her experience (with the viewers following her through the process), *Rosemary's Baby* is misleading in an important respect from the very beginning: it promises a film about a baby and then does not provide a single frame in which a baby appears.[14] We never receive direct visual confirmation of the child's moral status. But the evocation of ominous potential was certainly effective; in the years since its release, the film's title has come to serve as a flexible cultural reference for fetuses or other gestating human "conceptions" with perverted origins and potentially disastrous destinies.

Since the future mother is not nearly as warped as the fetus threatens to be, nor is she actually a mother until the film's concluding scene, frequent slippage between motherhood and its prologue—at least nominally—is a surprising thread running through critical discussions of *Rosemary's Baby.* Büssing, for instance, insists that "it is the perversion of motherhood which evokes the ultimate impression of horror within the spectator" (149). But this language implies that the enactment of motherhood is warped in this film; that is, that Rosemary is a horrifying, or at least unorthodox, mother. Quite the opposite is true, in fact, as it is Rosemary's desire for a baby and concern for her unborn child that lands her in the trap set by Guy and the Castevets. As Lucy Fischer points out, many of Rosemary's anxieties would likely encourage audience identification or sympathy since they are common among women pregnant with normal fetuses (422–23). Rosemary's selfless concern for her child prompts her to reject her husband, set out alone on a dangerous escape, and finally venture into a roomful of apparently sincere Satanists and threaten them physically; her terrified yet determined resistance provides the dramatic thrust of the film. Even though she suspects her child to be condemned (either to damnation or to a life irrevocably damaged by early trauma), Rosemary wants to care for him rather than abandon him to people who would not only care for but worship him. Rosemary's final choice to stay and mother the (devil's?) child is presumably the "perversion of motherhood" to which Büssing refers, and yet it occupies a small fraction of the film. Rhona Berenstein comes closer to the mark when she suggests that *Rosemary's Baby* is "centrally concerned with motherhood" (59). But in so doing, she implicitly conflates pregnancy with motherhood and col- lapses distinctions between the already-born and the not-yet-born. This is the same logic underlying the notion of "fetal personhood" that emerged partly from images like Nilsson's, which routinely frame fetuses as entities independent of the women carrying them (Petchesky 268). By maintaining a crucial distinction between pregnancy and parenthood, we can recognize that *Rosemary's Baby* horrifies us with the *potential* perversion of the unborn rather than the *visible* "perversion of motherhood."

Fischer more helpfully describes the film as "a skewed 'documentary' of the societal and personal turmoil that has regularly attended female repro- duction" (412). By "turmoil" Fischer presumably means that a woman's announcement of pregnancy tends to demand her submission to the atten- tions of well-meaning friends, relatives, and the medical community. As the fetus's needs augment and even potentially compete with the pregnant woman's, these attentions are just as often, if not more, focused on the former. Though Sharon Marcus refers to the novel, her suggestion that *Rosemary's Baby* "construes pregnancy as a hyperbolic invasion of Rosemary's privacy—the result of a rape, the pretext for constant surveillance by her husband, neighbors, and doctor, and an ongoing invasion of her body by a predatory, parasitical fetus," holds true for the movie as well (131). The key word here is "hyperbolic" though, since feeling the mother's stomach or draw- ing her blood were routine "invasions of privacy" committed by doctors in the 1960s in the name of fetal surveillance. Furthermore, all of these invasions are, at least on some level or at some point in the film, welcome: Rosemary explicitly and audibly wishes for children, she is glad to receive special atten- tion from the highly regarded obstetrician Dr. Sapirstein, and she initially (and accurately) takes the Castevets' proffered nutritious drinks and solicitous attention as an indication of concern for her health and that of her prospective baby. Such behavior is clearly perceived by Rosemary to be unassailably normal. The abnormality lies entirely within Rosemary's body in the form of a purported demon-fetus and her constant, debilitating pain. Thus, she must accept the burden of suffering or adopt the (socially untenable) position that the fetus itself is part of the invasion.

Rosemary has difficulty sorting her friends from her enemies because she is preoccupied with the fetus's health—she laments at one point, "I'm afraid the baby's going to die"—and because her enemies-in-disguise channel their efforts through her fear. But Rosemary's vision is clouded also by the fact that her fetus was conceived during a half-waking nightmare. After swallowing some of the "chocolate mousc" presented by Minnie Castevet, Rosemary falls into a drugged stupor that mixes her own guilt about her lapsed Catholicism with an apparent experience of being raped by Satan himself. One of the more horrifying moments of the film is when she cries out in fear and pain, "This is no dream! This is really happening!" The conception scene significantly relies on alternating visual perspectives and their unstable relationship with reality to frame Rosemary's fetus as a *potential* threat. While Rosemary must reach some conclusion about whether to trust her vision of Satan or not, the viewer must choose whether to trust the camera: when it presents Satan's face from Rosemary's perspective, it could be showing the film's reality or Rosemary's skewed perception. Dr. Hill later diagnoses Rosemary with hysteria, but the viewer's initial, visual access to her interior world makes it difficult to share his benevolent disregard for her anxiety. As Wells points out, "*Rosemary's Baby* playfully engages with empathy and identification in the sense that we are offered Rosemary's perspective" (83), in multiple senses. That is to say, the camera adopts Rosemary's viewpoint at crucial moments in the film: during the nightmare/ rape, when Rosemary rearranges the Scrabble tiles to reveal Roman's true identity, and when Rosemary, knife in hand, invades the Castevets' apartment. As a result, her concern for her baby becomes the audience's concern, and we also struggle, reluctantly, to accept the reality of both Satanists and conspiracy within the film.

Proceeding from this significant engagement with audience perspective, I concur with Fischer, Berenstein, and others who perceive a strong affect generated by how *Rosemary's Baby* portrays a pregnant woman as susceptible to manipulation by not just medical personnel, but also friends and family. As Berenstein suggests, Rosemary's lack of control over her pregnancy is a significant contributor to the film's nightmare-like effects (59) and may have prompted one contemporary reviewer to describe the viewing experience as being "like having someone else's nightmare" (Sweeney 6). Having witnessed her dreams and shared their destabilizing effect, the audience also experiences Rosemary's pregnant vulnerability, including the ways in which it silences her. She is even made vulnerable by her desire to become pregnant since her husband uses it as leverage to make a Faustian deal with the Castevets, to mask her drugging with a romantic evening, and then to explain away the injuries from her rape. As a result, we may be inclined to see the Satan-worshippers as "enemies." But Rosemary also is represented as carrying the monstrous fetus that plagues pregnant women's nightmares, so our sympathies are conflicted. Focusing entirely on Rosemary's experience would suggest that women alone are the target of this film's warning against empowered fetuses when in fact, this fetus's nominal destiny is to subjugate the entire world to Satan, whose "power is stronger than stronger" and whose "might shall last longer than longer," according to the Satanists' leader. If we cheer for Rosemary to survive and/or escape, we also potentially cheer for the survival of the hostile fetus. Its tremendous evil potential poses the widest threat in *Rosemary's Baby*.

Significantly, the film presents this dilemma against a cultural backdrop of developing medical imaging technology and imminent visual access to the womb. Images of fetuses had circulated widely in mainstream media at the time of the film's release, and the film draws on the emotional power of the visual that undergirds emerging notions of fetal personhood. But the technology for imaging fetuses *in utero* was far too rare and/or expensive to be a diagnostic tool. Cruelly, Rosemary cannot exploit any imaging technology that would reveal her fetus's true nature, though the prospect of visual confirmation hovers tantalizingly over Rosemary's belly: her own body either protecting the Antichrist or casting suspicion on an innocent and much-desired human fetus. The viewer is left with the sense that Rosemary is paralyzed by her condition and her ignorance about it. If only she knew the truth about her fetus, she would surely take steps to neutralize a confirmed threat, as did the Castevets' first victim, the suicidal Terry Gionoffrio. (We get the sense that Terry was aware of the plot when Rosemary overhears Minnie telling Roman, "I told you not to tell her in advance. I told you she wouldn't be open-minded.") But Rosemary is chronically reliant upon others for information about her own body, which reinforces her subordination to the contents of her womb: she needs Guy to inform her that her period is late; she needs doctors to confirm her pregnancy and assess her condition; and she needs friends to tell her that her constant pain is a health hazard. This scenario is undoubtedly familiar to many women who endure highly medicalized but normal pregnancies, particularly first-timers experiencing brand-new sensations. Rosemary's ignorance of her complicity with a malevolent plot is ensured by her ignorance about pregnancy, which leads her to surrender herself to Dr. Sapirstein. When he tells her, "Don't read books. Don't listen to your friends, either," Rosemary takes his advice and largely isolates herself with the enemy. The profound vulnerability of a pregnant woman is most painfully apparent when Rosemary seeks the aid of her first doctor, Dr. Hill, only to be delivered by him back into the hands of her enemies. The medical industry controls and then thwarts her efforts to learn more about her condition and the fetus within, even though it had previously promised diagnosis and information, albeit via blood tests instead of visual access.

Behind the interventions from "friends" and doctors, however, the being to whom (or to which) Rosemary is most vulnerable, and to whom we watch her submit herself, is the fetus she carries. The movie focuses on an embattled rather than a mothering Rosemary because the image of her bulging abdomen, pregnant with both potential evil and potential child, emphasizes her subordination to her unseen fetus and its external agents. Everyone who sees her comments on her wasted appearance, which suggests that the fetus really is a parasite that is consuming her—or as Karyn Valerius suggests, that the fetus has been cast into "the role of vampire, the traditional parasite of literary and cinematic horror" (131). The delivery scene reiterates Rosemary's subjugation to her fetus as well, a horrifying aspect overlooked by Fischer's consideration of "Parturition and Horror in *Rosemary's Baby*." Fischer describes how the delivery scene "subjectively replicates woman's experience of traditional hospital birth—of being physically restrained, anesthetized, and summarily separated from her baby" (424). However, focusing on how the film demonizes the medical industry in this scene deflects attention from this particular pregnant woman's demanding and potentially demonic fetus, to which she has already ascribed personhood by naming it. That anticipatory act of identification subtly reveals that despite the suspicions Rosemary has been harboring about her neighbors, doctors, and husband, she has already submitted to incredible social pressure to acknowledge her fetus as a separate entity, with needs and even perhaps a will of its own. As Rosemary is tied down for delivery, she calls for help and then fades into unconsciousness with the words, "Oh Andy, Andy or Jenny, I'm sorry my little darling. Forgive me!" This begging for forgiveness echoes her earlier dream-state request for absolution from the Pope, whose authority has apparently been surmounted, or at least equaled, by that of the fetus. Rosemary's change in allegiance, from the Pope to the fetus, significantly widens the threat posed by a purported fetal Antichrist. If she has indeed switched moral sides at that level, Rosemary herself is just the launching pad for a much larger campaign of destruction. At any rate, Rosemary seems to feel that she has failed to meet the fetus's demands. By the very end of the film, Rosemary's *involuntary* submission to its needs, predicated by its presence in her body and her ignorance about its nature, has been transformed into *voluntary* alliance with the destiny assigned to it by a Satanic cult. This choice is new to her precisely because the conditions of her pregnancy rendered her utterly dependent on the medical community but incapable of communicating with its members.

Rosemary's voice is restored by parturition, however, and she delivers our first clue to the baby's monstrous appearance when she wails, "What have you done to its eyes?" The heretofore-deferred authority of vision is reiterated by Minnie, who offers to show off his hands and feet, which are also presumably deformed. Rosemary finally, literally, *sees* how the inchoate fetus has resolved into the truth of her baby's situation. Then, as the Satanists stand aside, Rosemary chooses to mother rather than being forced to do so. However, the mere fact that she can choose is more important than the choice made. The novelty of options contrasts sharply with the previous lack of them since both Rosemary and the Satanists—she unwittingly and involuntarily, they by choice—were subjugated so intensely by this tiny, apparently helpless but (potentially) awesomely powerful baby while it was still in the womb. We in the audience are denied more than Rosemary's perspective—we are also left to ponder the moral valence of a choice based on visual access.

ALIEN AND THE DUBIOUS VALUE OF SEEING

David J. Skal comments that "[a]fter Rosemary had her baby, virtually all births in the popular media would be monstrous or demonic" (294) and identifies Ridley Scott's *Alien* as an heir to this tradition of exploiting "reproductive anxieties" (301). In the eleven years between the two films, reproductive technology developed quickly and produced correspondingly dramatic shifts in perceptions of fetal personhood and the cinematic reson-ance of represented fetuses. By the late 1970s, medical imaging technology had become accessible enough to lessen the awe originally associated with images of fetuses. But the result of these technological advances was a kind of media saturation, so that visible fetuses retreated from the realm of art into the less glorious and more ominous realm of the medical.

In *Alien*, the conspicuous visual lacunae of *Rosemary's Baby* are replaced by an insistence on the potential dangers of visual contact and a warning against pursuing access to fetal environments. Multiple scholars have recognized "the film's pervasive gynecological imagery," as John Cobbs put it, and he has even suggested that "the nature of the life-threatening, interior 'other' in *Alien* is of a particular sort: it is fetal" (201). I would like to reiterate the ways in which the film carefully characterizes the threat as specifically fetal, but I also would like to draw attention to the significance of transferring that threat to a future time and place. During a long-distance haul, the crew members of the spaceship *Nostromo* are sidetracked by unex-plored territory, and their obligatory investigation of the new planet includes a disastrous encounter with alien eggs. Over the protests of Officer Ripley (played by Sigourney Weaver), the medical officer Ash allows crewmember Kane, smothering beneath a large "face-hugger" parasite expelled by one of the eggs, to reboard the ship. This breach in protocol sets in motion a horrify-ing chain of events—including the famous scene in which a larvae-like alien "bursts" from Kane's chest—as the alien grows with supernatural speed and kills nearly every human who crosses its path. Ripley emerges as the sole survivor after she initiates the *Nostromo*'s self-destruct mechanism via a central computer ironically nicknamed "Mother"; in the dramatic final confrontation, she manages to expel the huge creature from her escape pod by daring to open the airlock. While Cobbs quite explicitly characterizes *Alien* as an "Abortion Parable,"[15] I would suggest that the film presents a fetal threat in ways that connote not only the abortion debate—nominally "resolved" by *Roe v. Wade* a mere six years prior to the film's release—but also the experiences of reproductive monitoring technology that so heavily influenced it.

This insistence upon a historicist reading is, I realize, an implicit rejection of the psychoanalytic readings that have dominated much analysis of horror in general and *Alien* in particular. A large part of my reluctance to employ a psychoanalytic approach to *Alien* is simply that I see no need to replicate the work that many have already accomplished, particularly that achieved by Creed in her landmark essay, "Horror and the Monstrous-Feminine: an Imaginary Abjection." Even there, however, direct references to the fetus-as-subject are limited to Creed's connection between Kane's invasion of the alien nest and "Freud's reference to an extreme primal scene fantasy where the subject imagines traveling back inside the womb to watch his/her parents having sexual intercourse, perhaps to watch her/himself being conceived" (57). I am motivated even more by the sheer confusion of fetal imagery offered by *Alien*, which—as many conflicting critical opinions would suggest—resists dissection and categorization. There is simply too much going on in terms of (")mothers("), gestation, wombs, and fetuses to extract a one-to-one allegorical correspondence to any discussion of Freudian or Lacanian psychoanalysis without resorting to either distortion (of theory or of the film) or self-contradiction. At the very least, as Catherine Constable has pointed out, in *Alien* 'the use of the womb as a key reference point clearly provides a break from the Freudian system in which the mother is encoded in relation to a phallic standard" (177). This is not to say that psychoanalytical approaches are not without considerable value; to the contrary, they surely offer as much insight into the film as they do into the minds of the viewing audience. The confusion of imagery in *Alien* seems, however, to reflect underlying social confusion and fear about gestation and fetuses, as well as an inability to articulate these concerns in conventional terms of sex and gender.

Even when focused on representing the unavoidably (female) physical human experience of pregnancy, science fiction can exploit the flexibility of an unknown future in order to explore horrific fears about bodily integrity, invasion, and rape in a way that decouples biological sex from reproductive roles. The film's success in this endeavor is manifested by critics' continuing disagreement about how to read the representations of sex and gender in *Alien*. Creed expounds at length on the monstrous-feminine in the guise of the "oral-sadistic mother" and "the phallus of the negative mother"

(138–39) while others insist upon the phallic qualities of the creature that inseminates Kane (Hermann 37), the chest-bursting infant alien (Hermann 39), and the alien's protruding and penetrating mouth (Cobbs 201). The alien is not assigned a sex during any phrase of its development, so its phallic imagery can be attributed to either a masculine or a feminine subject. A complementary bounty of womb-like spaces also have been identified by critics, with at least one male and several inorganic incubators further complicating the dynamic exchange between gender and embodiment.[16] The following chart not only summarizes some of the fetal and gestational imagery that previous commentators have identified in *Alien,* but provides a quick estimation of which impressions predominate:

Mothers/Fetal carriers	Wombs/Pregnant bodies	Fetuses
Mother (*Nostromo*)	Sleeping chambers	Crew
	Mess Hall	Crew
	Nostromo as a whole	Crew, alien
	Ripley's escape pod	Ripley, alien
Alien edifice	Nest/eggs	Aliens
Crewmember Kane	Self/torso	Alien

In the midst of these wombs-within-wombs, we easily can see that the alien is being incubated most often—unwillingly and/or unwittingly—by a series of host bodies, and this fetal alien is the most threatening entity in the film, in the sense of being a representation of *potential*, rather than fully unleashed, aggression and hostility. This is in significant contrast with the sequels, which inevitably incorporate Ripley's concrete awareness of the alien's destructive powers and also are much less invested in representing gestation because the cultural context had shifted in the interim.[17]

Precisely because she could not see her fetus and visually confirm its humanity, Rosemary was vulnerable to the machinations of medical professionals and neighbors channeled through her unborn child. In *Alien*, we see a similar imbalance of power registered by the female crewmembers' vulnerability to male crewmembers' curiosity about and authority over a dangerous alien fetus. In fact, the threat posed by embryonic inhabitants of the alien world is perceived by the female crewmembers first even though they do not serve as fetal carriers—Susan Jeffords points out that Lambert and Ripley are "the only crewmembers to show suspicion of the alien" as they "recognize before the men do the signs of reproduction" (77). The women intuitively react with resistance, exemplified by Lambert's repeatedly stated desire to "get out of here" while she and Kane explore the alien planet. Later, Ripley insists that the stricken Kane not be let aboard *Nostromo* without a regulation quarantine period; her command is overridden by the medical officer, who is actually a robot operating on behalf of their employers, a shadowy organization known simply as "The Company." He has been charged with bringing back alien life-forms at any cost of human life. To accomplish this end, he has been planted in a privileged site: the infirmary, where the physically vulnerable seek aid and medical authority trumps all others. Just as Rosemary's doctor could summarily dismiss her pregnancy-related anxieties to support the Satanists' campaign, the *Nostromo*'s medical officer can insist on bringing the alien-bearing Kane on board under the cover of compassion. His pivotal power over the main computer, "Mother," is similarly bound up in his role as her guardian. Mother had been surrendered to the care of Ash, the man of science, in much the same way that pregnant women routinely surrender themselves to their obstetricians. The computer can only blindly follow orders; after Ash's status as a Company "mole" is revealed and he is decommissioned, the computer is unable to resist Ripley's decision to initiate a self-destruction sequence. Ultimately, Mother merely serves as another example of how males, including a robotic medical professional literally made male by technology, consistently dictate access to the threatening entity.

Perhaps ironically, males' control over medical and imaging technology in *Alien* renders them more, not less, vulnerable. It is men who first literally *see* the alien/fetus, first when Kane invades the egg-strewn nest and then later when the medically trained crewmembers Ash and Dallas investigate the stricken Kane; this visual access is both a sign of and a channel for their power to unleash the fetal threat. Kane shines his headlamp onto a single egg to reveal pulsing movement within, and the shell refracts the light to make the incubating alien appear backlit, almost haloed. It is an act of visual penetration that bears an uncanny resemblance to those perpetrated by Nilsson and which also evokes the mixture of curious awe and vague unease associated with those first images of human fetuses *in utero*. The subsequent scene of Kane's "impregnation" clearly characterizes visual contact as a form of invasion or aggression in its own right, deserving of retaliation. Nor does he gain any informational power for his pains. In fact, imaging technology usually fails to augment human vision in *Alien*. When Ash and Dallas scan Kane with a futuristic x-ray, they cannot explain why Kane is still alive, much less use the visual information to deduce the creature's designs on his body. Later, Dallas succumbs to an alien attack when the crew's tracking device cannot register three-dimensional movement on a two-dimensional screen. Although Kane absorbs the most immediate counterattack, the entire human crew is implicitly punished for shining a light into a dark place of growth.

The ways in which the crewmembers actually "see" alien life, i.e., with the egg illuminated by Kane's headlamp, inside Kane's body via fluoroscope, and with motion-based sensing and tracking devices, strongly resembles the way in which people must rely on ultrasound to establish a (one-way) visual connection with a fetus that looks more amphibian than human. The crew's experiences with imaging technology encourage corresponding skepticism about the benefits of real-life counterparts, especially since sonograms and fetal photographs often present interpretive challenges as well. More simply, an "alien," particularly one with the sleek armor-like skin and acidic blood of a machine, serves as an excellent metaphor for the real difficulties that humans have confronted when making judgments about personhood. Fetuses, unlike babies who have evolved to pander to our most basic biological weaknesses, have an alien quality to their appearance that has drawn forth compensatory rhetoric to frame their images.[18] The film's substitution of fetus-like alien for fetal human undermines the rhetoric conventionally used to rehabilitate alien-looking images of human fetuses and recasts visual strangeness as a kind of physiognomic warning about aggression. And the fetus-alien is horrifying in large part because it is an unclassifiable *potential* of destruction, without natural boundaries. The Company knows this and is no doubt courting hubris in their plan to harness that potential for their weapons division.

As if to confirm the infectious power of its hostility, the fetus-alien actually brings out the hostile-fetus quality of the crew, which turns on the alien, the Company's robot emissary, and finally Mother. The film encourages us to draw parallels between their behavior and that of the alien (as my chart above demonstrates) by alternately positioning the crewmembers as fetuses. At no point in the movie does the crew fully abandon the womb-like space(s). Nor does the death of one fetal carrier eliminate the threats posed by the fetus(es) it once carried (loosely defined). At the same time that the alien threatens the crew, standing as the most obvious "fetus-as-bogeyman" (Skal 301), the crewmembers occupy fetus-like positions and threaten each other. Eventually, fetal-Ripley proves to be a lethal threat to Mother. It is Mother who implicitly allows Ripley to destroy the *Nostromo* since it is through Mother that Ripley learns that the Company has prioritized the alien's return to Earth over the crew's and deputized Ash to guard their interests. Indeed, Mother is ultimately subject to the autonomy of the fetuses within; shifts in the balance of power between them neither liberate Mother nor introduce new forms of subjugation since Ripley merely initiates irreversible processes of auto-destruction that were already programmed. And once Ripley is the sole survivor aboard the *Nostromo*, she still takes refuge in a womb-like escape pod and unwittingly brings the fetal threat of the alien with her. She finally beds down again in a yet another womb-like sleeping pod, and James Cameron's *Aliens* continues the theme with Ripley's (literally) nightmarish realization that the alien eggs have been incubating the entire time.

The nightmarish quality of the movie's fetal imagery is reinforced by the fact that the narrative begins and ends with sleep (Creed 140). We first see the crew as they emerge from their sleeping pods, and the final shot is of Ripley peacefully sleeping. The implication is that it might all have been a terrible dream, specifically a dream about futuristic reproduction gone wrong. The claustrophobic and metallic environment of the *Nostromo*, in which a computer named "Mother" governs life-support systems, frames both the alien and the crewmembers as fetal cyborgs, suggesting that humans are being overwhelmed by technology from without and within. Contemporary technological interventions may have been seen as producing more babies than ever while simultaneously turning fetuses into lab experiments and pregnant women into incubators.[19] This delicate relationship with technology at the time of *Alien*'s release is informed further by the recent advent of *in vitro* fertilization, heralded by the birth of the first "test-tube" baby in 1978. While Berenstein believes that *Alien* is "about a contemporary patriarchal dilemma, i.e., no matter how hard patriarchal culture tries, it still can't reproduce without mothers" (60), I would suggest the opposite: *Alien* expresses the fears that technology is assisting the fetus in rapidly gaining far too much autonomy and that men may also eventually serve as mothers, fodder for an invasive fetus/parasite.[20] As its encore presentation of traitorous medical practice would suggest, *Alien*'s reliance on fetal imagery capitalizes on a pre-existing fear of physical invasion rather than creating one. Moreover, it insinuates that the threat of unnatural impregnation is not limited to women since the alien's first victim is a male host and the movie is riddled with contradictory sexual imagery and deviations or omissions from conventional gender roles. Neither *Alien* nor *Rosemary's Baby* rely entirely upon female audiences for their continuing success, nor do I think we can assume that men viewing these movies are horrified or stimulated only by gore, Satan worship, or Sigourney Weaver in her underwear. Rather, the fear of being inhabited, i.e., raped and/or impregnated, is surely accessible to men for very much the same reasons that it frightens women: a state of submission with an unfortunate resemblance to demonic possession, it is an unfamiliar experience that distorts one's body and produces pain. However, in the real world, the battle is necessarily fought within a woman's body, as she submits to or resists the medical intrusion of reproductive and imaging technology. The movie's popularization of figures like the fetus-as-alien or the womb-as-spaceship dovetails with an available narrative and lexicon for discussing pregnant women's situations while making it possible for males to imaginatively experience their social and physical liabilities as well.[21]

CONCLUSION: PEEK-A-BOO TURNS GRIM

As a number of horror films have profitably suggested, a child's potential to cause harm is limited apparently (if not actually) by its visible physical boundaries. Cinematic representations of fetuses, on the other hand, suggest that their physical outlines are vague enough to stymie a sense of proportional power. In *Alien*, this anxiety about undefined borders translates into an alien that is larger-than-human-sized and subject to constant surveillance—but can still sneak up on its victims. In *Rosemary's Baby*, the amorphous threat is a literal fetus stowed in Rosemary's burgeoning belly for ninety percent of the film—and from this position, it still manages to draw upon enough human resources to overwhelm Rosemary's resistance. The growing visibility of the fetus generates more horrifying sights for the audience instead of vicarious opportunities to reassert control. This blatant cinematic focus on the gestation of hostile fetuses dramatizes the very specific fears of pregnant women besieged by the oppressive "options" of reproductive technology and by the privileging of fetal civil rights over pregnant women's, crucially reinforced by timing. Emphasizing the important role that visual access to fetuses has played as an ambivalent fulcrum of power, these movies bring into view the potential horror of a pregnant woman's situation at this particular point in history. As Duden also concludes, a pregnant woman who wants to retain primary agency must confront "the series of powerful suggestions that stamp her as the reproducer of a life" (54). Even preliminary interactions with the medical community may be a form of submission because mere contact naturalizes "social responsibility for the future of the life within her," and the momentum of "prenatal testing and the biotechnological care and management of her insides" inexorably guides pregnant women toward "the scientifically guided care of a modern infant" (Duden 54). Both films translate this empowerment of the fetus into settings that are somehow distanced from everyday reality: *Alien* propels us into the future and *Rosemary's Baby* invokes the supernatural. But rather than voiding the implied warning, these settings ground a dramatically resonant exaggeration of fetal agency. That is to say, by prioritizing the representation of emotion over realism, they can more vividly illustrate the consequences of empowering the unseen, critique the technology that renders it visible, and implicate all those who participate in such efforts.

We need not resort to psychoanalytic readings of sex and gender to concede that the most immediate threats, and the ones that remain unconquered, are those represented by fetuses throughout both films. Rosemary's fetus subjects her to demands from both inside and out, as the Castevets foreshadow the semi-voluntary intrusion of technology on pregnancy by invading Rosemary's personal space in all ways possible, feeding her chemicals and even dictating her medical care via Dr. Sapirstein. In *Alien*, the crew's clumsy invasion of the alien nest results in a reciprocal intrusion; they, too, invite a hostile fetus into their midst and provide its sustenance (unwittingly on all parts but that of Ash). By the ends of the respective films, Rosemary's baby has secured her devotion along with that of the coven, and although one alien has been banished, scores of them continue to incubate on the unknown planet. These films only nominally restore order at their conclusions by translating the fetus into a vulnerable and fully perceptible infant. The one time the alien can be clearly seen is when it clings desperately to an umbilical cord-like harpoon before being expelled into space. Similarly, Rosemary's baby is vulnerable to rejection only once it has been visibly exposed. But when framed by movies that acknowledge their visual slipperiness, hostile fetuses become identifiable threats to which women in the audience can cathartically respond. The films' portrayals of pregnant *and* typical adult bodies endangered by powerful fetuses and the responses to that threat—whether brave or submissive—are surely potent images for women who feel responsible for the fetuses they carry but also resent the ways in which social, political, and medical forces can turn their responsibility into servility.

Real horror stories abound in which courts have ordered women to submit their own bodies to the perceived health demands of their fetuses, for instance with coerced caesarian sections.[22] In her 1970 polemic *The Dialectic of Sex*, Shulamith Firestone called for "the freeing of women from the tyranny of their reproductive biology by every means available, and the diffusion of the childbearing and childrearing role to the society as a whole" (270). It was implied that technology would be one of these potential "means available," which indeed has offered motherhood to some who struggle toward pregnancy and preserved lives that otherwise might have been lost. In addition to freeing women, however, it also has spawned a fetus that is, as Ash describes the alien, "a survivor . . . unclouded by conscience, remorse, or delusions of morality." Advances in reproductive and imaging technology between 1965 and 1980 allowed for greater access to the fetus but also invited the projection of moral and legal debates into a space that had previously been relatively "unclouded." Thus, *Rosemary's Baby* and *Alien* respond to the increasing pressures on women to heed the voice of the fetus and subordinate their own bodies to its demands by recasting the helpless unborn baby as a power-hungry, dangerous, and barely human force biding its time behind a shield of human flesh. In an environment where the invisible and insatiable fetus has more power than the body it inhabits, women may find pregnancy just as unnatural or invasive as men would, and the hostile fetus becomes a far more potent cinematic image. More importantly, it gives an accessible form to fears that might otherwise remain undefined and unchallenged. Like Ripley in *Alien,* we are reasonable to maintain skepticism about humanity's ability—even that of remorseless and deceptive Company executives—to harness the destructive power of the alien(s) to their own ends. The fact remains that the fetuses themselves have no apparent thought but for their own survival. Shining light into the womb brings the fetus into view but does not necessarily diffuse the darkness that surrounds it.

NOTES

I am grateful to Dr. Greg Semenza for feedback on an early version of this essay.

1. I would argue that this is the case regardless of whether the child has "his father's eyes" because his father is Satan or because the Satanists have disfigured a normal infant—the film prevents its audience from confirming either possibility by withholding visual access.

2. In this respect, my interrogation in many ways complements Karyn Valerius's sociohistorical approach to the representation of fetal personhood in *Rosemary's Baby*.

3. As the need for this collection on "Evil Children in Film and Literature" demonstrates, critical attention to the popular image of horrifying offspring has lagged behind public consumption. When Sabine Büssing's *Aliens in the Home: The Child in Horror Fiction* was published in 1987, it could rightly claim to be "the only study of its kind" in terms of both breadth and depth. Even though she relegates "The Child in the Horror Film" to an Appendix, Büssing offers a still-rare instance of commentary on the frequent appearance of children in horror movies. Robin Wood and Gary Hoppenstand are perhaps other notable exceptions, but Wood's discussion of "the Terrible Child" in horror films stalls with identification of the "recurrent motif" and links it to a "unifying master figure: The Family" (83), while Hoppenstand's "Exorcising the Devil Babies" is a single article.

4. Ray Narducy usefully has pointed out that *Rosemary's Baby* "was influential in causing the horror genre to focus on the child as evil" (402) since it predates a rash of films with a similar theme, but accounts for the film as merely "a cultural reaction to the radical, protesting 'children' of the 1960s" (402–03). As many others have noted, *The Exorcist* might be seen as the culmination of a trend in representations of evil offspring initiated by *Rosemary's Baby*.

5. Larsen also briefly notes that scientific imaging would contribute to "anxiety" about the potential monstrosity of fetuses but declines to pursue a historical reading of this phenomenon (241). For a more recent discussion of "fetal monstrosity" that is similarly tangential in its approach to the cinematic representation thereof, see Andrew Scahill, "Deviled Eggs: Teratogenesis and the Gynecological Gothic in the Cinema of Monstrous Birth."

6. As Wells cogently points out, "The history of the horror film is essentially a history of anxiety in the twentieth century. . . . Arguably, more than any other genre, it has interrogated the deep-seated effects of change and responded to the newly determined grand narratives of social, scientific, and philosophical thought" (3).

7. Janelle Taylor's history *The Public Life of the Fetal Sonogram* discusses the pivotal role played by medical imaging technology in motivating pro-life political campaigns.

8. The issue remains pertinent in the specific context of fetal homicide laws; the Unborn Victims of Violence Act was signed into law by President George W. Bush on April 1, 2004. Pro-choice advocates like the National Organization of Women have continued to voice concerns about the need to distinguish between legal abortion and fetal homicide, fearing that such laws may be used as leverage to overturn *Roe v. Wade*.

9. *The Silent Scream* (1984) presents a sonogram image reacting to its helpless position and obviously relies heavily upon both technological "insight" and its ability to grant the fetus subjectivity. I would argue that *The Silent Scream* capitalizes on a pre-existing and growing acceptance of such imagery at the same time that it furthers it.

10. See also Chapter 7, "Prenatal Technologies: Ultrasound and Amniocentesis" in Farquhar's *The Other Machine*, pp. 161–77, and Cheryl L. Meyer's *The Wandering Uterus*.

11. For more on the rhetorical strategies that work to promote fetal personhood, see Newman, pp. 7–27, and Hartouni, pp. 1–66.

12. See particularly Chapter 4, "The Evil Innocent," especially "The Possessed Child," pp. 101–05, and Chapter 5, "The Monster," pp. 110–36.

13. Rabuzzi is particularly concerned with the unnatural quality of women's "prebirth visual encounter[s] with the fetus" via ultrasound: "Instead of the almost unconscious unity of the baby invisibly resting inside the body, this is a sudden dislocation. Now what has seemed part of one's self, albeit a new part, is suddenly 'other,' separate, before its natural time for separation" (65).

14. It is true that an extradiegetic projection of reptilian skin and yellow eyes appears onscreen. This image could be interpreted as a kind of "flashback" to her first glimpse of the baby. However, it could also be a flashback to her experience of conceiving the child, which included visions of Satan, and—in my opinion—does not settle the question either way. Instead, it reiterates our dependency on Rosemary's unreliable visual experience to draw such conclusions.

15. I would agree with his claim that the "final vacuum expulsion" of the alien strongly suggests a reference to abortion (201), but it seems to me that Cobbs stops short of acknowledging the ways that fetal threats loom throughout the film and broaden the scope of its social warning.

16. For example: "a womb-like chamber where the crew of seven are woken up from their protracted sleep" (Creed 129); "she expels the creature from the body of her spacepod" (Cobbs 201); "the gigantic womb-like chamber in which rows of eggs are hatching" (Creed 130); *Nostromo* as womb/mother-ship (Creed 130 and Skal 301); "the cozy womb-like atmosphere of the mess hall" (Bell-Metereau 15); "the dominant motif of [*Nostromo*] is the interior of the human body—the windings and curvings of organs and glands" (Cobbs 201); Kane as womb (Bell-Metereau 15 and Cobbs 201).

17. I am indebted to Dr. Karen Renner for pointing this out to me.

18. For an excellent reading of Nilsson's *Life* photographs and the rhetorical strategy of their captions, see Newman, pp. 10–16.

19. See Rowland, Farquhar, and Gena Corea's *The Mother Machine*.

20. Skal suggests that "the chest-bursting scene…became the seventies' surpassing evocation of reproduction as unnatural parasitism" (301).

21. Rowland testified to the currency of outer space metaphors prior to *Alien*'s release with her characterization of "the [medicalized] treatment of the fetus as both person and patient": "It is accompanied by the alienation of women, who now become merely the 'capsule' for the fetus, a container or spaceship to which the fetus is attached by a 'maternal supply line'" (121).

22. For additional discussion of such conditions, see "Woman as a Dissolving Capsule: The Challenge of Fetal Personhood" in Rowland's *Living Laboratories*, pp. 118–55, and "Reproductive Interventions" in Meyer, pp. 164–91.

WORKS CITED

Alien. Dir. Ridley Scott. Perf. Sigourney Weaver, Tom Skerrit, and John Hurt. 20th Century Fox, 1979. DVD.

Bell-Metereau, Rebecca. "Woman: The Other Alien in *Alien.*" *Women Worldwalkers: New Dimensions of Science Fiction and Fantasy.* Ed. Jane B. Weedman. Lubbock: Texas Tech P, 1985. 9–24. Print.

Berenstein, Rhona. "Mommie Dearest: *Aliens, Rosemary's Baby* and Mothering." *Journal of Popular Culture* 24.2 (1990): 55–73. Print.

Büssing, Sabine. *Aliens in the Home: The Child in Horror Fiction.* Contributions to the Study of Childhood and Youth 4. New York: Greenwood P, 1987. Print.

Cobbs, John L. "*Alien* as an Abortion Parable." *Literature/Film Quarterly* 18.3 (1990): 198–201. Print.

Constable, Catherine. "Becoming the Monster's Mother: Morphologies of Identity in the *Alien* Series." Ed. and intro. Annette Kuhn. *Alien Zone II: The Spaces of Science-Fiction Cinema.* London: Verso, 1999. 173–202. Print.

Corea, Gena. *The Mother Machine: Reproductive Technologies from Artificial Insemination to Artificial Wombs.* New York: Harper & Row, 1985. Print.

Creed, Barbara. "Horror and the Monstrous-Feminine: An Imaginary Abjection." *Screen* 27.1 (1986): 44–70. Print.

Curtis, Lindsay R., and Yvonne Caroles. *Pregnant and Lovin' It.* Los Angeles: Price/Stern, 1985. Print.

Duden, Barbara. *Disembodying Women: Perspectives on Pregnancy and the Unborn.* Trans. Lee Hoinacki. Cambridge: Harvard UP, 1993. Print.

Farquhar, Dion. *The Other Machine: Discourses and Reproductive Technologies.* New York: Routledge, 1996. Print.

Firestone, Shulamith. *The Dialectic of Sex: The Case for the Feminist Revolution.* New York: William Morrow, 1970. Print.

Fischer, Lucy. "Birth Traumas: Parturition and Horror in *Rosemary's Baby.*" *The Dread of Difference. Gender and the Horror Film.* Ed. Barry Keith Grant. Austin: U of Texas P, 1996. 412–31. Print.

Hartouni, Valerie. *Cultural Conceptions: On Reproductive Technologies and the Remaking of Life*. Minneapolis: U of Minnesota P, 1997. Print.

Hermann, Chad. "'Some Horrible Dream about (S)mothering': Sexuality, Gender, and Family in the *Alien* Trilogy." *Post Script: Essays in Film and the Humanities* 16.3 (1997): 36–50. Print.

Hoppenstand, Gary. "Exorcising the Devil Babies: Images of Children and Adolescents in the Best-Selling Horror Novel." *Images of the Child*. Ed. Harry Eiss. Bowling Green: Bowling Green State U Popular P, 1994. 35–58. Print.

Jeffords, Susan. "'The Battle of the Big Mamas': Feminism and the Alienation of Women." *Journal of American Culture* 10.3 (1987): 73–84. Print.

Kaplan, E. Ann. "Motherhood and Representation: From Postwar Freudian Figurations to Postmodernism." *Psychoanalysis and Cinema*. Ed. E. Ann Kaplan. New York: Routledge, 1990. 128–42. Print.

Kitzinger, Sheila. *Women as Mothers*. New York: Random House, 1978. Print.

Kristeva, Julia. *Powers of Horror: An Essay on Abjection*. Trans. Leon S. Roudiez. New York: Columbia UP, 1982. Print.

Larsen, Ernest. "The Fetal Monster." *Fetal Subjects, Feminist Positions*. Eds. Lynn M. Morgan and Meredith W. Michaels. Philadelphia: U of Pennsylvania P, 1999. 236–50. Print.

Leifer, Myra. *Psychological Effects of Motherhood: A Study of First Pregnancy*. New York: Praeger, 1980. Print.

Marcus, Sharon. "Placing *Rosemary's Baby*." *Differences: A Journal of Feminist Cultural Studies* 5.5 (1993): 121–53. *Project Muse*. Web. 9 February 2011.

Mehaffy, Marilyn Maness. "Fetal Attractions: The Limit of Cyborg Theory." *Women's Studies* 29 (2000): 177–94. Print.

Meyer, Cheryl L. *The Wandering Uterus: Politics and the Reproductive Rights of Women*. New York: New York UP, 1997. Print.

Narducy, Ray. "*Rosemary's Baby*." *International Dictionary of Films and Filmmakers: Volume 1. Films*. Ed. Christopher Lyon. 4 Vols. Chicago: St. James P, 1984. 402–03. Print.

Newman, Karen. *Fetal Positions: Individualism, Science, Visuality*. Stanford: Stanford UP, 1996. Print.

Nilsson, Lennart. "Drama of Life Before Birth." *Life* 30 Apr. 1965: 62–69. Print.

Petchesky, Rosalind Pollack. "The Power of Visual Culture in the Politics of Reproduction." *Feminist Studies* 13.2 (Summer 1987): 263–92. *JSTOR*. Web. 9 February 2011.

Rabuzzi, Kathryn Allen. *Mother with Child: Transformations through Childbirth*. Bloomington: Indiana UP, 1994. Print.

Rich, Adrienne. *Of Woman Born: Motherhood as Experience and Institution*. 10th anniversary ed. New York: Norton, 1986. Print.

Rosemary's Baby. Dir. Roman Polanski. Perf. Mia Farrow, John Cassavetes, Ruth Gordon. Paramount Pictures, 1968. DVD.

Rowland, Robyn. *Living Laboratories. Women and Reproductive Technologies*. Bloomington: Indiana UP, 1992. Print.

Scahill, Andrew. "Deviled Eggs: Teratogenesis and the Gynecological Gothic in the Cinema of Monstrous Birth." *Demons of the Body and Mind: Essays on*

Disability in Gothic Literature. Ed. Ruth Bienstock Anolik. Jefferson: McFarland & Company, 2010. 197–216. Print.

Skal, David J. *The Monster Show: A Cultural History of Horror*. New York and London: Norton, 1993. Print.

Squier, Susan M. "Fetal Voices: Speaking for the Margins Within." *Tulsa Studies in Women's Literature* 10.1 (1991): 17–30. Print.

Sweeney, Louise. "Polanski's Satanic Parody." *Christian Science Monitor* 23 June 1968: 6. *Academic Lexis-Nexis*. Web. 9 February 2011.

Taylor, Janelle. *The Public Life of the Fetal Sonogram: Technology, Consumption, and the Politics of Reproduction*. New Brunswick: Rutgers UP, 2008. Print.

Valerius, Karyn. "'Rosemary's Baby,' Gothic Pregnancy, and Fetal Subjects." *College Literature* 32.2 (Summer 2005): 116–35. *JSTOR*. Web. 9 February 2011.

Wells, Paul. *The Horror Genre from Beelzebub to Blair Witch*. London: Wallflower, 2000. Print.

Wood, Robin. *Hollywood from Vietnam to Reagan*. New York: Columbia UP, 1986. Print.

Extreme Human Makeovers: *Supernanny,* the Unruly Child, and Adulthood in Crisis

CATHERINE FOWLER
REBECCA KAMBUTA

In the cinema, there is little redemption for the evil child. As the perpetrator of crimes ranging from selfishness and bullying to wanton destruction and murder, the evil child threatens our belief in childhood innocence and goodness and is therefore made into a monstrous aberration. As sociologist Chris Jenks argues, children who do not display the appropriate characteristics (i.e., innocence, goodness, and sexual naivety) are symbolically expelled from the category of childhood (128).[1] Accordingly, since the evil children in such films as *The Bad Seed* (Mervyn LeRoy 1956), *Village of the Damned* (Rilla Wolf 1960), and *The Good Son* (Joseph Ruben 1993) show no remorse or ability to change, they must be destroyed at the end of the narrative. Fortunately, when it comes to television, redemption is more easy to come by; indeed, since 2004, thanks to the UK production company Ricochet and Mary Poppins wanna-be Jo Frost, the business of redeeming evil children, or tiny terrors, has become prime-time viewing material in the series *Supernanny*. While fictional evil children are often too evil to be redeemed, *Supernanny* insists that real tiny terrors can be changed—or, in reality TV speak, "madeover"—into little darlings.

In this essay, we explore the ways in which *Supernanny* accomplishes the redemption of the bad child through three easy steps. First, filtered through the conventions of makeover TV, badness is "converted" to unruliness; second, blame is passed from the children to the parents through an intricate structure built around five stages that establish Jo as our point of view and defer self-reflection (on the part of the parents) until the very end; and third—and underpinning steps one and two—via references to mythic notions of the child as innocent and good, *Supernanny* reinforces romantic views that badness is not innate and can be cured.[2]

The makeover format of *Supernanny* is crucial to each of these three steps, but the program also has to negotiate some areas of difference to earlier makeover shows. As we will see, *Supernanny* channels "crisis," pitting everyday expert Jo against the parents so as to involve us in its new kind of "extreme *human* makeovers" [our emphasis]. We borrow this phrase from journalist Sarah Werthan Buttenwieser, who coined it to express concern about what happens on the teenage bad behavior show *Brat Camp* (C4 2005). Werthan Buttenwieser argues that in airing personal problems for the audience's entertainment, *Brat Camp* is exploitative and ultimately "robs what is personal from unsuspecting minors for other's consumption." Furthermore, Werthan Buttenwieser contends that the show actually undermines the potentially positive effects of the therapy conducted at the ranch by turning the teenagers into celebrity brats.

Supernanny, we will argue, attempts to soothe any concerns that may be raised about the making over of children (particularly around the use of non-consenting minors in the program) by giving equal focus to the adults. Unlike in *Brat Camp* then, where the bad behavior, tantrums, swearing, and violence of damaged teenagers is center stage, in *Supernanny* the equal emphasis placed upon both Jo's strategies for teaching the parents and the adults' crises of authority is meant to displace any objections we might otherwise have to the making over of minors. One consequence of this displacement is that *both* the parents and the children are madeover. The double-makeover that *Supernanny* undertakes is executed by both drawing from and extending the well-established formulae of makeover television. Visualized as disorder, rowdiness, boisterousness, and disruptiveness, unruliness can easily be tamed, the show claims, by a few simple lessons in competent parenting from Jo Frost.[3] Therefore, as well as attempting to displace concerns about the exploitation of minors, *Supernanny* also dismisses suggestions that the children Jo has come to help are in any way related to the monstrous evil children found in the cinema.

EXTREME HUMAN MAKEOVERS

Whether transforming our bodies (*Extreme Makeover* ABC 2002–2007; *The Biggest Loser* NBC 2004–; *The Swan* Fox 2004), our homes (*Changing Rooms* BBC 1996–2004; *Extreme Makeover Home Edition* ABC 2003–), our wardrobes (*What Not to Wear* BBC 2001–2007; *Queer Eye for the Straight Guy* Bravo 2003–2007; *How to Look Good Naked* UK Channel 4 2006–), our gardens (*Ground Force* BBC 1997–2005), or even our cars (*Pimp My Ride* MTV

2004–2007), "making over" predominantly involves cosmetic improvements to appearances, be it surgery to reduce a large nose, or carpentry to increase the size of a room, the right style of clothing to flatter one's body shape, or the use of landscaping to revive a tired-looking backyard. The spread of make-over TV testifies to its appeal to audiences; however, for critics this spread has not been unproblematic. June Deery and Misha Kavka highlight the slippage that has occurred as home improvement programs have developed into self-improvement programs. Precisely because *The Swan* follows the formula set out for homes, Deery argues that the show "makes being (e.g., unattractive) more equivalent to having (e.g., an unattractive room)" (162). In other words, for Deery, *The Swan* seems to imply that one is not born attractive or unattractive; one is made so by one's cosmetic choices. Mean-while, in an essay that traces the development of makeover shows, Kavka makes a similar point when she observes that "a distinction can be made between an emphasis on doing and on being, between madeover subjects . . . and the madeover self" (215).

This particular emphasis sets makeover TV aside from straight docu-mentaries, in which people's problems are interrogated, and talk shows, through which people confess their sins, shame, and sorrow. In makeover TV, then, change happens with little contextualization of, or interest in, underlying problems. Deery acknowledges the surface tendency of make-over TV when she comments on the plastic surgery show *The Swan* that "while psychological therapy is offered to participants, this kind of alteration is hard to detect on film and is therefore largely ignored" (166). Deery's comment explains the production choices taken in the makeover genre to prioritize changes that can be seen over changes that are below the surface, whether psychological, emotional, ethical, behavioral, or attitudinal. It is not so much that makeover TV precludes the latter kinds of changes, but more that its conventions construct the changes we can see as more fascinating and more significant than changes that we can't. Even on *Extreme Make-Over: Home Edition,* in which the families chosen for the program's benev-olent acts of home-building are given more back-story, the articulation of that story happens in a fragmented manner in and around the real business of building them a new home. It is clear from this prioritization that the series is not really about the family; it is about the transformation of a house into a spectacular home. By remaining on the surface and avoiding analysis of causes, the makeover genre is staunch in its belief that what the chosen sub-jects need is not counseling or the talking cure but rather to consume, to shop, and to be made better, "betterness" being measured in terms of the lavishing of "improvements" upon their surface environments.

At first glance, *Supernanny* would seem a very different type of make-over show in both form and content. For one, the series is far more complex in structure than most makeover television. Deery articulates that the typical "dramatic process" (162) of these other programs occurs over three stages, beginning with the "cataloguing and display of problems and inadequacies," followed by the "dramatic intervention and transformation," and then closing with the "before-and-after revelations displaying the new" (162). By contrast, *Supernanny* has an intricate structure built around five stages. First, in a direct address to the camera, the parents describe the problems they are having. These descriptions (sometimes, but not always, drawn from their audition tape) are accompanied by shots of the offending behavior. Once the family has been introduced to the viewers at home, Jo travels to the family home (in the U.S. version she watches clips of the family on her portable DVD player while being chauffeured around in an English black cab), ready to begin her "rescue mission." In stage two, Jo arrives and instructs the parents to "carry on as normal" so that she can observe the household dynamics and in her own words "take mental notes" about the issues that need addressing. Jo's observation period (usually a couple of days) is followed by stage three, in which she sits down with the parents, talks through what she has observed, and advises them on how to address their problems. Jo then teaches them new techniques and remains with the family during the parents' initial implementation of her parenting plan. In stage four, Jo leaves the family alone to continue the implementation of her advice. Finally, in stage five she returns, shows the parents footage of stage four on her laptop, discusses where they are still going wrong, provides further advice, and then leaves again. The program closes with a shot of the family together, madeover and happy.

Supernanny's extension to the tri-part formula typical of most makeover TV is produced to cope with the problem of the "human turn" which, again, Werthan Buttenwieser's concerns might be said to address. With its dedication to the transformation of familial dynamics, involving changes in attitudes, beliefs, emotional connection, and expression that manifest themselves in more harmonious behavior, it would seem that *Supernanny* poses a challenge to the superficiality of the makeover format. With this in mind, we want to suggest that *Supernanny* has initiated a third wave of makeover programs. While the first wave madeover our living spaces and the second wave our bodies, this third wave turns its corrective lens to our social/familial interactions. Programs in this third wave include: *Brat Camp* (UK Channel 4 2005–2007; USA ABC 2004–), *Nanny 911* (Fox 2004–), *Demons to Darlings* (BBC 2004), *The House of Tiny Tearaways* (BBC 2004–), *Little Angels* (BBC 3 2004–2006), *Bad Behaviour* (UK Channel 4 2005), *Ladette to Lady* (ITV 2005–) *Driving Mum and Dad Mad* (ITV1 2005–2006), *Redemption Hill* (NZ Channel 2 2005–2006), and *The World's Strictest Parents* (BBC 2008–2009). It is not our intention to discuss these programs here. Rather, we include this list to indicate the necessity for further engagement with the makeover genre's "human turn" that might follow from our own analysis of *Supernanny*, the originating show.

The third wave of makeover TV serves competing demands. On the one hand, it provides new opportunities for reflection and learning while, on the other, it sustains the entertaining and enticing attractions of the first two waves. To illustrate the new emphasis cited above, compared to many make-over series, *Supernanny* is rigorous in the opportunities it gives the subjects and the viewers to reflect on what needs to change and how the changes might happen. As if to acknowledge that working with children and families requires more care and consideration than other makeover shows, *Supernanny* devotes more time to the teaching and learning process. However, as much as this difference might seem to separate *Supernanny* from other makeover shows, the series still incorporates many of the features that have made the first two waves so successful with audiences. For example, because the focus is on making over family relationships, there is even more justification for the invasion of private lives that has been so central to the appeal of the makeover genre. For, as with most makeover TV, in *Supernanny* we are given complete "scopic access" (Deery 169) to the subjects, in this case family life in the home. In stage one, for example, we witness shocking scenes that titillate and grab both our and Jo's attention.

Furthermore, for all its focus on rehabilitation, *Supernanny* ultimately does not allow for the sort of deeper psychological explorations that such changes would necessitate. For one, it focuses on the behavior of the children rather than any root causes of their behavior, thereby discarding psychological explanations for their conduct. The emphasis on unruliness rather than psychological issues works to the program's advantage, for unruliness suggests actions, deeds, and performance patterns, surface features that can be corrected. In addition, the structure of the show is such that any self-reflection on the part of the parents is deferred until the end. In this way, *Supernanny* closely resembles *The Swan*, in which, as Derry has noted, subjects are not allowed to look in mirrors or have family members around them while they are undergoing their procedures. Instead, it is Jo who comments on and guides us through this initial judgment. As we discuss later, the elongated structure of the program is designed to ensure that it is not until parents see themselves on Jo's laptop that they realize that she is right and they are wrong. This delay in self-reflection on the part of the parents means that Jo's insights and facial expressions become our main point of identification: we see the family through her eyes and judge them through her words. Echoing makeover television's growing "dependence on outside ... agencies" (Deery 161), it makes "expert" Jo's role pivotal to successful change. Jo becomes charged with identifying and eliminating surface disorder rather than diagnosing and treating emotional and psychological problems.

Jo's role here is significant, for it allows the series to produce a "quick fix" that can be easily accomplished within the pre-set, one-hour format. Systems of point of view are crucial in convincing us that transformation has occurred. First, our relationship to Jo is established in the sequences in which she comments upon the opening scenes of family disorder, then, we observe the family once they are left alone, and finally we watch video footage with the parents and witness how their change of perspective leads to the figurative "reveal" we have come to expect from makeover TV. Similar to the denials of personal reflection (in both senses of the word), *Supernanny* saves the moment of revelation for the camera. More importantly, it also universalizes the family's problems and invites engagement from viewers who may be experiencing the same challenges with disorder, disobedience, and discord. This emphasis on a journey toward rehabilitation enables the series to act as a teaching tool for viewers, who in some episodes are able to follow tips that appear on the screen.

The quick fix is crucial if the makeover is to keep viewers' attention. It is also a further example of the visual rather than verbal nature of the makeover format and its mediated nature, as we need to see rather than be told of the transformation that occurs in family dynamics. Just as how in *The Swan*, it is crucial that revelation happens "on camera" and is "seen" by viewers at home, *Supernanny* uses its expert figure, Jo Frost, to both foreground and delay the mediation of the process of making over. Similarly, *Supernanny* delays the moment of revelation in order to keep viewers engaged until the end of the program. These delaying tactics re-confirm that the entertainment values of makeover TV remain a priority for *Supernanny*. Turning to some concrete examples from the program, we will also see how the double makeover (of both children and adults) comes about.

FROM UNRULY CHILDREN TO UNRULY ADULTS: ADULTHOOD IN CRISIS

Stage one of *Supernanny* performs various important maneuvers. The family is introduced, and we are given visual images of the children. We see them kick, scream, bite, punch, swear, jump on the furniture, rip the wallpaper, and generally refuse to do what they are told. The parents then give their views on what they think are their problems. It is important that we hear the parents' perspective on their children because the language they use establishes their belief in badness rather than unruliness. Their opening words conjure up a familiar image of the Dionysian child, who is devilish and self-centered and wreaks havoc wherever s/he goes. According to Jenks, this image "rests on the assumption of an initial evil or corruption within the child—Dionysus being the prince of wine, revelry and nature. . . . The child is Dionysian in as much as it loves pleasure, it celebrates self-gratification" (62). The Dionysian image owes much to the Judaeo-Christian doctrine of original sin and was popular in the sixteenth and seventeenth century. The fear of hell and eternal damnation for the child gave rise to a particular model of parenting, one that was harsh and often cruel. As Jenks puts it, "in the tradition of this image, a severe view of the child is sustained, one that saw socialization as almost a battle but certainly a form of combat where the headstrong and stubborn subject had to be 'broken,' but all for its own good" (63).

The language used by the parents on *Supernanny* to describe the problems they are having with their children echoes Jenks's language, for it suggests that childrearing is a battle of equals in which the child, rather than the parent, has the power. For example, in one episode, Wendy tells us that her daughter Maryanne is "like a *bomb* waiting to *explode*" and that her "tantrums are getting worse." Wendy is shown cowering in a corner while her seven-year-old daughter hurls abuse at her, calling her a "fat bitch" ("Agate"). Likewise, Tami tells us that dressing her four-year-old daughter Maile in the morning is "impossible" and that it often "takes up to two hours to win the *battle*" ("Keilen"). In another episode, dad Alex tells us that mealtime "is like a *war*" and that he would "rather stick needles in [his] eyes" than endure another one ("Bixley"). The language used by these parents evokes a powerful image of warfare.

If the parents talk about their children as if they were warriors who have waged battle against them, the images show the parents basically surrendering. These purposely shocking images are followed by the parents' verbal expressions of desperation. Most of the parents on *Supernanny* admit they have "given up" or "given in" to their children rather than enforce any type of discipline. Kelly, a twenty-five-year-old single mother, tells Jo that she "can't be bothered" with discipline because the constant fighting between her two children Sophie (five) and Callum (four) has worn her down. For Kelly, just making it through each day is hard enough: "I don't know how much attention they think I can give both of them. You know, there's other things I'm trying to do. Even like if I'm cooking dinner they'll play up. Just day to day things I have to do" ("Steer"). Giving up is often likened by the parents to defeat in battle. In another episode, Shaun and Tami tell Jo that when it comes to their four children, they have "conceded defeat," they have "waved the white flag." Tami reveals that she often gives in to four-year-old Maile "so that everybody else can have a better day," despite the fact that this strategy is clearly not working ("Keilen"). Karen, mother to four energetic children, expresses similar sentiments, revealing to the camera that "over time [the children's bad behavior] has sort of drained me. I feel like I've got no energy to kind of fight and argue with them. So it's easier to give in to them most of the time" ("Collins"). Clearly, the language chosen by the parents in *Supernanny* echoes Jenks's, and opening sequences are edited to underscore this view, in preparation for the change that will occur in both the parents' attitudes and the children's behavior by the end of the program. Indeed, returning to our opening point, the parents could be said to adhere to the cinematic view of the evil child as beyond redemption.

The time given over to the parents' enunciation of the destruction perpetrated by the child upon the household in the opening sequences assumes extra weight once we consider our earlier observation that unlike documentaries or talk shows, makeover television does not privilege explanation and confession. Typically, in *Supernanny* talk and reflection are largely Jo's domain (although as we will see later they are also gifts that she bestows on the parents in stage five, when she invites them to view footage of their first failed attempts to implement her rules and techniques). Stage one thus provides the first step toward an implementation of the ideological view of the child that underpins the program, that is, that children are not devils (as the parents see them) but are instead, at heart, angels.

A tension is set up between the parents and Jo in terms of differing beliefs in the child as innately good or bad, and Jo is established as a key point of identification for viewers. In stage one, the parents despair at the unchangeable deviltry of their children. According to the parents, this behavior is beyond their control, but according to Jo, it is not. It is very clear from the language Jo uses and the visuals chosen that she does not endorse the Dionysian view of the child; rather, her advice and practice seems to stem from quite the opposite end of the spectrum: the Apollonian child. Drawing from Jenks's work once more, we can see how the Apollonian child is to goodness as the Dionysian is to badness. Apollonian children are "angelic, innocent and untainted by the world which they have recently entered," and they possess "a natural goodness." Accordingly, models of parenting that embrace such a belief are also conceived of differently: "within this model . . . we honour and celebrate the child and dedicate ourselves to reveal its newness and uniqueness" (Jenks 65). The Apollonian view of the child rejects the doctrine of original sin and, as Jenks points out, is associated with the work of Jean Jacques Rousseau and other Romantic novelists/poets. In this model, "children . . . are not curbed nor beaten into submission; they are encouraged, enabled, facilitated" (Jenks 65). Jo's view of the child as essentially Apollonian and therefore deserving of encouragement and nurturing as well as order and boundaries creates the tension that drives the series. It sits in contrast to the view of the parents that their child is innately bad and that consequently there is nothing that they can do to curb bad behavior. What is more, and leading us to stage two of redemption, the opening sequences make it apparent that *Supernanny* features not one protagonist to be madeover but two: the children and the parents, for it is the parents, not the children, who are responsible for the chaotic state of the family.

Camera, editing, and dialogue throughout Jo's observation period in stage two and the advice session in stage three swiftly pass the blame for the unruliness of the child to the parents. The importance of Jo's point of view is established during the observation period. Despite the implication of her chosen word "observation" that she will be an unobtrusive fly on the wall, Jo actually comments directly to the camera as well as pulling faces, allowing the viewer to gain insight into what she is thinking and reinforcing her dominant view of the unruliness of the children and ineffectiveness of the parents. After observing a chaotic breakfast time at the Jeans' house, Jo says disgustedly, "Jessie this morning had chips for breakfast. Leah did not have anything" ("Jean"). On another occasion, having witnessed a typical meal-time in the Bixley household that ends with seven-year-old Brandon running away from the dinner table screaming, Jo steps out for a breath of fresh air. She shares her thoughts with the viewer: "I can't believe the drama that went on over dinner time. They'd all lost control. We have a little boy who's screaming and freaking out, because he was being forced fed by a sausage being jammed in his face. It was absolutely disgusting" ("Bixley"). Finally, while watching Debbie, a single mother of three, struggle to maintain control over her three young daughters in a busy car-park, Jo remarks, "This is absolutely crazy. This mother knows what's going on here—she is totally out of control when it comes to her children being in public and something needs to be done ASAP" ("Seniors").

This theme of children and adults needing to be put back in their proper places extends into stages three and four. At a family meeting, for example, Jo informs Steve and Lucy that their two-and-a-half-year-old son controls the household: "What Charlie says goes. He's running the household. This little boy is doing what he wants, when he wants and not being told any-thing... for how he's behaving." The evening prior to the meeting provides a snapshot of his controlling behavior: Charlie refuses to eat his dinner (he eats Smarties later in the evening), he turns the television off while his older brother Billy is watching it and then throws a tantrum when Billy tries to turn it back on, and after a two-hour struggle to get him into his pajamas, he refuses to go to bed. Jo tells the Woods that she's been a nanny for fifteen years and has "never seen a boy run riot and control his Mum and Dad... like [she] has in this household." According to Jo, Steve and Lucy have lost sight of their "proper" roles as parents: "I don't see a Mum and I don't see a Dad. I see mates and one little chief and four Indians" ("Woods"). In another episode, Jo tells Chris and Colleen to "grow up" and recognize their responsibilities as parents: "You guys are the parents here and when they're misbehaving *you act like teenagers*. . . . I suggest the pair of you grow up right now and get real with the responsibilities you have in front of your face" ("Christiansen"). In another episode, Jo tells Debbie that she needs to disci-pline her own children rather than running next door to her Dad's house whenever the girls misbehave: "Every time you call Dad you undermine yourself and *become one of the kids*" ("Seniors").

Several parents even readily admit they have relinquished power to their children. This issue of parents behaving like children resurfaces when parents acknowledge that they have lost control of their children. David, father of three young girls, admits, "I'd like to be the boss [but] I don't feel that I am right now or that I have ever been." David is shown struggling to get his four-year-old daughter strapped into her car seat—she has lost her *Care Bear* book and is screaming at the top of her lungs ("Jean"). Likewise Kevin, also a father of three, tells us, "I'm sick of being pushed around by the kids." Like most other nights, all three of Kevin's children have climbed into their parents' bed, causing mayhem and disrupting sleep ("Charles"). In all of these examples, the problem to be remedied is the loss of parental control. *Supernanny* links familial disruption to a problematic reversal of the parent/child roles. In the examples provided above, the adults are acting childishly, scared of their children, while the children have too much power over the adults.

Jo's solution to this problem is to prompt the parents to use their "authority." In order to take back control of their households, Jo believes parents must learn to take responsibility for their actions and their children. In every episode, Jo implements a strict new household routine and system of discipline designed to help the parents reassert control. Whether tackling how to control the household, ward off chaos, offer structure and organization, achieve a work/home balance, deal with conflicting parenting styles, foster effective communication, provide a healthy diet, or institute one-on-one time or fun activities to make the family work together, everything comes back to restoring children and adults to their proper places. In stages three and four, then, blame is passed from the children to the adults, who continue to fail in their duties, and Jo's expertise is put into action. In stage four in particular, we see much evidence of the crisis of adulthood as the parents try to take back control. We might suggest, then, that the opening sequences of *Supernanny* accomplish what Jenks terms a "conceptual eviction" (128) of adulthood that has to be righted by Jo, who will restore adults and children to their proper places, a solution that is meant to benefit both the children and the adults.

Jo's carefully chosen words above make it very clear that, though she may judge the families, she also sympathizes with their despair. This typically occurs at moments in which Jo's incisive vision allows her to see what lies behind the parents' "brave faces." Thus, in one episode she tells Carolyn Pandit, mother of four, highly independent children:

> ...how you haven't already had a breakdown, I do not know. But because you put on a brave face, because you want to do the best you can, because you're a Mum and you love your children it makes you carry on every day. ("Pandit")

Similarly, Jo tells forty-three-year-old Barbara, mother of three, that the lack of discipline and the resulting chaos in the household is visible in her demeanor: "I see a Barbara who's emotionally drained, that actually wants to be Barbara and not Mum 24/7" ("Jean"). Jo is also not fooled by Lorraine's performance. She tells viewers "The first thing I noticed about Lorraine was this great big smile that she had painted on her face. But it was fake and I could see right through that" ("Amaral"). In *Supernanny*, the parents' "makeover" is shown to be beneficial not only for themselves but also for their children.

In stage five, Jo provides the final apparatus of reflection: the DVD footage of the family when left alone. After witnessing a variety of footage (both good and bad), Jo returns to the family home to show the parents where they are still going wrong. According to Jo, the DVD footage plays a crucial part in the transformation process, as it allows the parents to "see with their own eyes the mistakes they have made" ("Wischmeyer").[4] Rather than leave it up to the parents to evaluate their "performances," Jo stops the footage at particular moments to point out when they fail to use the techniques correctly. Jo effectively acts as a parent, both to the children involved in the program and to their caregivers who have failed in their duties. While watching the DVD footage, many of the parents cover their heads in shame or embarrassment. Jenn tells the viewers that she was "really surprised at how many times [they] messed up, "cause [she] really thought things were going much better" ("Ririe"). Likewise, Joanne also says, "Watching the DVD was a real eye-opener. Some of the things that Jo told us before we were still doing" ("Burnett"). Finally, Deirdre realizes that she only sees the bad things her daughters do. She tells Jo that she is "ashamed of [herself] for . . . putting blinders on . . . to their good behavior and just focusing on the bad" ("Facente"). Thus, the DVD footage provides the tool for self-reflection.

It would be easy to see this ritual of viewing the footage as just another way of implementing the makeover's tendency for the unmediated to become not just "mediated but mediatized" that is, to translate unmediated reality into "media-worthy . . . media image[s]"(Deery 160). Yet there seems to be more going on here. The footage is the last in a number of apparatuses for reflection that begins with Jo's facial expressions and asides to the camera and continues with her first sit-down session with the family and her advice as they try to implement strategies in her presence. Jo's commentary throughout the show situates her as an "expert eye" that sees exactly what is wrong. Her on-screen persona is such that viewers are encouraged to frown with her at the noise and mess created by the unruly child and stare open-mouthed at the incompetence of their parents. Jo's commentary gives her an authority that she otherwise would not deserve. After all, Jo has no formal qualifications and doesn't arrive complete with theories about how the family might be improved. Instead, she relies on her nineteen years of experience working with children. She watches, comments on what she sees, and then draws from tried and tested strategies (tried and tested on the various episodes of *Supernanny* as much as in her nannying career) that are appropriate for the needs of each family. Also, as more than one reviewer of the show has pointed out, she has no children of her own. Jo's inexperience has been cited often by those who disapprove of her methods: one respondent to an online forum wrote, "I have seen some 6–7 episodes and I'm disgusted by this show. Putting people's problems in front of a camera where a woman who [doesn't] even know what it's like to be a mother is just making money [out of] people's problems" ("Forums"). Clearly, Jo's persona does not work for this viewer, and we might see the acts of looking and listening that Jo undertakes as an attempt to win over those who don't immediately warm to her.

CONCLUSION

In *Supernanny,* as in much makeover television, we watch as the parents "capitulate...to the rule of the expert" (Deery 169).[5] The breach between Jo and the parents is evident in the opening sequences, but it is not far-fetched to suggest, as we do, that this breach can also be thought of in terms of how Jo and the parents position themselves in relation to the Apollonian to Dionysian spectrum of the child. In common conceptions of adulthood, the child is seen as being incomplete and adulthood as the much-desired state.[6] With its emphasis on the teaching and learning of parenting, however, *Supernanny* would seem to imply that adulthood is a state one might learn. As the narrator of the US version tells us, "children don't come with instruction manuals!" the implication being that this knowledge is exactly what Jo will provide.

For if *Supernanny* emerges out of current thinking on child-raising to be found in books such as Diana Loomans's *What all Children Want their Parents to Know* (2005) and E. D. Hill's *I'm Not Your Friend, I'm Your Parent* (2008), then this literature is in turn informed by centuries of debate about the boundaries between the child and the adult and the roles of children and parents in functional society. Over the previous five centuries, the concept of the child underwent a radical transformation: once thought of as little more than chattel (with virtually no legal protection), children are now seen as an investment in the future, one that must be vigilantly guarded and expertly tended if it is to yield a good result.[7] Today, childhood continues to be strictly policed with various government strategies designed to curb juvenile delinquency and other social problems, such as child obesity, youth drinking, teen pregnancy, and child abuse. Children are seen as worthwhile investments, with parents spending significant amounts of time and money on their children's education and other pursuits. Families today are child-centered whereas in the past children were largely invisible.

Supernanny intervenes in this history and these debates over child-rearing by conceptualizing the unruly adult as well as the unruly child. Although much discussion has taken place about childhood and the child being in crisis, less has occurred about adulthood in crisis. If in *Supernanny*, children are unruly when they stop acting like Apollonian angels, adults are unruly until they start acting like a very specific sort of parent. Essentially, then, *Supernanny* pivots on a common assumption—that childhood and adulthood are so intimately linked that, as Jenks argues, we cannot understand one without the other: "the child...cannot be imagined except in relation to a conception of the adult, but essentially it becomes impossible to generate a well-defined sense of the adult and indeed adult society, without first positioning the child" (Jenks 3). Jenks's assertion that the child must be and more usually is positioned "first" before the adult can be defined perhaps explains the need for the double makeover in *Supernanny*. Therefore, just as it is not possible to define the adult without first defining the child (since theory dictates that the adult is what the child "becomes"), so it is not possible to makeover the child without also making over the adult: the two are so entangled as to be interdependent and mutually supporting.

Yet *Supernanny's* redemption of the bad child is accomplished not only through shifting blame to the adults but also thanks to an expansion of the makeover's tri-part structure. *Supernanny's* intricate five-stage structure delays the parents' self-reflection until the very end of the show. Jo Frost provides the dramatic arc to this journey. She acts as our eyes and ears, sympathizing and criticizing, supporting and cajoling, reinforcing Apollonian rather than Dionysian views of the child, and ultimately restoring children and adults to their proper places. These underlying references to mythic notions of the child as good or bad help us to understand both the dramatic arc of the program and its ideological underpinnings.

At the end of the reinforcement period, Jo leaves the family for the final time, but not before she has had her chance to sum up the changes that have taken place. Standing outside one home, Jo remarks: "I'm really proud of the family. I mean, just over three weeks ago, everyone was in tears, including myself, but now I feel like crying for the opposite reason. You know it's priceless to see the changes—it's overwhelming!" ("Ball"). On many levels, Jo is right. It *is* overwhelming to see the changes that happen to family dynamics, largely because they happen so relatively quickly and easily. Having redeemed not just unruly children but also unruly parents, Jo Frost moves on to her next family. But the makeover television genre and the evil child on television will never be the same again. The former has undertaken a "human" turn that has challenged the overly superficial nature of transformation upon which it has relied for its success, and although *Supernanny* does not quite manage to probe the emotional or psychological reasons for the family crises it examines (we may have to wait for a fourth wave for that), it does provide new opportunities for reflection and learning (as opposed to mere consuming). Meanwhile, the evil child is redeemed. Downgraded to unruliness, the child's problems are recognized as stemming from the adult ineptitude, and although this maneuver suggests a crisis in adulthood, the parents in question seem to emerge from the experience with more insight and understanding. *Supernanny's* biggest reveal of all, then, is not the making over of Dionysian devils into Apollonian angels or of childish parents into responsible adults. Instead, it is the transformation of reality television into a space for entertainment, drama, crisis, and a superficial place of *teaching and learning*.

NOTES

1. Karen Corteen and Phil Scraton argue that the notion of childhood is inherently flawed: "No issue reveals the contradictions within the politics of childhood as starkly as that of sexuality, its definition and regulation. As 'non-adults,' children are assumed to be asexual. While they are socialized into gender-appropriate roles from birth, a universal feature of patriarchal societies, they are expected to retain a sexual naivety. Yet the images which surround them, implicit and explicit, of hegemonic/dominant masculinity and emphasized/subordinate femininity are all pervasive and all persuasive. The daily experiences of children and young people are contextualized by constructions of masculinity and femininity which are both gendered and sexualized" (76).

2. Because of the large number of episodes broadcast, we examine only seasons one and two of *Supernanny* (both the UK and U.S. versions). These seasons were chosen largely for their availability: US seasons one and two are available on DVD. The UK episodes were purchased directly from Ricochet. Please note: the episodes contained on the DVDs may differ from those broadcast on television.

3. Here we draw upon Ron Becker's observation that "regardless of the family, all problems are rooted in incompetent parenting" (184).

4. The U.S. version utilizes split screens so that the viewers are able to see the parents' reactions as they watch the footage.

5. Deery argues that the participants of makeover television "capitulate . . . to the rule of the expert and the power of the camera." We will discuss the latter when we turn to the shifts in point of view that underpin the learning journey of *Supernanny*.

6. See Hoyles, Postman, and Jenks.

7. See Zelizer, Hays, and Stearns.

WORKS CITED

"Agate Family." *Supernanny*. Season 2. UK. Ricochet, 2009. DVD.

"Amaral Family." *Supernanny: Season 2*. US. Roadshow Entertainment, 2005. DVD.

"Ball Family." *Supernanny*. Season 2. UK. Ricochet, 2009. DVD.

Becker, Ron. "Help is on its Way: *Supernanny, Nanny 911*, and the Neoliberal Politics of the Family." *The Great American Makeover—Television, History, Nation*. Ed. Dana Heller. London: Palgrave Macmillan, 2006. 175–91. Print.

"Bixley Family." *Supernanny*. Season 2. UK. Ricochet, 2009. DVD.

"Burnett Family." *Supernanny: Season 1*. US. Ventura Home Entertainment, 2005. DVD.

Werthan Buttenwieser, Sarah. "Fame Undermines Therapy in Reality TV's *Brat Camp*." *Usatoday.com*. Gannett, 16 Aug. 2005. Web. 19 Mar. 2011.

"Charles Family." *Supernanny*. Season 1. UK. Ricochet, 2009. DVD.

"Christiansen Family." *Supernanny: Season 1*. US. Ventura Home Entertainment, 2005. DVD.

"Collins Family." *Supernanny*. Season 2. UK. Ricochet, 2009. DVD.

Corteen, Karen, and Phil Scraton. "Prolonging 'Childhood', Manufacturing 'Innocence' and Regulating Sexuality." *'Childhood' in 'Crisis'?* Ed. Phil Scraton. London: UCL Press, 1997. 76–100. Print.

Deery, June. "Interior Design: Commodifying Self and Place in *Extreme Makeover, Extreme Makeover Home Edition* and *The Swan*." *The Great American Makeover—Television, History, Nation*. Ed. Dana Heller. London: Palgrave Macmillan, 2006. 159–74. Print.

"Facente Family." *Supernanny: US Season 2*. Roadshow Entertainment, 2005. DVD.

Hays, Sharon. *The Cultural Contradictions of Motherhood*. New Haven: Yale UP, 1996. Print.

Hill, E. D. *I'm Not Your Friend, I'm Your Parent: Set the Boundaries they Need and Really Want*. Nashville: Nelson Thomas, 2008. Print.

Hoyles, Martin. *The Politics of Childhood*. London: Journeyman, 1989. Print.

"Jean Family." *Supernanny: Season 1*. US. Ventura Home Entertainment, 2005. DVD.

Jenks, Chris. *Childhood*. London: Routledge, 2005. Print.

Kavka, Misha. "Changing Properties: the Makeover Show Crosses the Atlantic." *The Great American Makeover—Television, History, Nation*. Ed. Dana Heller. London: Palgrave Macmillan, 2006. 211–29. Print.

"Keilen Family." *Supernanny: Season 2*. US. Roadshow Entertainment, 2005. DVD.

Loomans, Diana. *What All Children Want Their Parents to Know: Twelve Keys to Successful Parenting*. Tiburon, CA: New World Library, 2005. Print.

"Pandit Family." *Supernanny*. Season 2. UK. Ricochet, 2009. DVD.

Postman, Neil. *The Disappearance of Childhood*. 2nd ed. New York: Vintage, 1992. Print.

"Ririe Family." *Supernanny: Season 1*. US. Ventura Home Entertainment, 2005. DVD.

Scraton, Phil. *'Childhood' in 'Crisis'?* London: UCL Press, 1997. Print.

"Seniors Family." *Supernanny*. Season 2. UK. Ricochet, 2009. DVD.

Stearns, Peter. *Childhood in World History*. London: Taylor and Francis, 2005. Print.

"Steer Family." *Supernanny*. Season 1. UK. Ricochet, 2009. DVD

"Forums: *Supernanny*: She Doesn't Even Have Her Own Kids!" *TV.com*. CBS Entertainment, 17 Nov. 2007. Web. 19 Mar. 2011.

"Wischmeyer Family." *Supernanny: Season 1*. US. Ventura Home Entertainment, 2005. DVD.

Zelizer, Viviana. *Pricing the Priceless: The Changing Social Value of Children*. 2nd ed. Princeton: Princeton UP, 1994. Print.

Index